Before the Curse

BEFORE THE CURSE

THE CHICAGO CUBS' GLORY YEARS
1870–1945

Edited by Randy Roberts
& Carson Cunningham

University of Illinois Press

URBANA, CHICAGO, AND SPRINGFIELD

A portion of chapter 4 is reprinted from David L. Porter, "Cap Anson of Marshalltown: Baseball's First Superstar," *Palimpsest* 61:4 (1980). Copyright 1995 State Historical Society of Iowa. Used with permission of the publisher.

A portion of chapter 5 is reprinted from James A. Cox, "When Fans Roared 'Slide, Kelly, Slide!' at the Old Ballgame," *Smithsonian* 13:7, 1982, pp 120–31.

"Three-Fingered Immortal" reprinted with permission, copyright SPORT Gallery Inc.

George Monteiro, "Grover Cleveland Alexander in 1918: A New Kansas City Piece by Ernest Hemingway," in *American Literature* 54:1, pp 116–18. Copyright 1982 Duke University Press. All rights reserved. Used by permission of the publisher.

"Ronald Reagan: Above All, the Gipper was a Good Sport," © McClatchy-Tribune Information Services. All rights reserved. Reprinted with permission.

"Wrigley Spent Fortune to Make Cubs Champs," "Hack Wilson Fined $100," "M'Carthy Likely To Go; Hornsby Rumored for Job," "All World Thrilled By Big Series," and "Back Cubs with Heavy Betting" reprinted courtesy of Sun-Times Media.

"Busher Joe McCarthy" reprinted from *The Saturday Evening Post* magazine © 1939. Saturday Evening Post Society. Text by Joe Williams.

"Gabby Likes 'Em Hot" reprinted from *The Saturday Evening Post* magazine © 1939. Saturday Evening Post Society. Text by Warren Brown.

"The Decline and Fall of the Cubs" reprinted from *The Saturday Evening Post* magazine © 1943. Saturday Evening Post Society. Text by Stanley Frank.

"Home Runs by Ruth, Gehrig Beat Cubs 7–5" from Chicago Tribune. © 1932 Chicago Tribune. All rights reserved. Used by permission and protected by the Copyright Laws of the United States. The printing, copying, redistribution, or retransmission of the material without express written permission is prohibited.

"Well-Spent Dime" © The Courier-Journal.

Library of Congress Cataloging-in-Publication Data
Before the curse : the Chicago Cubs' glory years, 1870–1945 / edited by Randy Roberts and Carson Cunningham.
p.   cm.
ISBN 978-0-252-07816-3 (pbk.)
1. Chicago Cubs (Baseball team)—History. I. Roberts, Randy. II. Cunningham, Carson.
GV875.C6B44   2012
796.357′640977311—dc23   2011018433

To the bleacher bums and box-seat suits
and all the rest of the Chicago Cubs fans past and present.

Contents

Part II. From the Colts to the Dynasty

Acknowledgments

THE VINTAGE ARTICLES FOUND IN *Before the Curse* come from a wide array of sources: the *Chicago Times, Outing* magazine, the *Chicago Tribune*, the *Saturday Evening Post*, and the *Spalding Guidebook* to name a few. We're grateful to all of the periodicals and authors who have agreed to share their work with us here.

Every baseball fan at some point thinks about visiting Cooperstown. We had the good fortune of doing so for this book, and the nostalgic feel of both the town and its celebrated National Baseball Hall of Fame put us in the right mood to work on *Before the Curse*. It also helped that the Hall of Fame has a world-class library, which we drew upon heavily. Thank you to Cooperstown and to the National Baseball Hall of Fame.

We also benefited from the Chicago History Museum's archives, especially its impressive collection of old-school Chicago Cubs photographs, and the fine libraries of DePaul University and the University of Chicago. Thank you all.

For decades now, the University of Illinois Press has supported the game of baseball and its illustrious past. *Before the Curse* is yet another example of its commitment to the national pastime. So we offer a big thank you to the University of Illinois Press and to its editorial maestros who helped this book come alive, director Willis Regier and senior editor Tad Ringo.

Most of all, we'd like to thank the fans of the Chicago Cubs, as well as the team's players, managers, and owners of years past and present, for making the franchise one of the world's most storied professional teams.

The Chicago Cubs: From Early Excellence to the Golden Age to That Darn Goat

THE CHICAGO CUBS were a team to be reckoned with back when Teddy Roosevelt was President of the United States, and they continued to be the club to beat during the early administration of William Howard Taft. They forged a golden age for the record books, providing their fans with enough stories to keep them warm during many a cold Chicago winter night.

But here's the problem with golden ages: everything afterward savors of anticlimax. This is particularly true when the golden age took place in the distant past. You don't have to go back to the Greeks and Romans, either. Spain was on top of the world in the sixteenth century. The Dutch could buy and sell just about anyone in the seventeenth century. The French had a Sun King in the seventeenth century and gave England a good game in the eighteenth century. Great Britain ruled the waves in the nineteenth century. The United States, in a fit of wisdom, saved its best for more recent times. Sadly, the Chicago Cubs took their cue more from Spain than America. In four generations of baseball history, the Cubs have been accused of many things, but never of saving the best for last. Not yet, anyway. Quite the opposite, they burned like a comet during their first generation and then promptly and unceremoniously fell to earth.

Back in the Golden Age, at the birth of the Cubs, baseball looked different than it does today. It was like a child, changing and maturing by the year, and it was difficult for anyone living though the game's awkward, gawky stage to predict what it would look like when it grew up. Baseball during the 1870s and part of the 1880s resembled fast-pitch softball. The pitcher employed a stiff-armed, underhanded delivery from forty-five feet away from the batter. The ball the pitcher tossed was soft and loosely wound, and the batter could not hit it very far, but he did have the right to request high or low pitches, and his batting average was bolstered by the fact that until the 1880s few fielders wore gloves. To make matters even more complicated, the number of balls it took to walk a batter varied over the years. In some years a walk required nine balls. The game, then, featured short hits, frequent errors, and high scores.

In the later 1880s and 1890s, the sport's teenage years, baseball began to more closely resemble its adult form. After changing the number of balls that constituted a walk seemingly every year, for the 1889 season the rules committee settled on four, a number that both seemed fair and speeded up the game. Pitchers won the right to throw overhand and batters lost the right to request high or low pitches, though perhaps as a humanitarian concession for a few years batters were permitted to use a flat, cricket-like bat. Gloves arrived en masse, errors dipped to respectable levels, and many of the refinements of the modern game took shape. It became a game for Americans on the make, a game novelist Mark Twain described as "the very symbol, the outward visible expression, of the drive and push and rush and struggle of the living, tearing, booming nineteenth [century]." Gone were the trappings of the mid-century gentleman's game, replaced by the swell of immigrant players, crush of rowdy fans, smell of stale beer, and bloody-nose fights for pennants.

Through these evolutionary waters, the Chicago Cubs steered the boat. Of course, they were not called the Cubs back then. For more than thirty years of the team's history it went by different monikers. Originally, in addition to being referred to as the Chicagos or Chicagoans, the team took the name White Stockings—not to be confused with the South Side team and never called the White Sox. During the late nineteenth century and early twentieth century, sportswriters and fans pinned other names to the team. They were dubbed the Colts, Orphans, Microbes, Remnants, Spuds, and Zephyrs. Not until 1907 did the Cubs become, formally and eternally, the Cubs.

Perhaps all the name changes left deep-seated psychological scars, the kind that burrow into the soul and never really go away, resurfacing every few decades with a sudden unprovoked ax murder or singularly maladroit play. Whatever the case, during the team's wonder years it enjoyed tremendous success, a result of outstanding ownership, innovative management, and the best talent money could buy.

In October of 1869 a group of well-heeled Chicago businessmen formed the team that became the Cubs. They acted out of civic pride, instilled with the belief that some city would be the home of the finest baseball team in the country and it would be a sign of Chicago's preeminence if it were that city. The all-professional team took the field in 1870 and defeated the Cincinnati Red Stockings, the team that had drubbed another Chicago nine the year before. Encouraged, in 1871 Chicago joined the National Association of Professional Base Ball Players (NAPBBP) and competed successfully against the best teams in the country.

Competed successfully, that is, until Mrs. O'Leary's cow, so the legend goes, kicked over that damn lamp and started a fire that consumed much of Chicago. In the aftermath, few Chicagoans thought much about baseball, and the White Stockings disappeared from the sports pages and baseball diamonds of the city. Gone but not entirely forgotten, the team was re-formed for the 1874 NAPBBP season. In fact, a better team emerged out of the ashes of the Great Fire, rising like a Phoenix from the charred bones of Chicago.

The driving force of the new White Stockings was William A. Hulbert, a wealthy member of the Chicago Board of Trade who believed that he could personally improve any business deal. For several years he observed the workings of the NAPBBP and reached some hard conclusions. Not to put too fine a point on the matter, he concluded that the player-managed and player-run league was a mess. As gentlemanly as baseball was supposed to be, the league lacked propriety and integrity. Players drank too much alcohol, gambled and fought to an excess, and displayed a marked tendency to jump team fences when the grass looked greener in some other (ball)field. Fixed games, rowdy players and fans, and economic unrest were hallmarks of the league.

Hulbert's idea was to transform professional baseball from player-centered to owner-centered. He believed that owners should act more like bosses and players like employees. In early 1876, the same year that future Cubs pitching great Mordecai Peter Centennial "Three Finger" Brown was born, Hulbert and a handful of other influential club executives founded a new league, the National League of Professional Baseball Clubs. Henceforth the owners would run the show and the players would limit their games to those on the field. Immediately, the new barons of baseball doubled ticket prices from twenty-five cents to fifty, banned Sunday baseball, stopped selling alcohol in the parks, and generally attempted to serve a cleaner, more Christian product to their patrons. Their second American revolution, coming conveniently one hundred years after the first, set a pattern for professional sports in the country. When players said they were playing a sport, the owners answered that they were engaged in a business. And when players complained that they were working in a business, the owners responded that they were playing a game.

Business or sport—or business and sport—Hulbert wanted to be on top at both ends. As a result, he began to purchase the best players he could find. A century before George Steinbrenner and the New York Yankees, Hulbert showed America how to buy a team. The key addition was pitcher and baseball great Albert G. Spalding, who not only left the Boston Red Stockings for the Chicago White Stockings for more money and a piece of the action, but also convinced a number of other premiere players from the NAPBBP to join him. Adrian Anson, still a few years away from being called "Cap," was among Spalding's recruits. With Spalding on the mound, Anson at first base, and other talented hitters and fielders, Chicago immediately became one of the National League's better teams. They won the pennant in 1876 but finished out of the running during the next three years.

But better was not the best, and Hulbert, Spalding, and Anson were not interested in second place. During the next few years they added even better players, and in 1879 "Cap" Anson became manager. An innovative baseball mind, he implemented the nascent hit-and-run play, developed a pitcher rotation, began using a third-base coach, experimented with signs, and is credited as one of the creators of the tradition of spring training. After the 1879 season Chicago acquired Mike "King" Kelly, a marvelous baseball talent who could do everything in the game except stay sober and make a curfew. The team also picked up a few superb pitchers, making up for the hole in the team left by Spalding, who was more interested in developing a sporting goods and publishing business than actually playing baseball.

In 1880 Chicago soared above their competition in the National League, winning almost eighty percent of their games. The team was as unbeatable as a major league baseball team has ever been, and they were seldom boring. Kelly and his teammates might not always have played sober, but they played with heart and imagination. Even future evangelist Billy Sunday, who joined the team a few years later, found it difficult to play in Chicago and follow the straight and narrow path. The players' off-field activities angered Hulbert and Spalding, but the management found no complaint with the action on the field. Chicago followed their 1880 pennant with championships in 1881, 1882, 1885, and 1886.

It seemed like Chicago would go on winning for years. But they didn't, and there were, of course, reasons. There are always reasons. Hulbert died in 1882, and Spalding, the new president, seemed more interested in making money from baseball than working in baseball. He left most of the day-to-day operations to Anson. And both Spalding and Anson grumbled about the behavior of the players. Increasingly players showed up at the park hungover and sometimes drunk and, in an end-of-the-season series against American Association champion St. Louis, the players added another infraction to their rap sheets: fixing games. Chicago was on the verge of becoming less a team than a dysfunctional Alcoholics Anonymous meeting.

Something had to change. Heads had to roll. At a time when a wave of prohibition was sweeping across the land, Spalding and Anson began dealing their worst drunks—and often best players—to other teams for less-talented players who would sign the club's new pledge on abstinence. Seeing his drinking buddies discarded, Kelly revolted. He refused to sign any pledge that severed him from the bottle, and he demanded to be traded to a town where saloons suggested conviviality, not frostiness. He wanted to go to Boston, whose 1886 team had finished distant from Chicago. For a hefty price, Spalding complied.

The team that Chicago fielded in 1887 was comprised of mostly males between boyhood and manhood, lads with peach-down chins and rose-milk cheeks, clean-cut and innocent and fresh as the morning. Journalists accurately referred to Anson's new team as the "Colts." They played with enthusiasm but not always with skill. The team marked the beginning of Chicago's gradual fade into baseball mediocrity. For the next decade the team that would ultimately become the Cubs began each season talking about winning a pennant and finished each season out of the race.

During those years baseball changed. Players, angered at management's dominant position in the game and the emergence of the reserve clause, revolted and formed the Players' League. The league provided a nice product but failed in a year. Even worse, black players were barred from organized baseball. Behind the virulent racism of Cap Anson, who never saw a black player with whom he wanted to share a field, the National League drew a color line that would last until Jackie Robinson erased it. Without any black players, the National League struggled into the new century, dodging charges of racial and anti-labor biases.

Both were true. Unfortunately for the league, it could not add monopoly to its list of abuses. In 1900 Ban Johnson rechristened his Western League as the American League and declared war on the National League. Not only did Johnson go head-to-head against the senior circuit for the best players, he set up teams in prime National League markets. In Chicago a new team appeared, owned by Charles Comiskey and calling themselves the White Stockings. Although Comiskey eventually agreed not to use the name, he felt no qualms about raiding the talent of the older team. As one player after another deserted the National League Chicago team, sportswriters began to call the remaining players the Remnants.

Slowly, in the early years of the century, baseball in America and Chicago achieved peace, order, and prosperity. In 1903 the baseball war between the National and American Leagues ended with the National Agreement, a covenant that committed both leagues to honor the contracts of the other. The agreement also opened the way for a World Series as we now know it. In Chicago the National League team began to rebuild. Led first by manager Frank Selee (1902–1905) and then by their peerless manager Frank Chance (1905–1912), the team replaced the older players who had either defected to the Chicago American League franchise or retired with a young, energetic crop of players whom local sportswriters dubbed the Cubs. The name, which first appeared in 1902, had legs, outlasting such others names as the Colts, Zephyrs, and Microbes. In 1907 "Cubs" became the official name of the National League team.

By 1907 the Cubs had also become the best team in baseball. The squad had everything. Led by their hard-hitting manager Frank Chance at first base, the Cubs combined superior pitching with exceptional hitting, base-running, fielding, and intelligence. Their best pitchers were Ed Reulbach and Mordecai "Three-Finger" Brown. As a young boy Brown had lost the forefinger and part of the middle finger of his right hand in a farming accident, but he overcame this disability, developing an array of pitches that jumped, curved, and dropped. At his best—and he was often at or near his best—he was virtually unhittable. In 1906 he had an ERA of 1.04 and in 1908 he won 29 games. Stellar players behind Reulbach and Brown included the legendary double-play trio of shortstop Joe Tinker, second baseman Johnny Evers, and first baseman Frank Chance. Combined with other outstanding players—including pitcher Orval Overall; outfielders Harry Steinfeldt, Jimmy Sheckard, Mike Donlin, Frank Schulte, and Jimmy Slagle; and catcher Pat Moran—the Cubs, for a short time, played like grizzlies.

In 1906 the Cubs were close to unbeatable. They far outdistanced their National League rival, the Christy Mathewson–led New York Giants. Winning 116 regular season games and establishing an all-time record .763 winning percentage, the Cubs ran away with the pennant. Matched in the World Series against the cross-town White Sox, labeled the "hitless wonders" for their ability to manufacture runs with few hits, the Cubs swaggered with understandable overconfidence. The problem for the 1906 Cubs was that they had had too much time to develop their swagger. From mid-June it had been clear that they would win the pennant, and the second half of the season was little more than an exhibition tour. All the while the White Sox had been battling to win the American League pennant. By the October World Series the south-side team was scarred and battle hardened, ready to fight tooth and spikes for a victory. For Cubs fans the series proved a bitter disappointment. Their peerless team finished the season as the second best team in Chicago and America.

The 1906 World Series defeat made the 1907 campaign all the sweeter. The Cubs won twenty-four of their first twenty-nine games and never looked back. They finished the season with 107 victories, a full seventeen games ahead of second place Pittsburgh. In the World Series they faced the Detroit Tigers, whose star, Ty Cobb, was the greatest player of the dead-ball era. But not even the hard-charging Cobb was a match for the Cubs. After the opening game finished in a 3–3 tie (called because of darkness), Chicago won the next four in convincing fashion. The Cubs, for the first time but not the last, were World Series Champions. Not only had they captured a pennant and a World Series crown, they had made it look easy.

No one accused the Cubs of running away from the pack in 1908. It was one of the most thrilling seasons in baseball history. The Cubs fought relentlessly. On the field they were locked in a three-way pennant race with the Pittsburgh Pirates and the New York Giants, a contest that immortalized Fred Merkle's boneheaded base running, Johnny Evers' clearheaded decision-making (so legend has it), and a pennant-deciding call by an umpire who grew up in Chicago that was affirmed by the National League's front office. The infamous play occurred on September 23, the day after the Cubs swept a doubleheader against the Giants to keep any hopes of a pennant alive. With the game tied 1–1 in the bottom of the ninth with two outs, the Giants managed to put runners on the corners. Al Bridwell came to the plate and drove a single into center field, scoring the runner on third. Bridwell glided to first, touched the bag, watched the winning run score, and continued to run toward the clubhouse in center field. Merkle, on first, broke for second when Bridwell hit the liner, but as the run scored and fans stormed the field, he made a sharp right turn and joined Bridwell in a sprint toward the clubhouse.

Evers watched the entire play unfold. A few weeks before, the exact same play had taken place in a Cubs–Pirates game. On that occasion, Evers had called for the centerfielder to throw him the ball, stepped on second base, and demanded that umpire Hank O'Day rule a force out at second and no run scored. O'Day had not seen the play at second and ruled that the run had scored and the Pirates had won the game. The Cubs protested the call to the league president, who promptly upheld O'Day's decision. But Evers had been technically correct. O'Day had missed the call. Evers knew it, and what is more O'Day knew it. (Interestingly, though, as readers will see, in 1914 O'Day claimed that other Cubs players deserved more credit for recognizing Merkle's mistake than Evers.)

Now Evers called for the ball again. At the time it was in the hands of one of the Giants' faithful who was dancing in celebration on the field. After a bit of strong-arming and some minor fisticuffs, Evers got the ball and tagged second. Umpire O'Day, watching and waiting, made the call. "Merkle didn't run to second; the last run don't count," he announced. The inning was over. The day was late, tempers were hot, and O'Day's life was in serious jeopardy. He ruled the game a tie and the entire affair was soon thrown onto the plate of the National League officials.

Being half politicians to begin with, and hoping to remain on good terms with citizens in both New York and Chicago, the officials believed the most prudent course of action was to do as little as possible and hope that the game would not matter in the race for the pennant. In short, they collected affidavits, cogitated a bit, and did and said nothing of importance. But when it was clear that the season was not going to end without a league decision, they, mix-metaphorically, stepped up to the plate and swallowed their medicine. The game would have to be replayed, which meant that the National League pennant would be decided by a one-game playoff in New York.

The Cubs took an overnight train to New York, defeated the regal Christy Mathewson (thanks largely to Mordecai Brown's relief work) in the playoff, and then boarded another train back to the Midwest for the first game of the World Series in Detroit. By the time they reached Detroit they were train-lagged, dog tired, semi-hungover, and walking on air. They believed they were destiny's team, and they played like it. Detroit, despite still having Ty Cobb, who had led the American League in hits, doubles, triples, and RBIs, never had a chance. The Cubs won the Series 4–1, capping a year that can only be described in superlative terms. It was a true *annus mirabilis. Chicago Tribune* sportswriter I. E. Sanborn was right on the dime when he wrote "What those gray clad modest young warriors have accomplished will be remembered longer than any of them lives."

Were the Cubs' National League and World Series victories somehow written in the cards, a playing out of some cosmic scorekeeper's grand design? Has the last century been all payback, a balancing of accounts for the Giants' collapse, Merkle's baserunning mistake, the National League office's close call, taming the Tigers in the World Series, and more? Has everything that has happened since 1908 all been karma: the late-season slumps, World Series stumbles, playoff collapses, billy goat curses, Bartman deflections? Of course not, but it sure has seemed that way.

At the end of 1908 the Chicago Cubs were one of the premier teams—perhaps *the* premier team—in professional baseball. The New York Giants were great and the Boston Red Sox had a storied past, but the Cubs had been the cornerstone of the National League, a pivotal and innovative franchise, and the first back-to-back World Series champion. What is more, there was every reason to believe that they would continue to win National League pennants and World Series crowns. But they didn't. The Frank Chance teams won only one more pennant, in 1910, and then disappeared as a contender.

If excellence characterized the first generation of the Cubs existence, near misses denoted their second. Pennants in 1918, 1929, 1932, 1935, 1938, and 1945 raised hopes for another Series championship, but each year's hopes ended in bitter disappointment. However, the second generation of Cubs and Cubs fans witnessed their own miracles: the opening of Weeghman Park (later to be known as Wrigley Field); the innovations of William Wrigley Jr., Philip K. Wrigley, and Bill Veeck Sr.; Ruth's called shot in the 1932 World Series; and Bill Sianis' alleged "billy goat curse" in the 1945 World Series. The teams of the World War I era, Roaring Twenties, Great Depression, and World War II years were also blessed with great and often colorful players—consistent Charles Leo "Gabby" Hartnett, erratic Lewis Robert "Hack" Wilson, dependable Charlie Root, supremely gifted Rogers Hornsby, and hometown hitter Phil Cavarretta among them.

Before the Curse traces the joy and pain of being a Cubs fan from 1870 to 1945, through roughly the first two generations of the glorious—and occasionally exasperating, frustrating, and infuriating—franchise. We have collected writings by journalists and historians—some lovers, others haters, and a few a bit of both—about the Cubs. They tell the story of wins and losses and what might have been, if only. It's the story of great players and greater personalities from the beginning of the organization until the end of World War II. It's the tale of hundreds of people, players famous and infamous, owners seen and unseen, managers imaginative and hide-bound, and one beautiful, transcendent ball park. Finally, it's about the fans that lived and endured—and continue to endure—the rocky road of the Chicago Cubs.

PART I

FROM "LET'S PLAY BALL" TO KING KELLY

Season	Wins	Losses	Winning Percentage	Games Behind	Attendance	Ballpark	Owner
1871	19	9	0.679	2		Lakefront Park	George Gage
1874	28	31	0.475	18½	66,000	23rd Street Grounds	George Gage
1875	30	37	0.448	35	60,323	23rd Street Grounds	George Gage
1876	52	14	0.788	—	65,441	23rd Street Grounds	William Hulbert
1877	26	33	0.441	15½	46,454	23rd Street Grounds	William Hulbert
1878	30	30	0.500	11	58,691	Lakefront Park	William Hulbert
1879	46	33	0.582	10½	67,687	Lakefront Park	William Hulbert
1880	67	17	0.798	—	66,708	Lakefront Park	William Hulbert
1881	56	28	0.667	—	82,000	Lakefront Park	William Hulbert
1882	55	29	0.655	—	125,452	Lakefront Park	Albert Spalding
1883	59	39	0.602	4	124,880	Lakefront Park	Albert Spalding
1884	62	50	0.554	22	87,667	Lakefront Park	Albert Spalding
1885	87	25	0.777	—	117,519	West Side Park I	Albert Spalding
1886	90	34	0.726	—	142,438	West Side Park I	Albert Spalding
1887	71	50	0.587	6½	217,070	West Side Park I	Albert Spalding

1. Title Time?

AS A FRANCHISE KNOWN FOR unmatched futility, it seems odd that, in what was arguably its inaugural season, the 1870 Cubs—known then as the White Stockings or Chicagoans—won the championship. But even that championship came with a caveat, because the New York Mutuals, who had the best record, protested the controversial ending of its late season series with the White Stockings. The controversy erupted in front of more than 7,000 fans in Chicago when the Mutuals' pitcher, Mac Wolters, became so upset that he'd thrown twelve straight pitches to the plate which neither the batter nor umpire liked that he stormed off the field. Chicago fans then rushed onto the field to celebrate. By the time everyone got cleared away it was too dark to finish. (Negotiations between the teams to replay the game failed.)[1]

Counting the Mutuals series as a victory, the Windy City's title, as the *Chicago Times* reported, arrived a short time later when the White Stockings won a wildly popular end-of-season series over Cincinnati, making the Chicagoans the "champions of the country."[2]

This championship occurred several years before the formation of the National League and thirty-three years before the first World Series. Still, a crowd of some 15,000, "larger by thousands than any that ever before witnessed a game in America" according to the *Times*, turned out to watch the game, which was played on the South Side in Dexter Park. Hundreds of the spectators were from Cincinnati.

The White Stocking's victory in this 1870 series came at an early period in the evolution of modern professional sports, not to mention a much different time in America. Only five years before this championship, the Civil War ended. And, though booming, the city of Chicago—yet to be nicknamed the

"Windy City"—was constructed largely of wood and boasted a population of fewer than 300,000. The Great Chicago Fire was still a year away.

The White Stockings, depending on the day, played at Dexter Park, which was next to the South Side's Great Union Stockyards, or at the lesser-regarded Ogden Park, on the near-north side. The team was yet to move to their brand new home field, the Union Base-Ball Grounds, between Michigan Avenue and the Illinois Central tracks north of Madison Street. (The fire would wipe out the new park in its first season).[3]

Still, despite Chicago's relative modesty, by 1870 areas like Englewood, Hyde Park, and Calumet had already formed, and the people of Chicago already loved professional baseball.[4] So too did folks in Cincinnati. Indeed, fans from both cities did not hesitate to show their zeal for the home team with a wager.[5]

Along with the *Times*' reportage of the closely followed series, in this selection, readers get a sample of the Cincinnati papers' reactions to their team's loss.

Comments of the Cincinnati Press
on the Late Base-Ball Match

Chicago Times, October 15, 1870

THE LATE CHICAGO-CINCINNATI GAME.

The following comments of the Cincinnati press indicate the feelings of that city over the late Red Stocking defeat:

FROM THE GAZETTE.

We were beaten! We know it, we feel it, but how could we help it? The umpire was against us, the weather was against us, the crowd was against us, the heavens were against us, the ground was against us, the pestilential air of the Chicago river was against us, the Chicago nine was against us, and last, but not least, the score was against us.

Chicago is joyful to-night. She has achieved the dearest wish of her heart in having taught Cincinnati, at Dexter Park, in the presence of 15,000 people, that she at last can play base-ball. The contest between the White and Red Stockings was close and bitter, and ended in victory well and honorably earned by the recognized nine of the Chicago club.

Fortune and the vast crowd were with the latter, in the fact that the fielding errors of the Reds were fatal ones, while those of their opponents did not materially affect the issue. In this fact, indeed, is told the whole story of the game, for the wild applause which the crowd bestowed upon the good plays of the local favorites, and its contrast with the seemingly feeble cheer which the 400 Cincinnatians, and they alone, sent up whenever the Red Stockings did anything brilliant, could not unnerve the victors of 200 fields, especially as it was the result of a partisan feeling more than usually devoid of ruffianism.

The game here to-day between the Red Stockings and White Stockings went against the Cincinnatis by 16 to 13. The White Stockings are the first club in the United States to win two games from the Reds. The Mutuals hold the nominal championship, but the victory of today makes the Chicagoans the champions of the country. The game this afternoon was wrought with the greatest determination on both sides, as it proved one of the most intensely exciting ever played. Superior weight at the bat enabled the White Stockings to win. Their batting the last three innings has never perhaps been equaled in an important contest. The Reds and their friends conceded the entire fairness of the defeat. Ferguson, captain of the Atlantics, umpired the game superbly. He was the right man in the right place.

The feeling in Chicago before the game was that the Red Stockings would succeed. No even bets could be obtained this morning. The Cincinnatians, of whom about 500 came up, were almost certain that their favorites would win by a handsome score. Their feeling to-night is one of surprise at the excellent work of which the Chicago nine is capable. The White Stockings had not the same spur to win as the Red, having already scored the first of the series, which is one reason why their friends were reluctant to stake money on the result, but they fought their best, far excelling their display of skill in the Cincinnati game. Before the game commenced it was informally arranged that in case the Reds won to-day, the third and deciding game should be played in Chicago next Monday. . . .

The crowd at Dexter Park this afternoon was enormous, and larger by thousands than any that ever before witnessed a game in America. The number is estimated at 15,000. Not more than 500 ladies were present. At least 1,000 carriages and other vehicles accommodated the dense multitude. For an hour after the game closed there was a blockade of carriages in the avenue leading from the grounds. The weather was clear, though a steady wind made it slightly too cold for comfort. The grounds are level, and in satisfactory condition.

The conduct of the crowd was highly creditable. Their club was in the rear most of the game, but they made no spiteful demonstrations. When their favorites forged ahead, they cheered loudly, and in the ninth inning, when the White Stockings made the remarkable number of eight runs, they cheered furiously. The Cincinnatians rewarded the good plays of the Reds with hearty applause. Hundreds of strangers from Iowa and Wisconsin were present, and to a man they sympathized with the Reds, and were ready to back them with money. The Reds also had thousands of backers among Chicagoans.

FLY CATCHES

It is estimated that $20,000 changed hands in this city on the result of the late Chicago–Cincinnati game.

2. Baseball, Celebrated and Lampooned

WITH NO TIMEFRAME governing a baseball game's length, playing fields that feature "bullpens" and fences, and a playing season in-step with that of planting and harvesting, symbolically and mythically baseball echoes America's rural past. Yet baseball in the late nineteenth and early twentieth centuries—especially professional baseball—was strongly urban. It represented, as Mark Twain put it, "the outward and visible expression of the drive and push and struggle of the raging, tearing, booming nineteenth century."[1]

Surprisingly, though, in 1881 the *New York Times*—which sometimes showed support for baseball—ran a scathing op-ed about the sport, saving its choicest barbs for the professionals. The paper called on Americans to shun baseball and turn to the more refined game of cricket.

The second article presented here, written in 1888 in *Outing* magazine, reflects how near the turn of the twentieth century baseball not only made Americans giddy, it could unite classes and represent America's "verve."

In 1888 the industrial revolution roared and European immigrants came to America in droves. The two-year-old Statue of Liberty stood as a beacon of hope and Victorian mores were giving way to a more liberated cultural attitude. These changes brought their own issues, though, as cities with exploding populations like Chicago sometimes saw tensions arise and social problems multiply. Still, steam, steel, and electricity had already made significant inroads in changing how cities looked, felt, and functioned, and how people worked. Indeed, the increase in leisure time that came with the industrial revolution fueled the startling growth of professional baseball.

This article shows that, through all the rapid changes in America, the National League managed to appeal to thousands upon thousands of Americans—Americans that reveled in baseball. We also get a glowing report on the evolution of baseball as a business and the ballplayer as a professional.

This National Game

New York Times, August 30, 1881

There is really reason to believe that baseball is gradually dying out in this country. It has been openly announced by an athletic authority that what was once called the national game is being steadily superseded by cricket, and the records of our hospitals confirm the theory that fewer games of baseball have been played during the past year than were played during any other single year since 1868.

The history of the development of baseball is a curious and interesting one. It has existed in a rudimentary form in England ever since the latter part of the twelfth century, and it is believed that the young Plymouth Pilgrim played this inchoate game, then known as "rounders," on Good Friday as a public protest against the Church of Rome. Undoubtedly the game of "rounders" was developed from the still older and simpler game of "two-old-cat." The latter game, in the opinion of our best archaeologists, was invented by the Egyptians during the period of the Third Dynasty, and afterward introduced into Greece, whence it spread throughout the Mediterranean basin. It formed part of the Olympic games, and is believed to have been played by the Pythagorian neophytes as part of the initiation ceremony of the mysterious brotherhood founded by the great enemy of the bean school of philosophy—a school which was the forerunner and antitype of the modern Concord school. "Two-old-cat" has always held its place among the small-boys of all nations, and it is the germ whence all other games of ball in which "runs" are counted originate. Its extreme simplicity has prevented it from ever attaining the proud position of a national game, but it will always retain the reverence of ball-players as the primitive game of remote antiquity.

About twenty-five years ago there was an effort made to induce Americans to play cricket, but it failed. We were not, at that time, worthy of the game, and in our ignorance and indolence we said, "Give us something easier." It was then that certain unknown persons resolved to take the old game of "rounders," which had gradually become known by the name of baseball, and to make of it an easy substitute for cricket. To the latter game it bore much the same relation that the frivolous game of euchre bears to the grand science of whist. The base-ball conspirators said to their fellow-countrymen, "Here is an easy game which everybody can learn. Let us play it and call it our national game." The suggestion met with a warm response, and base-ball clubs sprang up all over the country.

Of course, the national game soon lost the simplicity of the familiar base-ball of country small-boys. Elaborate rules were made, and these were so constantly changed and so many additions were made to them that the study of base-ball jurisprudence became a gigantic task. When objection was early made to the national game that it was really fit only for boys, the conspirators hit upon the plan of using a ball about as hard as a ten-pound cannon-ball and much more dangerous, and then proudly asked if they had not taken away the reproach that base-ball was a small-boys' game. From that time it became rather more dangerous to play base-ball than to fill lighted kerosene lamps or to indulge in any other of our distinctively national sports. It is estimated by an able statistician that the annual number of accidents caused by the base-ball in the last ten years has been 37,518, of which 3 per cent have been fatal; 25,611 fingers and 11,016 legs were broken during the decade in question, while 1,900 eyes were permanently put out and 1,648 ribs were fractured. Had not the popularity of the game begun to decline some two years ago it would undoubtedly have been demanded by Western Democrats that base-ball cripples should be pensioned by the Government, a measure which would at once bankrupt our national Treasury.

During the halcyon period of the national game a number of enthusiastic players went to England in order to introduce it in that benighted land. They played several games in public, but the Englishmen refused to take any interest in the matter. They said: "Ah! yes. Very nice game for little boys, but it's only our old game of rounders, you know." The American missionaries returned disappointed and somewhat disheartened, and from that time base-ball began to show signs of waning popularity.

Then appeared the "professional players," [that] fell upon the game. They made a living by hiring themselves out to base-ball clubs. They made of what was originally designed to be a sport a matter of business. Worse than this, they made the national game a national instrument of gambling, and gradually succeeded in placing it on a level with the game of three-card monte. Games were won and lost in accordance with previous "arrangements." In other words, one set of players sold the game to their opponents before it was played, and the unfortunate people who had bets on the result were thus systematically robbed. Of late years base-ball has been rather more disreputable than was horse-racing in the days before the existence of Jerome Park. The honest young men who dressed themselves in ridiculous uniforms, called themselves "Red-legs," or "White-legs," and broke their fingers by playing matches in public, found that they were ranked in public estimation with professional black-legs, and one need not wonder that they are now abandoning the game wholly to the professional players.

Probably the time is now ripe for the revival of cricket. The day has gone by when Americans looked upon athletic sports which really required muscle and endurance, and upon games of cards in which intellectual effort was a more important element than chance, as something which they had no time to attend to. Whist has to a large extent superseded euchre, and the latter has been banished from the drawing-room to the railway smoking car. Our experience with the national game of base-ball has been sufficiently thorough to convince us that it was in the beginning a sport unworthy of men, and it is now, in its fully developed state, unworthy of gentlemen. Cricket will probably become as popular here in the course of a few years as it is in England. And we shall be contented to play a game worth playing, even if it is English in its origin, without trying to establish a national game of our own.

America's National Game

Harry Palmer, *Outing, An Illustrated Monthly Magazine
of Recreation*, July 1888

Long live the National Game! Of all the games and field sports that have been introduced into civilized countries from time immortal, not one, so far as history has kept account, has ever awakened the same enthusiasm, attracted the same following, or enjoyed such steady progress along the highway of public favor as the national game of America. It will not be necessary, so far as the American readers of *Outing* are considered, to refer to figures or data in support of this assertion. The average American boy, although he may be rather ignorant as to how delegates are elected to the national convention, the number of electoral votes apportioned to the different States in the Union, or the date of Lee's surrender, can call the names of eminent professional ball-players off-hand, or with equal ease give the principal events of Captain John Ward's history as a pitcher and short-stop, and Adrian C. Anson's record from the date upon which he left Philadelphia to play ball with Deacon White, Col. McVey, Ross Barnes and Al. Spalding in the Chicago team.

It is a great sport, this game of baseball, involving directly and indirectly, as it does, the exchange in investment of nearly $10,000,000 of money annually; occupying, as it does, thousands of columns of room in the great daily papers and magazines of the country, and receiving, as it does, the support of business man and mechanic, clerk and capitalist alike.

Fifteen years ago the future of baseball was a question which comparatively few were sufficiently interested to entertain. It had begun to don a professional garb, to be sure, but salaries were small, backing was of a dubious character, and patronage was—well, in its infancy. Captain John Ward, of the New York team; Michael J. Kelly, of the Boston team; and Albert Spalding, the now wealthy head of the Chicago team, have at divers times related some interesting reminiscences of the game as it was in the old days, during the first stages of its existence. Fancy John M. Ward indulging in a ride on a freight train through New York State to secure an engagement with a ball club that really did not know how much longer it would be privileged to live. Imagine Michael J. Kelly, the great player for whose release the Chicago club received $10,000 in hard cash, striking for an advance of $5.00 from the old Columbus (O.) club, with which to buy a pair of shoes, as he was then playing in his stocking feet. Fancy Al. Spalding, the millionaire president of the Chicago club, playing ball for the old Rockford team at a salary of $60.00 a month. Those were anxious days for the men who played ball for a living, and doubtless few, if indeed any one of them, ever anticipated the great improvement that has taken place in the affairs of the national game during the past decade—aye, mostly since 1884.

In America of to-day, the game is the recognized national sport of our people, the turf alone comparing with baseball in point of attendance, grounds and money invested therein. Within the past three years the game, which had previously been confined to the Northern, Western and Eastern States of the nation, has penetrated the South. It has also crossed the line and entered Canada, and in both sections of the country to-day it is enjoying great and rapidly growing popularity. Further than this, from present indications the game will, ere another year has passed, extend beyond the shores of our own continent. Mr. A.G. Spalding has already outlined his plans for introducing the game into the antipodes. It is altogether likely that similar steps will be taken in the near future to popularize the game in Great Britain. The reported determination of the Australian Cricket Eleven, which recently arrived in England to school itself in the science of baseball playing, will also tend to familiarize Europeans with the game of all games.

"Why is it," asked a distinguished subject of Queen Victoria upon a recent visit to this country, "that your people support with such astonishing liberality the game of baseball?"

"Because," rejoined the equally distinguished Yankee (Governor Hill, of New York), "baseball, like the average American, has more dash, more enterprise, more vim and more 'git-up-en-git' to it in a minute than anything else of its kind that any other nation on earth ever attained to in a lifetime. That's the secret of the national game's success in the United States, and in every other enterprising country in which it has been introduced."

Without calling into question the spirit of national pride and that well-known admiration for the game that may have prompted the distinguished politician's reply, it is certainly true that the game of baseball owes its popularity in a large measure to those elements in it which are identical with the crowning characteristics of the average American. Clean, vigorous, honest, and spiced with just enough of the element of risk and danger to make it intensely interesting, baseball presents none of the tiresome features of cricket as played under established rules; is free from the demoralizing effect of the pool box and book-maker, that makes many shun the race-track; has none of the roughness of football, as demonstrated in many a college game upon record; presents no opportunity for juggling, "sellouts" and crooked work; and is to-day governed and controlled in the majority by men of high social and business reputation, who could not, for obvious reasons, afford to identify their names with an enterprise of questionable character.

The growth of the game in popular favor soon rendered necessary the employment of more businesslike methods in the conduct of its affairs. Prior to 1871, the different professional clubs were really under no organization. No such thing as a prearranged schedule was ever heard of or ever suggested, and not infrequently the receipts secured at a game, when it was not practicable to play within enclosed grounds, were obtained by popular subscription, or, as it was known in those days, by "passing the hat."

In 1871 the first steps toward organization were taken, and through the efforts of the veteran, Henry Chadwick (now on the editorial staff of *Outing*), the old National Association came into existence, and nine teams played through the season for the pennant, which was won by the Athletics of Philadelphia. I say they played through the season, and so they did—after the style of pennant contests, peculiar to those days. Games were *forfeited* without penalty to the club which forfeited, and, indeed, the offending club was not always to blame, for the walking between towns was not always good, and anticipated receipts, through unfavorable weather or other causes, were not always realized! In those days, the players did as they liked, and the clubs had no redress. If a man chose to sit up and play cards until daybreak, or indulge in a "toot" with convivial companions, his club meekly put some other man in the recreant player's place for the game of the following day, or played with eight men when they were unable to find a substitute. Why not discharge a drinking player, or at least fine him? Well, fines did not go in those days, and a man discharged from one club could easily find work with another.

Dating from 1871, however, the affairs of the game began to assume a healthier complexion, although the systematic and perfect business methods of the present day were then never dreamed of. The first steps toward organization had been taken, and the action began to bear good fruit in the better conduct of players, the increased interest of the public in the games, and the growth of confidence in baseball as a promising field for investment on the part of moneyed men. From the time when the old National Association was organized, Boston was the centre of interest in baseball affairs. She came into the field in that year with a pennant-winning team, and managed to capture the championship every year thereafter up to the season of 1876. Of the thirteen teams in the Association at the close of the season of 1875 Boston had the pick of the ball-playing talent of the country, the stars of the team being Al Spalding, Ross Barnes, George Wright, Colonel McVey, and the then sprightly "Deacon" White. No club could face the Red Stockings, as they were called, with any well-grounded hope of winning, and Boston had begun to take a municipal pride in its seemingly invincible ball-team.

Unfortunately for Boston, however, it had among its players a Western man, whose heart was in the West, and whose mind often reverted to the good old days when he played with the old Forest City team for fun, and with the old Rockford team for a salary of $60 a month upon the broad prairies of far-off Illinois. What happy inspiration led William A. Hulbert to communicate with Albert Spalding as the man best able to help him in establishing the game upon a firm footing in the West, probably no one save the now long-departed Hulbert himself ever knew. Certain it is that the opening of the negotiations at that time between these two pillars in the baseball structure laid the first stone in the solid foundations upon which the great baseball enterprises of to-day stand.

The Chicago Club, of which Hulbert was president, had entered the National Association in 1874. For two years it had struggled against misfortune and adversity. The game in the West was still comparatively in its infancy, and the gate receipts of the club did not nearly meet its running expenses. That baseball would ultimately prove a paying investment in the West as well as in the East, however, was one of the things which William A. Hulbert had never for one moment doubted. He anticipated the time when baseball interests in America would shape themselves into one or more great organizations, the West arrayed against the East in battle for the annual championships, with both sides possessed of sufficient playing talent to raise the game and the struggles of the contesting teams to a position of national importance in the minds of the American people. How unerring his judgment proved, and how completely his hopes have been realized, the history of the game since 1876—the year in which the present National Baseball League of America was founded—will tell. It is a question, however, whether Mr. Hulbert would have succeeded in his undertaking had he not enlisted Albert Spalding—at the time the great strategic pitcher of the Boston Club—in his behalf. Spalding was anxious to return to the West, and when Hulbert wrote him that unless he (Spalding) aided him in securing a winning team for Chicago for the following season, professional baseball, in Chicago at least, would die a natural death, the present head of the Chicago Club grasped the opportunity tendered him, and took the step that has since made him a millionaire and raised the game to its present important position in the Western States.

The situation, in a nutshell, was this. The old Association of 1875 consisted of thirteen clubs, nine of which were located in eastern cities, and the remaining four in western cities. The East had the crack players of the country on its teams. The West had secured what the East did not want.

Thus public interest in the game was to a great extent confined to that section of country beyond the Alleghanys, and only through the infusion of some of the vigorous blood of the Eastern teams into the weak arteries of the West, could the foundation be laid for that spirit of sectional rivalry which has since grown up, and to which the national game is largely indebted for its success. "Leave Boston," said Hulbert, in a letter to Spalding, in the winter of 1875–6, "and bring with you to Chicago the pick of the Eastern club talent, or as much of it as you can induce to come, and I shall be in a position to offer you such inducements as I think will be more than satisfactory to yourself, and fully so to the players you bring with you."

The result of this correspondence was that some days after Hulbert quietly took the train for Boston, and before his presence in "the Hub" had been discovered, he had seen Spalding and arranged with him the details of what subsequently proved to be the greatest sensation in the history of baseball up to that period of its existence. Colonel McVey, A.G. Spalding, "Deacon" White and Ross Barnes, of the Boston club, and Adrian C. Anson and Ezra Sutton of the Philadelphia club—the Athletics—agreed to leave their clubs and don the uniform of the Chicago club for the season of 1876. When the news of this great combination was flashed over the country, it shook the baseball world to its very centre.

The directors of the great Boston club were wild with chagrin and anger, and offered their deserting players extravagant salaries to remain with them. Philadelphia also felt mortified, but took the loss of Anson more philosophically, as in those days "the big fellow" was not possessed of the great reputation as a ball player that is his to-day. With the single exception of Sutton, however, none of the seceding players went back upon their agreement. Anson weakened and offered to buy his release from the agreement he had entered into, but Spalding and Hulbert stood firm, and the big captain has probably never regretted coming west. Sutton deliberately refused to join the party and remained in the east, an action which he has since doubtless regretted.

When the season of 1876 opened the good results of the transfer began to manifest themselves. The National League was organized, by which eight clubs, Hartford, Boston, Philadelphia, and New York in the east, and Chicago, St. Louis, Louisville and Cincinnati in the west, were bound together under a mutual agreement to respect a constitution and by-laws for the government of the clubs and players of League. This was but a single one, however, of the many steps that have since been taken toward securing the permanent existence of our national game as an institution.

In 1882 the American Association sprang into existence, and has since become a formidable rival of the National League. For a time the prospects for a cut-throat game between these two bodies were excellent, but reason ruled where war would have inflicted untold injury to the game.

From a joint discussion of the questions at issue grew the existing national agreement, governing and controlling the employment, release, suspension and penalties of players; protecting the clubs in the circuit of one organization from the rapacity of those in its rival organizations; providing a Board of Arbitration to which all differences between organizations, party to the agreement, are submitted for settlement, and in other ways securing for professional baseball in America such methods and understanding as will protect both clubs and players, the players from arbitrary and unjust rulings upon the part of the clubs, and the clubs from unreasonable demands and dishonorable actions upon the part of their players. The establishment of the national agreement, which has since taken under its protection every reputable baseball league and association in the country, was unquestionably a great step in the direction of reform. The next step was the formation of a joint schedule committee, by which the schedule committees of each organization met upon an appointed date, after each had prepared its schedule of games for the season, for the purpose of comparing their schedules, and so altering them that there should be as few conflicting dates as possible in cities wherein there was located an Association as well as a League club.

Up to the fall of 1886 each of these great organizations possessed their own code of playing rules. The awkwardness of this condition of things was becoming more and more apparent each year since, during the interchange of exhibition games during the spring and fall months, prior to and after the championship seasons, a question arose in many instances as to which rules would govern the games. In November of 1886 representatives of the League and Association met in the City of Chicago, and after organizing what is now known as the Joint Rules Committee, proceeded to frame the code of rules which now govern the play of every professional ball club in America. This reconstructed code was subsequently submitted to both the League and Association at their respective annual meetings, and adopted by them as the National Playing Rules of Professional Baseball Clubs, governing all clubs party to the National agreement. Thus was a uniform code secured for the guidance of every professional ball club in the country from Maine to California.

It has been our purpose in the preceding pages to give as briefly as possible, and in a general way, some idea of the growth and development of the game in America since it donned the garb of professionalism, as well as to show how, at the present time, its interests are protected, and its affairs directed by methods as systematic and businesslike as those governing the greatest commercial and manufacturing institutions of the country. As in many other enterprises, where capital and labor are brought into contact for mutual benefit and profit, those who work at baseball by no means lack the advantages of organization. The Brotherhood of Ball Players, organized and maintained chiefly through the efforts and intelligence of Captain John M. Ward, of the New York club, has, through wisely chosen methods, secured much to afford protection to its members, as well as to elevate the character of the professional ball player, and command for him that respect which such an organization alone can secure, and which individual effort would require years to accomplish.

The relations existing between the National League and the Brotherhood are to-day of a frank and friendly character, and it is sincerely to be hoped not only that such a condition of things may continue, but that the Brotherhood may increase in power and influence, always provided that it exercises such influence for the general good and advancement of its members, and for the good name and reputation of the national game.

There can be no question in the mind of any well informed lover of baseball, but the *personnel* of the average professional ball team, so far as intelligence, good behavior and gentlemanly address are concerned, has improved greatly from that of fifteen years ago. The causes are plainly apparent.

Without organization discipline was out of the question, and as in all classes of men, the ranks of professional ball players have, ever since the game has been played, contained an element that can be governed only by discipline. Then too, in its earlier stages baseball was at best an experiment.

Its great future, it is safe to say, was anticipated by no one, so that there was little, if any, inducement to able, intelligent, well-bred men to select it as a profession.

There were some, however, who, through force of circumstances or an ungovernable love for athletic sport, did so, and to the influence exerted by such men as A.C. Anson, John M. Ward, John Morrill, John Clarkson, Edward Williamson, James O'Rourke, Thomas Keefe, Arthur Irwin, and a score of others, whose records have been equally bright and honorable, the elevation of the profession is in a great measure due. The wide-spread popularity of the game, and its subsequent establishment upon business principles, enabled professional clubs to remunerate their players at a rate which such professions as the law, medicine, surgery, the ministry, and others to which the eyes of the average college student are taught to look, were unable to offer to one in one hundred of their followers. The result is just what might have been expected. The ranks of professional ball players to-day embrace men who were once intended for the bar, the pulpit, the operating table, the sick-room and the dental chair, and while these men no doubt possessed the ability to one day shine in the professions for which they had been trained, it is a question whether they would have so quickly obtained such a pecuniary reward as their efforts upon the ball field have earned.

In the minds of some people who still regard ignorance and immorality as the leading characteristics of the ball player, the men who wear the uniforms of the professional are classed as objectionable people of ordinary mental and undeveloped moral caliber. Gradually, however, this erroneous idea is being dispelled, for the shining lights of the ball field to-day are men of more than ordinary ability and intelligence, possessed of a keen regard for the amenities of social life, and whose morals in many instances might be proven far in advance of those of their critics, A quick mind, strength of purpose, close application to work, the ability to grasp constantly changing and unexpected situations, power of execution, and, above all, abstemious and exemplary habits are the requisites of a ball player.

Many of them have wives and children whom they have surrounded with all the comforts, and not a few of the luxuries of life; many of them own their own homes, purchased with the proceeds of their own industry and attention to work; and others have striven nobly under the burden of helpless fathers, mothers, sisters and brothers, that they might render happy the declining years of the former, and educate the latter.

3. Measuring Fielders

MANAGED BY ALBERT G. SPALDING, who also pitched for the club and would later become a sporting goods titan, the 1876 Chicago White Stockings won the first ever National League championship. The club finished 52–14 and attracted droves to its 23rd Street Grounds ballpark (bounded by State Street and present-day Cermak).

Only five years removed from the 1871 Chicago fire that had caused the White Stockings to halt play for two seasons, the 1876 National League championship showed that Chicagoans not only loved their squad but followed baseball closely. This seems evident in the following *Chicago Times* article, which championed new statistical methods for measuring fielders' and base runners' performance. Baseball is a sport known for statistical analysis, and as early as the 1870s readers of daily papers seemed interested in using statistics to measure players' work. The method the *Times* advocated for assessing a fielder's performance is still in use. This method measures "the fielding record . . . upon the only true and equitable basis—that of fielding chances."

Fall Field Sport

Chicago Times, October 1, 1876

BASE-BALL

A GLANCE AT THE RECORD

The past week has brought the Chicago season of base-ball to a close, and has settled the championship race in favor of the home nine. At length the multitude of base-ball lovers in this city who have sighed and groaned

Leading nine for the Cubs in 1877—coming off of the National League pennant win of 1876. Working clock-wise from center-top and then ending with Spalding in the middle: Ross Barnes, John Peters, Cap Anson, George Bradley, Charlie Waitt, Paul Hines, Cal McVey, John Glenn, and Al Spalding.

for the possession of the champion nine are unmeasurably gratified at the realization of hopes which have outlived the failures of half a dozen years to win the coveted trophy. *The Times*, on last Thursday, simultaneous with its account of the closing game, published a full and accurate summary of all the championship games played by the White Stockings this year. A general glance at that summary and a few comments upon some of the most prominent features which it set forth will not be uninteresting to the Sunday readers of this paper. In the first place it may be necessary to refer to those points in the summary which have originated with *The Times* and are, perhaps, not thoroughly understood by the general reader of baseball statistics. Those who have studied the summaries of the several series which have appeared in the paper from time to time must have noticed that a player's fielding record or his [batting record show us how players are doing].

AVERAGE ERRORS WERE NOT COMPUTED on the basis of the number of games in which he has participated, as is still the custom with papers which have not advanced to an accurate and scientific treatment of base-ball records. Time was when the average of base hits was computed by dividing the number of base hits by the number of games in which a player had played. It gradually dawned upon base ball scorers that the results so obtained were not a fair criterion of a player's batting ability. It was observed that some players came to bat oftener than others, that is, they had more batting opportunities. It was found that a computation of a player's batting average upon any other basis than the number of his times at bat was unfair, and scorers now [do compute] that feature of the game. Why is not the computation of a player's average of errors based upon the number of games in which he has participated similarly unfair?

IT IS REALLY AS ERRONEOUS a method as basing a player's batting average upon the number of his games. *The Times* has introduced a system which entirely overcomes this difficulty and gives each player his true and exact average. A glance at a fielding record computed upon the number of games instantly shows the unfairness of the old method. For instance, in a table of the Athletic and Chicago series, made up after the old fashion, [Oscar] Bielaski's average of errors is but 25 per cent, while [Deacon] White's, who stands at the bottom of the list, is 112 per cent, yet Bielaski put out but four men and assisted but once, while White put out 88 men and assisted nine times. Bielaski stood in the field, and it was but seldom that the ball was knocked his way, while White, on the other hand, was constantly handling the ball, or, in other words, having constant opportunities to make errors and yet [in] his record made up by dividing the number of his errors by the number of his games he stands far below Bielaski. Bielaski, in the same table, stands ahead of Anson, Spalding, [Paul] Hines, [John] Peters, [John] Glenn, [Ross] Barnes, [Bob] Addy, and White, a circumstance which hardly accords with the fact that the White Stockings have dispensed with his services. [Cal] McVey in the same table is shown to have put out 71 men; that is, he had that number of fielding chances in each of which an error might have been made. Notwithstanding this he [averages] eight per cent better in his fielding record than Bielaski, who had but five chances to make errors.

THE TRUE WAY is to compute a player's fielding average upon his number of fielding chances. *The Times* has introduced the method, and it will eventually be adopted, as the computation of batting upon the number of times at bat has been adopted. A player's fielding chances are made up of the number of times he has put out opponents, the number of times he has assisted in their being put out, and the number of his errors. Whenever he does either of these he handles the ball—has a fielding chance. Now, by adding the "put outs," "assisted," and "errors" together, the number of a player's fielding chances is arrived at: in other words, the number of his opportunities to commit errors. If his errors are now divided by this total his exact fielding average will be obtained. Every player will accordingly be judged, not by the number of games he has played, in some of which the ball hasn't been his in his direction at all, but by the number of opportunities he has had to make misplays. The justice and correctness of this method will recommend its general adoption. It has already been taken up by *The Boston Herald*. It will be seen that "fielding chances" is not a matter of mere speculation, but one of mathematical precision.

ANOTHER FEATURE introduced in *The Times* tables is that of base-running. A word in the way of speculation. Runs are made up of base-hits on the one side, and errors on the other. A total of these gives the number of chances a club had for making runs. In the summary of the season the

Chicagos made 146 base-hits against the Athletics, and the Athletics made 99 errors. In other words, the Chicagos [had] 245 chances. Divide this by the number of their runs, 105, and the result is 2.33, which constitutes their average number of chances necessary to produce a run. In this manner an estimate of their base-running is arrived at. . . .

ANOTHER IMPORTANT FEATURE brought out by *The Times* is "the percentage of runs to times at first base." A player may make a base-hit, but it does him no good if he gets no further than first. He may reach first base either by a base-hit or on account of an error by his opponents. The aggregate of base-hits and first base on errors shows the number of times at first base. Divide the number of runs by this sum and the percentage of runs to times at first is obtained. . . .

The average fielding record showed the percentage of errors which the Chicagos individually made in playing with every other club, computed, of course, on their fielding chances. McVey leads the list, and it will be seen that his play was very even throughout. Peters' stands next and shows very even play.

4. "Cap"

IN THE EARLY 1920S, sportswriter Grantland Rice called long-time Cub and eventual Hall of Famer Adrian "Cap" Anson the "Grand Old Man" of baseball. In 1939 Cooperstown labeled him "the greatest hitter and the greatest National League player-manager of the nineteenth century." And in the first selection here, a 1980 biographical article from *Palimpsest,* David L. Porter calls Anson baseball's "first superstar performer."

Anson's career lasted twenty-seven seasons, ended with a batting average of .333, and included five pennants in the 1880s as a player and "captain-manager" of the Chicago White Stockings (Cubs). It also saw him get at least partial credit for such baseball innovations as signaling batters, using fielders to back up one another, rotating pitchers, and utilizing a third base coach. Anson was also an early innovator of what became known as the hit-and-run. In addition, some credit him, along with White Stockings President Albert Spalding, with initiating pre-season training for baseball teams in a warm climate.

Yet, as Porter notes, Anson's racial views have scarred his legend.[1] Anson held disdain for African Americans and Irishmen, among others. Baseball Hall of Famer Hugh Duffy, who played for the Cubs in 1888 and 1889, complained to the *Chicago Tribune* that Anson had "no use for the players who had Irish blood in their veins and never lost an opportunity to insult those men who have played with him in the past."[2] As was the case with teammate Jimmy Ryan, Duffy came to "despise the leader that he had once so admired."[3] Though it's hard to say with certainty, Duffy's Irish heritage might very well have been the key thing that kept him from continuing to play in Chicago (and it was Chicago's loss, for Duffy tallied 100 or more RBIs in eight seasons in Boston and, in 1894 with the Beaneaters, won the Triple Crown while registering the best batting average in Major League Baseball history, .438).

An "Old Judge" baseball card depicting Cap Anson. New York City's Goodwin & Company became one of the nation's first firms to use baseball cards to advertise product—in this case, its popular "Old Judge" and "Gypsy Queen" cigarettes. Cap Anson did smoke "ten or twelve cigars a day" up to the early 1880s but then, he claimed, quit tobacco altogether (David L. Fleitz, *Cap Anson: the Grand Old Man of Baseball* [Jefferson: McFarland & Company, 2005], 232).

Even with Anson's many on-field successes and innovations, the second selection here shows that by 1897, in the rough-and-tumble world of sports, the legend faced fans who were clamoring for him to retire. In this instance, "Charley Horse," a pseudonym taken on by the anonymous baseball fan who penned the selection, argues for Pop to hang 'em up. As it happened, his last job in the majors, a brief one with the New York Giants, came less than a year later.

Incidentally, the choice of the name "Charley Horse" by this anonymous fan was fitting in a way since a number of things suggest that the phrase—which is still used to describe muscle cramps—was conjured by Cubs player Joe Quest in the latter part of the 1880s. He used the phrase for the hobbling muscle tightening that he and fellow Cubs base-runners would endure.[4]

Sadly, Anson's sunset years were marked by destitution, disappointment, and failure. His firing eventually led to a bitter falling out with his old friend Albert Spalding, and in 1920 he lost out on the new job of baseball commissioner to Judge Kenesaw Mountain Landis. But the discipline-minded Anson remained married to his wife and continued working into his final days. Anson's career stats and contributions to baseball remain noteworthy, and his impact on the early history of the Cubs was considerable.

Cap Anson of Marshalltown: Baseball's First Superstar

David L. Porter, *Palimpsest* 61: 4, 1980

Lo! From the tribunes on the bleachers comes a shout,
beseeching bold Ansonius to line 'em out;
and as Apollo's flying chariot cleaves the sky,
so stanch Ansonius lifts the brightened ball on high.

Nicknamed "Cap," "Unk," "Pop," and even "Pappy," Adrian Anson of Marshalltown was baseball's first superstar performer. The "bold Ansonius" of sportswriter Eugene Field's verse earned fame on baseball diamonds and in clubhouses at a time when the game became America's national pastime. Indeed, for better or worse, Anson and a few of his contemporaries gave professional baseball much of its modern character.

Born in 1852, young Anson learned the fundamentals of the game from his father, an amateur third baseman who organized the first Marshalltown Baseball Club. After a brief stint at the University of Iowa, he transferred to Notre Dame University in 1869; there he excelled as a second baseman. Anson was a poor student, however, and soon quit school. Returning to Marshalltown in 1870, Anson continued to play baseball for his father's club, which also included Adrian's brother Sturgis. Marshalltown in 1870 attracted considerable publicity by playing an excellent team from Rockford, Illinois in a exhibition game. The Rockford club was one of the nation's premier teams, having an outstanding pitcher in Albert Spalding, and often scored over 100 runs a game. Marshalltown astonished the visitors from Illinois by losing only 18–3, as Adrian played well both at bat and in the field. "They put up a rattling game, especially the two (Anson) sons," Spalding commented, "and they were the hardest fighters I ever saw in my life."

Launching his professional baseball career while still a teenager in 1871, Anson signed a contract for $66.66 per month with a newly-founded Rockford, Illinois team. "It was a fairly good salary for a ball player," Anson recalled in his memoirs, "and especially for one who was only eighteen years old and a green lad at that." Anson played third base and led Rockford in batting, but the club finished in last place in the National Association and disbanded at the end of the 1871 season.

From Rockford, Anson traveled east in 1872 to play for the Philadelphia Athletics of the same National Association. Here he received a more lucrative contract of $1,250 annually, which was boosted to $1,800 after he performed well in the club. Although primarily a third baseman, Anson played all infield and outfield positions and frequently even caught.

In Philadelphia Anson became embroiled in baseball's first contract dispute. When the National League was formed in 1876, Chicago entered a club named the White Stockings. The previous year, club president William A. Hulbert had secretly signed six players from the rival National Association, including Anson of Philadelphia. He had agreed to play for the White Stockings for $2,000—$200 more than he was receiving from the Athletics. Hulbert hoped to keep the signings secret because the players legally were still under contract to their National Association clubs, but the *Chicago Tribune* published the story in late summer 1876.

Before the 1876 season began, however, Anson sought a release from his new contract with the White Stockings, for the Athletics had offered to increase his salary from $1,800 to $2,500. It was a raise that he simply could not refuse. Explaining that his fiancée Virginia did not want to leave Philadelphia, Anson requested but was denied a release from the Chicago contract. Anson journeyed to Chicago twice to persuade Hulbert and team friend Albert Spalding—another of the six ballplayers jumping to the Chicago club—to release him from the agreement. On his second trip Anson even offered to pay the Chicago club $1,000 in return for his release. The offer astonished both Hulbert and Spalding, but they still declined to release Anson. "A man who will give a thousand dollars rather than break his word," Hulbert commented, "must be a good man to have."

Still determined to secure his release, Anson watched the White Stockings in the first practice dressed in a Prince Albert coat, striped trousers, and fashionable hat. Anson grew impatient after watching for a few minutes and asked hurler Spalding to throw him a few pitches. Spalding refused to honor the request until Anson took off his coat and hat.

Cap Anson not only practiced in the remainder of practice that day, but stayed with the White Stockings for the next twenty-two years. In his rookie season with Chicago, Anson continued as a third baseman and helped the White Stockings win the National League pennant. The 1876 club still ranks as one of the best in baseball history, winning 52 of 66 games or nearly 79 percent of its contests. Pitcher Spalding won 47 of those games while Anson compiled an impressive .343 batting average with 59 runs batted in.

Over his entire career, Anson had a remarkable .333 batting average. In 27 seasons he had 3,041 hits, a figure surpassed by only eleven players. [There is some discrepancy over his total number of hits.—Ed.] He holds a major league record for hitting at least .300 in 25 of 27 seasons, including his final season at age 46. The first player to make 3,000 hits, he won the National League batting title twice and finished second four times. Anson was also a power hitter, pounding 96 home runs and driving in over 1,700 runs in a dead ball era. Larger physically than most of his contemporaries, the six-foot, 227-pound Anson menaced his opponents with a 44-ounce bat to the end of his long career.

With his good eye and his strength, Anson became one of the great hitters in the game's history. He proved himself competent in other playing categories as well. Although a slow runner and only an average first baseman, he nevertheless enjoyed great moments in the field. He led National League first basemen in fielding six times and was the first player to make two unassisted plays in the same game.

For all of his contributions to the game, unfortunately Anson also established an unwritten rule banning black players from organized baseball. His rigid belief in the segregation of black and white players and his enormous popularity discouraged other owners from recruiting blacks. While managing the White Stockings in 1884, Anson threatened to remove his team from the field during a game against a Toledo team that included a black player, Moses Fleetwood Walker. The Toledo management insisted that Walker play even if it meant a forfeit by the White Stockings for refusing to play. Several years later, however, Anson again threatened to take his squad off the field, this time against a Newark minor league club unless its black pitcher, George Stovey, left the field. Later Anson persuaded the New York Giants to cancel plans to promote Stovey to the major leagues, and—according to baseball historian David Quentin Voigt—used "all the venom . . . of a Tillman or a Vardaman" to achieve his end. (Benjamin F. Tillman of South Carolina and James K. Vardaman of Mississippi were rabid segregationists in the United State Senate in the late nineteenth century).

As manager, Anson was a strict, gruff, outspoken taskmaster; he disciplined players for drinking violations, required top physical conditioning, and even made legendary night bed checks. He insisted that his players wear suits, abstain from liquor and tobacco, and stay at reputable hotels. Although well-respected, he was regarded as a domineering manager by many players. A serious-minded team leader, Anson also stressed honesty and dignity among his players. After his team lost one very erratically played game, a suspicious spectator telegrammed Anson inquiring whether the contest was "on the level." "I would not disgrace my players by showing them your telegram," Anson tartly replied, "nor degrade myself by answering your question."

Anson managed and captained the Chicago White Stockings from 1879 to 1897, and is considered the premier manager of the late nineteenth century. His apprenticeship for the post took place between 1876 and 1878, when he served as the team's captain and player-coach. Ranking in tenth place among baseball managers, Anson won nearly 1,300 games and compiled a .575 lifetime won-lost percentage. In the years 1879–1886 Anson directed the White Stockings to five National League pennants: the club won consecutive championships from 1880 to 1882 and won again in 1885 and 1886. During the next five seasons, the White Stockings finished in second place three times and in third place twice.

Stressing aggressive team play under Anson's leadership, the White Stockings compiled other impressive records as well. In 1880 they set a yet-unsurpassed record of winning 67 games, or nearly 80 percent of their contests. In September 1883, the team sent 23 players to the plate in one inning against Detroit, scoring 18 runs on 18 hits. The next year Anson's club hit 140 home runs, the highest team total until Babe Ruth's legendary 1927 New York Yankees. Considered an exceptional judge of baseball talent, Anson developed many important players, including pitchers Larry Corcoran, John Clarkson,

Jim McCormick, and Clark Griffith, as well as outfielders Mike "King" Kelly, Ed Williamson, William Lange, and fellow Iowan Billy Sunday.

Anson made several innovations in the game during his career. In 1886 the White Stockings manager required his players to train for three weeks in the South before beginning the regular season. Soon other major league baseball clubs were employing spring training seasons. Anson also introduced the daring "hit and run" strategy—having the batter try to advance the runner an extra base without concern for his own average. Besides encouraging base stealing, he developed the baseline coaching box and invented both offensive and defensive signals. Anson's idea of rotating pitchers encouraged opposing teams to try the strategy, especially when Anson's club won five pennants in seven years.

Throughout his years as a player, Anson served as a goodwill ambassador for baseball abroad. In 1874 Anson's Philadelphia Athletics made a thirty-day tour of England, playing fourteen exhibition games against the championship Boston club. Although not familiar with cricket, the American players had such batting skills that they defeated the premier Marylebone All-English Eleven and another British team. Fourteen years later, the Chicago White Stockings and ten National League All-Stars made a six-month tour playing numerous baseball exhibitions around the world. Accompanied by their wives, the players visited Hawaii, Australia, Ceylon, Egypt, Italy, France, and England, and received a cordial welcome everywhere. "[They] created interest in the game," tour organizer Spalding said, "in countries where it had never been seen before."

In the 1890s Anson began to experience an increasing number of problems as a player-manager. During the late 1880s, the White Stockings sold stars Mike Kelly and John Clarkson to Boston. The formation of the rival Players' League in 1890 further depleted Anson's once-stellar team, which was renamed the Chicago Colts. The hapless Colts did not finish above fourth place for the rest of the decade. Chicago sportswriters chided "Old Man Anson" for the failings on the field and boldly hinted that he should retire as a player. In a game on September 4, 1891, the 39-year-old Anson retaliated by wearing broad, long whiskers covering the letters on the front of his uniform and made three hits. He insisted on being awarded first base in the second inning after one pitch hit his whiskers, but the umpire refused to oblige. "And even if it had hit them," umpire Tom Lynch replied, "they aren't really yours and you couldn't take first base just because somebody else's whiskers got hit." The *Chicago Tribune* remarked that "the grand old man of baseball was hurling defiance into the teeth of age by aping its appearance." Although Chicago sportswriters and spectators became increasingly disenchanted with the team's declining performance over the years, manager Anson continued playing first base until 1897, when he quit at age 46 after 28 years as a player.

(The whiskers incident was not the only humorous escapade involving the usually very serious Anson. In a home game against Louisville during the 1890s, a Louisville player hit a sharp ground ball to Chicago shortstop Bill Dahlen. Dahlen threw the ball wildly over first baseman Anson's head. After hitting the base of the stands, the ball bounced toward right field. Anson chased the ball into right field until a sway-backed horse owned by a Chicago grounds keeper escaped from a fenced area behind the clubhouse and galloped toward the first baseman. Anson promptly gave up on retrieving the ball and ran for safety, while the runner circled the bases and scored the winning run. No ground rule existed limiting the number of bases that a runner could take when a fielder was being chased by a horse.)

Quarreling with umpires was another Anson trait and he often used "brawling, bullying tactics" against game officials, according to the *New York Times*. Anson has "a voice in his impassioned moments like a hundred Bulls of Bashan," and—as sportswriter Ira L. Smith noted—"the spectators love to see him face up the umpires" and "go wild when he clashes with the officiators. Whenever there is the slightest cause for a difference of opinion, he leaves his place at bat, on the coach's line, or at first base and roars into a presentation of his argument." National League President Nicholas E. Young, who fined Anson $110 for misconduct in 1886, said "he has walked a hundred miles up and down the first base path in mild deprecation of the umpire's decisions."

Anson also frequently engaged in spirited conflicts with team officials. He strongly disliked James A. Hart, a businessman named by owner Albert Spalding as White Stockings club President in 1891. Previously Spalding had given Anson a free hand in field operations. After all, the manager was in the fourth year of a ten-year contract and owned 130 shares of stock in the club. Anson aspired to become club president and now insisted that the younger Hart not infringe upon his managerial authority. In an attempt to placate Anson, Spalding assured Anson that Hart would only be a figurehead and that Anson would be retained as manager. In truth, Spalding intended to let

Hart operate the club, and increasingly during the 1890s Hart compromised Anson's control over daily operations. To Anson's dismay, Hart repeatedly blocked player deals and did not back his manager in disciplining players. And to make matters worse, Anson's once powerful club continued to founder in the standings. Writers and fans were growing more and more impatient.

In February 1898, Hart fired Anson. Anson's ten-year contract had expired a month earlier, and Hart had concluded that Anson was no longer useful to the club. He needed only Spalding's consent to remove the veteran manager. Spalding hoped to retain Anson, but Hart already had committed the club to name Tommy Burns as replacement and threatened to quit unless Anson was replaced. Spalding considered Hart a very able businessman, and thus reluctantly consented to the dismissal of Anson and named Burns as manager. In a fitting gesture, the Chicago Colts were renamed "the Orphans" to symbolize the departure of their nineteen-year manager.

Spalding meanwhile offered Anson an opportunity to establish and preside over a baseball college for training young players, but the veteran manager rejected the offer. Spalding also arranged with the Chicago Athletics Club a testimonial dinner designed to raise a pension worth thousands of dollars for Anson. On the day prior to the event, however, Anson learned of the dinner and ordered Spalding to cancel the testimonial. "This I refused to accept," Anson stated, "for the reason that I was not a pauper, the public owed me nothing, and I believed that I was still capable of making my own living."

That same year, Anson made a fruitless attempt to become the controlling stockholder of the Chicago team. On February 15, Spalding agreed to sell Anson 1,000 shares of stock at $150 per share and set a sixty-day deadline for the transaction. Anson worked diligently to raise the amount by the April 15 deadline, but failed to acquire the needed funds for the purchase. In his memoirs, Anson charged "there was never any intention on the part of A.G. Spalding and his confrères to let me get possession of the club." Anson claimed that he had trusted Spalding too much and thereafter did not continue cordial relations with his once close friend.

Ousted from his Chicago Club, with little chance of assuming front-office responsibilities, Anson did not remain in baseball much longer. The New York Giants selected Anson as field manager with the guarantee that he would have full control of the team, but Anson resigned after three weeks charging that owner Andrew Freedman had interfered too much in daily operations.

Later he attempted to revive the American Association, an older baseball league, but was unable to convince his former colleagues in the Orphans front office that the city of Chicago could support two rival franchises.

Anson remained active in sports nonetheless, operating both a billiard hall and a bowling alley in Chicago. Himself an outstanding bowler and billiards player, the former major leaguer captained a team in the 1904 American Bowling Congress Championships. When his businesses faltered—because of strikes by workers and because business associates often took advantage of him—Anson turned to politics and enjoyed brief success in public life. Elected City Clerk in 1905, Anson gleefully told reporters, "I'm just as pleased as I'd won another pennant." After serving two years, however, Anson met defeat in a bid for re-election.

His hard times continued. In January 1909 Anson was summoned to appear in municipal court for owing $111 to a Chicago wrecking company. Admitting that he was "busted," Anson told the judge that he was "getting on as best as he could, and wasn't going to worry because he never got anything." The judge, who had watched Anson play baseball years earlier, dismissed the citation. Leaving the courtroom, Anson remarked, "There is still another inning," and received a round of applause from spectators. Despite this temporary reprieve, Anson eventually saw his Chicago home foreclosed.

Anson managed a semi-professional baseball team that toured the Midwest in 1909 and 1910, but this endeavor likewise was unprofitable. In an attempt to restore his assets, Anson starred in a much-criticized play entitled "The Runaway Colt." He also appeared in a slapstick vaudeville act, during which he wore green whiskers and sang chorus, "We're Ten Chubelin Tipperary Turks." National League President John K. Tener attempted to establish a pension fund for Anson, but the former Chicago manager rejected the plan as another charity move. More insulting, perhaps, in 1920 baseball club owners chose Judge Kenesaw Mountain Landis over Anson for the newly created position of Commissioner of Baseball.

Two years later, while managing Chicago's Dixmoor Golf Club, Anson was stricken with a glandular ailment and had to be rushed to the hospital. Surgical efforts to relieve his painful condition proved unsuccessful and on April 18, 1922 the legendary slugger was dead.

News of Anson's death spread quickly throughout Chicago and then across the nation. Players and fans looked back on his career with both awe and affection, all of them aware of his immense impact on the sport. Albert Spalding lauded him as "one of the greatest ballplayers that ever lived . . . a man who was as good as his bond," while pitcher Cy Young claimed "they never made any greater or better players." Sportswriter Grantland Rice praised Anson as "The Grand Old Man of Baseball" and lamented that "there is none in sight who will ever quite take his place." A year after his death, Anson's friends erected a monument in his honor at Chicago's Oakwood Cemetery, where he is buried.

The ultimate tribute came in 1939 when Anson was elected to the National Baseball Hall of Fame in Cooperstown, New York. According to his plaque in Cooperstown, the young man from Marshalltown had become "the greatest hitter and greatest National League player-manager of the nineteenth century." Anson's innovative leadership and aggressive style put him in the select company of the game's great pioneers—including Connie Mack and John McGraw—men who helped transform a sandlot sport into the national pastime.

Open Letter to Anson

"Charley Horse," *Chicago Daily Tribune*, July 5, 1897

BASEBALL FAN THINKS VETERAN MANAGER SHOULD RETIRE

———

**Tells the Colts' Leader He Has Had a Long and Honorable Career, but Should Now Give Way to a Younger Man—
Says the Poor Showing of the Team is to Be Laid Solely to Anson's Door—
Has Prejudices Concerning Players.**

———

Chicago, July 4—A. C. Anson, Manager Chicago Baseball Club—Dear Sir: You also want to know "What's the matter with the Chicago club?" It appears. In this interrogative conception you have at last come into touch with the baseball public. The latter has been asking the question of you for several weeks without receiving a satisfactory answer. Now you join in the chorus yourself, and ask of the winds, "What's the matter with the Chicago club?"

Well, what is the matter? If you, the sole responsible manager of the club do not know, you must expect to be told, with more candor, perhaps, than you will relish. It will be the sole object of this open letter to express frankly that which you should know, if baseball is to continue to prosper in Chicago, and if the stock holders who pay you a large salary are to continue to receive returns on their investment.

You have seen the aggression of stars under your management lose game after game without apparent reason. A constant dwindling of public interest in the club and a falling off in attendance at games have cut you to the quick, and you suddenly develop a vituperative facility heretofore unknown to your close friends. You abuse members of the club indiscriminately, roast some of its most deserving members unmercifully, and then go to bag No. 1 with an air of uninjured innocence and lose another game.

Has it ever occurred to you that the other fourteen members of the team are not wholly to blame for the disgraceful record made this spring? Has it ever occurred to you to consider your own qualifications as player and manager? Second basemen, pitchers, and others have their day and become back numbers. Do first basemen and managers ever go through the same experience?

Says Anson Has Seen His Best Days.

The writer has been and is now one of your most sincere admirers. In common with the Chicago baseball public I have the greatest respect for your sterling qualities as a man and a sportsman. Your individual career, ever characterized by honest and earnest endeavor, has been, perhaps, the most potent single factor of all in making the American national game what it is today. And you have won laurels as batsman and baseman which few will ever merit. But, sir, while we hold you in the highest esteem for your past achievements and for your present admirable qualities, we have long known—though reluctant to declare it to you—that you have seen your best days. For one of your age you are a magnificent specimen of the manly virtues. But neither in temperament nor muscular activity are you qualified to retain longer the place you have filled with much credit to yourself and your adopted city.

That there may be no mistake about your responsibility for the Chicago baseball club you will pardon me for calling your attention to one or two facts about which you knew well enough, but of which many are ignorant. First, and above all, you are the sole and absolute manager. James A. Hart is nominally your superior. So is Mr. Spalding. But you know that Hart is engaged in other business ventures with Spalding, that it is a part of your contract that you shall have absolute control of the team, that you can release, buy, sell, fine, suspend, and do what you please with them, and furthermore, that you have had, and continue to have, such absolute control without hindrance of any sort—even advice—from your employers.

ALLUDES TO INDIVIDUAL CASES.

You can blame no one but yourself. If the team is a failure it is your own doing. You may blame them individually or collectively, as you please. But if they are what you have said why did you get them and why do you keep them?

The fact of the matter is that now you are not a good judge of ball players—if you ever were. You would not trade Walter Thornton for the whole league. Yet Thornton has been a miserable failure. You stick to him because he is a gentlemanly fellow, faithful in morning practice, and one to whom you have taken a personal liking.

On the other hand, you want to get rid of Dahlen. You are willing to trade him, sell him, almost to give him away. We all know Dahlen's weak points. He may sulk at times, but every baseball man in the country except yourself knows he is a star at short, and nearly indispensable if Chicago hopes to have a winning team. If Dahlen would truckle to you it is good betting that you would value him above Thornton. Would you?

It is well enough to have your personal likes and dislikes in private affairs, but when you are employed by the stockholders of the Chicago baseball club to look out for their interests you should lay personal prejudices to one side, and do your duty like a man of intelligence.

The most competent critics all over the country admit unanimously that the Chicago club as individually constituted should be a winner. It may be that you were "gold bricked" by Herbert Briggs with his lame back, and that Friend should have known better than to let you exile him to Kansas City for several weeks, but the team is as well off, or better, than any in the league as regards the condition of its players, and hard luck stories don't go. If the team were to put up at auction today it would bring more than several which are higher in the percentage table.

LACK OF SPIRIT IN THE TEAM.

In one word, there is a lack of "espirit" in the team—a listlessness and don't-care feeling which has lost game after game. For this no one but yourself can justly be held responsible. The Chicagos run bases like wooden men. You sit idly on the bench yourself, without caring, apparently, whether there is any one on the coach lines or not. Often there is no one there unless the bleachers yell for it. Even the enthusiasm all comes from the spectators.

Line your men up at practice this morning, Mr. Anson, and put the question to them. They will answer frankly, if they answer at all, that they don't care much whether the team wins or not. Each has a certain regard for his professional records, but there is nearly an absolute disregard of team play, and the former suffers through the dry rot engendered by the latter.

Why is it you have ceased to inspire your men with confidence and enthusiasm? Because, sir, chiefly, of injustice toward deserving members of the team and your favoritism towards others, I have mentioned Thornton and Dahlen already. Allow me to name another instance. You have criticized McCormick, and the baseball public and McCormick's fellow-players know him to be as earnest and conscientious a worker as there is to be found on the field.

As to your own qualifications on the field, you no longer bat with your old vigor, you can't run bases, you can't play first as well as Decker, and certainly you can't manage the Chicago club much longer without the stockholders making a row.

There is one thing you can do, however, with good grace. That is, retire on the comfortable fortune you have amassed in the business and give a younger and more nimble man a chance to pull the club out of the slough of despond into which you have led it. Sincerely your friend,

CHARLEY HORSE.

5. The $10,000 Beaut!

ACCORDING TO AUTHOR JAMES COX, Michael J. "King" Kelly was Babe Ruth before Babe Ruth. This larger-than-life figure and one-time White Stocking played hard and dirty, lived fast and demanded exorbitant salaries, churned out magnificent seasons and popularized the slide. A song about him is considered one of America's first "pop hits." He was one of the first athletes hounded by fans for his autograph. He even starred on stage.

Kelly's rise to fame was swift and great, but he drank too much and his demise came about quickly. Still, here from Cox we get a picture of a burly Irishman that Chicagoans and Bostonians loved virtually to a man, even if umpires and baseball managers (on the field and in the front office) endured their fair share of "kicks" from Kelly, and even if he proved his own worst enemy.

Kelly moved from Chicago to the Boston Beaneaters in 1886 thanks to a record-setting overture from the eastern club and to Kelly's acrimonious relationships with Albert Spalding and Pop Anson. Part of the problem was Spalding practiced temperance, while Kelly certainly

An "Old Judge" baseball card depicting Mike "King" Kelly, and denoting his legendary price tag—paid by the Boston Beaneaters to bring him to *The Hub.*

did not. As an indication of Kelly's footloose ways, when he had first come to Chicago he moved into the Palmer House—where the good times were known to roll. Still, before leaving the Windy City, Kelly produced aplenty, winning two batting titles and leading the league in runs three times in a row from 1884 to 1886. During that time he saw the club move from Lakefront Park (1878–84), the same site as the one previously destroyed by the Chicago fire, to the "West Side Park I" (in which it played from 1885 to 1891).[1]

Following Cox's article is the *Boston Globe*'s 1894 coverage of Kelly's all-too-soon death, which came at the age of thirty-seven and at a time when "King Kel" was broke. Nonetheless, Kelly stoked the passions of baseball fans the world-over (he went on Spalding's world baseball tour in 1889). His life shows that before the "Sultan of Swat," before the United States' more complete break with its Victorian past, Americans celebrated the raucous "King of Steal" . . . only Kelly didn't know when to stop celebrating.

When Fans Roared "Slide, Kelly, Slide!" at the Old Ballgame

James A. Cox, *Smithsonian* 13: 7, 1982

He was a scourge of umpires and a miscreant on the base paths,
but no one ever played baseball with more verve—or more creativity.

It's the 12th inning in Boston and the score is tied. The Beaneaters have the bases full, with two outs. Any kind of a hit will score a run and win the game. But twilight is slipping into darkness. And if Cap Anson's champion Chicago White Stockings can get that last out, the game will be called on account of darkness.

The Chicago pitcher goes into the windup. In the grandstand, the "kranks"—as baseball fans were called in the 1880s—lean forward and squint their eyes to see in the thickening dusk. Bat meets ball with a *crack!* A grayish blur rips on a line toward right field and disappears into the gloom. The Chicago right fielder—a fellow named Kelly—leaps high in the air, grabs with two hands, gives a great shout of exultation and trots off the field to the clubhouse.

"Three out!" cries the umpire. "Game called on account of darkness!" In the clubhouse, the White Stockings compliment Kelly on his catch. One of them asks where the ball is. "How the hell would I know?" he answers with a grin. "It went a mile over me head!"

Now it's the ninth inning in Chicago, Detroit at bat, two down, a runner at second, and the White Stockings ahead by a run. The Detroit batter slaps a shot up the alley in left. The base runner rounds third as the left fielder retrieves the ball. It will be a whisker-close play. But what's this? The Chicago catcher—Kelly again—drops his glove and turns away from the plate, as if the outfielder has caught the ball for the third out. Taken in, the runner slows to a trot. Whereupon the devious catcher whips around, catches the incoming throw, and slaps the ball on the runner for the out.

Chicago again, with Kelly, the White Stockings catcher, on the bench this day, nursing a monumental hangover. His team is ahead and needs one more out to clinch the victory. The St. Louis batter swings and squirts a low foul fly in the direction of the White Stockings bench. The substitute catcher starts after it but gives up—he hasn't a prayer of catching it. The lad with the headache leaps to his feet, shouts to the umpire, "Kelly now catching for Chicago!" and gathers the pop fly in. The St. Louis players scream and so does the outraged ump, but the grinning Kelly cites the rule book: a player can be substituted at any point in the game, simply by notifying the umpire. The play stands, the game is over—and shortly thereafter the rule book is changed.

We have just witnessed three highlights (if they can be called that) from the career of Michael J. (for Joseph) "King" Kelly, the most colorful, audacious, electrifying, daring, crafty, and *creative* player ever to drive an umpire batty in baseball's formative years.

As Alfred P. Cappio points out in his monograph, "Slide, Kelly, Slide," it may be hard for those weaned on Frank Merriwell and Horatio Alger to believe, but Kelly—the antithesis of almost everything the moralistic writers of the Victorian age held up as the American ideal—was the greatest sports hero of his day. A darkly handsome, burly Irishman with thick hair, a fierce handlebar mustache and a wild, uninhibited personality, he was, writes one historian, "totally unfettered by English conceptions of good sportsmanship."

A MONOPOLY ON FANS' HEARTS UNTIL THE BABE

He was also a cigarette-smoking hot dog in pointy, high-button shoes who wore a tall hat tipped far enough over his eye so that any man would know at a glance that there was one hell of a fellow under it. Like so many star players of the early days, good times, good companions and good booze were the joys of life—and there came a time when the booze didn't have to be good, it just had to be there.

But he was also so fun-loving and generous, so sunny of disposition, that he found it difficult to make enemies. Men and small boys rushed up to him on the street just to touch his hand. Kranks everywhere turned out in droves to see him play. Even people who knew little about baseball, and cared less, crowded into the ball park when "King Kel" came to town. He dominated baseball in the 1880s, and would continue to do so in legend until Babe Ruth, another swaggering hero—known as the "Sultan of Swat"—came along to capture the hearts of the fans.

Part of King Kel's attraction was based on possibilities. You never knew when he was going to pull another outrageous trick that would set the whole baseball world buzzing. And on the other hand there was certainty that when the King got on base, excitement would follow. Mike didn't invent the slide. Other players had flopped down on their bellies or backsides in attempting to elude a baseman's tag. But it was Kelly who developed sliding into a fine art, to the delight of Chicago fans and the frustration of opposing infielders.

There is a stirring in the grandstand as Kelly approached the plate . . . a bubble of excited conversation as he takes his place in the batter's box . . . a *whoosh* of pent-up breath as the big right-handed hitter swings mightily and misses for a strike . . . a howl of delight as he knocks the next pitch over second for a single . . . and now for a roar of anticipation, for the King is on first and the next act in the drama is ready to unfold.

Every eye is on Kelly as he stands, a picture of studied casualness, on the base. No false starts, no jigging for him. Shoulders up, head back, a look of bland innocence on his face, he stares at the pitcher, who shows all the nervous signs of a man suddenly possessed with a case of the willies. Ten thousand throats create a waterfall of sound, half of them shouting at the pitcher to throw the ball, half of them beseeching the King to GO!

At last the ball spins toward the plate, and Kelly is off! The roar from the crowd is deafening. With fierce determination the catcher plucks the ball from his glove and hurls it to second. The shortstop spears the ball and turns grimly as Kelly thunders toward him. The kranks are on their feet, screaming the three words that have become the slogan of Chicago baseball: "Slide, Kelly, slide! Oh, slide, Kelly, S-L-I-D-E!" And Kelly does just that. Suddenly his body drops and a cloud of dust roils towards the base. The shortstop lunges. But Kelly's body isn't where it should be—it's off to one side—and his toe has hooked a corner of the bag. "Safe!" cries the umpire and the crowd cheers.

We call it the "hook" slide today, and even Little Leaguers know how to do it. Back then it was dubbed the "Chicago" slide, and the infielders sweated for months before they figured out how to handle it. And by that time the inventive King Kel had added some refinements, like sliding wide and late, and catching the bag with his hand when he went by. Or piling right into the baseman, feet jabbing his defenseless victim like a boxer's fists.

On one such occasion, Kelly roared into second, feet flying. "You're out!" shouted the umpire. Mike reached under his body, held up the ball—knocked loose by his famous slide—and inquired sweetly, "If I'm out, then what's this?"

But Kelly on second after a steal is only the start of the fun. Kranks who have seen him in action before seize the arms of their neighbors and cry excitedly, "Watch close. Now! You ain't seen *nothin'* yet!"

HIS WILES DROVE POOR UMPIRES WILD

The next batter hits a long single to right, Kelly starts for third, but is looking back over his shoulder. Why? To see what the umpire (there was only one in those days) is doing. If he is watching the play in the outfield, or running to first to call a play there, the King suddenly cuts past the pitcher's box (there was no mound then) and streaks for the plate. Everybody sees it but the hapless umpire, who hears the cries of rage from the opposing players and screams of delight from the stands. He *knows*, but he can't do anything about it because he didn't *see* it.

Kelly was also known to take a shortcut from first directly to third via the pitcher's box if the umpire's attention was directed elsewhere, and there is even an account of how he once scored from first without going within spitting distance of either second or third. Such tales credit his audacity but, for ingenuity (and causing the umpire fits), nothing can match the incredible play he created one afternoon in Detroit.

Once again, it's the ninth inning. The score is tied, there's one out, and Mike is at bat. He reaches first on a single. The next batter, shortstop Ed Williamson, draws a base on balls. The pair then executes a successful double steal and Kelly, as usual, slides into third. He leaps up clutching his arm and yowling in pain. All the White Stockings, including Williamson from second, rush over to see what's wrong. In the confusion, Kelly whispers some hurried instructions in Big Ed's ear, then breaks for the plate. Alertly, the Detroit third baseman zips the ball to the catcher, who has plenty of time to tag Mike out. But just before he reaches the plate, Kelly stops short and spreads his legs far apart. And as the catcher leans forward and tags him for the second out, Ed Williamson, running hot on his heels, dives through the King's outstretched legs to score the winning run! That one also kept the rule makers working overtime.

Mike Kelly was born in Troy, New York, an early baseball town, on December 31, 1857. His father died when he was still a boy, and his mother moved the family to Paterson, New Jersey. Young Mike left school early and got a job as a bobbin boy in one of the "Silk City's" many mills, but he spent every spare minute out on the sand lots, playing ball.

At 17, he joined the Paterson Olympics, the dominant semipro team in the area. In rapid succession he quit his job, signed with the Port Jervis, New York, team, moved quickly to play in Columbus, Ohio, then on to the Cincinnati Redlegs. As a rookie, he won a silver bat for the first home-park home run, and went on in 1879 to bat .348, alternating between catcher and outfielder.

A year later, Cap Anson signed Mike to a Chicago White Stockings contract. With a good team to back him, his legend took shape. Over the next seven years, the White Stockings won five league championships and Kelly was unofficially crowned "King Kel."

There were feelings of shock and betrayal when Albert G. Spalding, president of the White Stockings, sold the King to the Boston Nationals in 1887 for $10,000. It was a regal sum, an unbelievable sum for the period, probably ten times what the average man earned in a year. It was so unbelievable, in fact, that the Boston owners had the sales agreement reproduced in the newspapers. Sportswriters dubbed Kelly the "Ten-Thousand-Dollar Beauty," borrowing from the publicity releases of a stage lady of the time, and the city of Boston, teeming with Irish immigrants, went wild with joy.

King Kel, on the other hand, publicly wept and protested that he did not want to leave Chicago. But that was window dressing. Mike had no doubts about his huge value as a drawing card: he demanded a salary of $5,000, twice what Chicago had been paying him. The league owners, hungry for profits, had just established a $2,000 upper limit on player salaries, but the King was something special. Boston got around the new rule by giving him a $3,000 bonus for their right to use his picture in advertisements.

During his first ten days with the new club, Alfred Cappio writes, Kelly "made more hits, scored more runs, and stole more bases than the rest of the team put together." A few years later, Boston fans showed their jubilation over obtaining the greatest player of the age—and an Irishman, to boot!—by presenting Mike with a house, stable and land in Hingham, and a spiffy wagon and horse.

Even more touching was the "Welcome-home-we-miss-you" of the Chicago fans when the Beaneaters visited the Windy City for the first time that season. An enormous crowd filled the street around the hotel where the Boston team was to stay, waiting for the King to make an appearance. Kelly, true to form, had spent the long train ride cradling a whiskey bottle in his arms. He was probably still sleeping it off when the team carriage arrived at the hotel, but he woke up long enough to dazzle the crowd with his big smile during at least a part of the festivities. A local reporter enthused that "President Cleveland, or even the Queen herself, could hardly have had a more flattering ovation."

Festivities concluded, Mike's debut as a Beaneater in Chicago brought more than 10,000 people out to the park that June afternoon in 1887. It would be stretching the truth to say that, with two hits, he starred in the game, for the final score was Chicago 15, Boston 13. But the King went on to have his finest year, batting .394 and stealing 84 bases, even though his team straggled home in fifth place.

Win or lose, Kelly continued to reign as King of the Diamond during his years in Boston. Two years later, a song called *Slide, Kelly, Slide!* was published in his honor. It concluded: "If someone doesn't steal you,/and your batting doesn't fail you,/They'll take you to Australia!/Slide, Kelly, slide!" Despite the "spectacularly banal" lyrics, as they have been generously described, the song became as popular as the contemporary comic ballad, Ernest L. Thayer's "Casey at the Bat." In fact, included in the many versions of "Casey" are several that substitute "Kelly" for the hero's name and Boston for the storied town of Mudville. (Some years later, in 1927, *Slide, Kelly, Slide* again served as the title for a work honoring the King, this time an MGM film starring William Haines.)

Meanwhile, back in the real baseball world of Boston in the 1880s, Mike was, according to one observer, the sole center of attention for the fans who packed the park daily. And he seldom disappointed them.

There was the time, for example, when the Beaneaters were involved in a crucial game. The score was tied, there were two outs, and the winning run was at third, where the King was coaching. The Boston batter, no slugger, was laboring under a count of no balls and two strikes. Kelly signaled that he wanted to examine the ball. The pitcher ignored him. Kelly signaled again, adamantly. The umpire took a step and the pitcher underhanded the ball to Kelly—just as the King shrugged and turned away. The ball dribbled over to the stands, the runner on third scored, and King Kel made another entry in the book of baseball legends.

His creativity extended in more constructive directions, and he has been credited with establishing or popularizing enough baseball innovations to guarantee anybody a place in the Baseball Hall of Fame, to which he gained admission in 1945. The fact is, however, that his bronze plaque in Cooperstown, New York, does not list any of these supposed contributions, and some serious baseball historians consider them apocryphal. Nevertheless, they are a part of the King Kelly legend and, as such, until someone can make a better claim, they deserve at least this qualified mention. Here are the most important ones:

- First outfielder to back up his infielders.
- First right fielder to take a line drive on the bounce and throw out the batter at first base—a rare and exciting play still.
- First catcher to set up battery signals with his pitcher, and to signal the fielders what the pitcher would throw next.
- Inventor of the hit-and-run play (this was erroneously credited to the old Baltimore Orioles, who made good use of it but didn't create it).
- Innovator of the practice of having pitchers and catchers back up infielders to protect against overthrows to the various bases.
- First catcher to intentionally drop the new "birdcage" mask on the plate, or toss it in the path of an incoming runner to trip him or scare him or at least slow him up—not a glowing accomplishment, but a typical Kelly ploy that won a few games.

ON BILLBOARDS, THE LOOK OF SUCCESS

In Boston, the world seemed to be Mike's oyster. In addition to his $5,000 salary, money flowed in from streetcar companies, cigar companies and other enterprises for the right to plaster his good-looking Irish face on billboards in the nation's major cities. He was lionized wherever he went, and in the pubs and saloons his rendering of "Casey at the Bat" was superior even to that of comedian DeWolf Hopper, who had recited the poem in New York City in the late 1880s and was still at it in 1932.

For all his bad habits, Mike showed the kind of man he was in 1890, the year of the players' revolt. The owners had passed another rule limiting and reducing player salaries, and the athletes responded by joining together in the Players' Brotherhood and forming the new Players' League. Mike, the player-manager of the Boston entry, built a team that won the pennant.

Under severe financial duress, the National League owners commissioned Chicago's Albert Spalding (who three years earlier had sold Kelly to Boston) to "persuade" him to return to the field, on the assumption that his defection would break the back of the strike. At a secret meeting, Spalding offered Mike a certified check for $10,000 as well as a three-year contract with blanks which he could fill in with his own figures. The total bribe was said to have amounted to $25,000. Mike asked for some time to think it over, took a walk, returned in half an hour and said, "Aw, I want the $10,000 bad enough, but . . . I can't go back on the boys."

Impressed, Spalding shook Mike's hand, then lent him $500 when he learned that the man who had just turned down 25 grand was broke.

Other players weren't cut from the same kind of cloth, and the Brotherhood broke up. Mike returned to the Beaneaters, but his playing days were drawing to a close, the decline brought on as much by drink as by the passing years. Booze had been the King's weakness since his earliest days in the majors, and there are almost as many anecdotes devoted to his drinking habits as to his playing exploits.

Mike was not a social drinker. He drank to get drunk, and worked at it faithfully. On a world tour in the 1890s, he remarked to a British journalist that he had "got home at 6 A.M. with as fine a jag as you could get in any country in the world." The reporter asked if he drank during a game, and Mike replied, "It depends on the length of the game."

He did, in fact, drink during many a game, as well as before and after. The *Sporting News* once complained that he had held up an exhibition game while he "quaffed beer with disreputable characters in the grandstand," according to Harold Seymour's *Baseball, The Early Years*. But beer was not Mike Kelly's drink, not when he could get a scupper of red-eye for a paltry 15 cents. There were times, especially later in his career, when he had "trouble with his feet" running the bases or chasing a fly ball, occasionally getting so tangled that he fell flat on his face. He also sometimes experienced difficulty following the flight of the ball through the air, and after he muffled a catch—but not by much—he would shake his head and mutter, "By Gad, I made it hit me glove."

The end of the trail came for Mike in 1893. He was sent on loan to the financially pressured New York Giants in hopes that the fame of his name would bring the crowds through the gates. Trying to keep him in the lineup, the Giants sent him to sober up in a Turkish bath before each home game. But there happened to be a saloon next door . . .

Shipped back to Boston, where he was no longer wanted, the King then moved on to manage Allentown in the Pennsylvania State League. Even there, in the bushes, the cheers turned to boos and catcalls when the fans realized they were seeing only a bloated shadow—and a tipsy one at that—of the hero who had once been King Kel. Still, Mike led Allentown to a winning season. He played his last game with Allentown-Yonkers (the teams had merged) against the Giants. Yonkers won and Mike was so pleased, he had a drink on it.

THE HUMILIATING SLIDE TO BURLESQUE

The stage came next. At the peak of his fame he had been paid fat fees to take on minor roles, and he remembered the applause that used to follow his renditions of "Casey." But those successes had taken place in hotel barrooms where, usually, he was picking up the tab. Ticket-buying theatergoers were a tougher audience; the slide to burlesque was short and bitter.

Mike opened a saloon in New York with "Honest John" Kelly, the famous umpire, as partner (it was called "The Two Kels"), but he still yearned for more exciting times. Early in November 1894, he headed by boat for Boston, hoping his vaudeville act would receive kinder treatment in the city where he had been so recently a favorite son. On the trip, a head cold worsened and by the time he had arrived in Boston, a doctor called it pneumonia. In the doorway of Boston Emergency Hospital, one of the stretcher bearers stumbled and Mike slipped to the floor. "This is my last slide," he whispered hoarsely.

It was. Three days later, on November 8, just short of his 37th birthday, the King was dead. "At 9:55 last night," the *Boston Globe* sermonized, "'King Kelly' heard the decision of the great umpire from which there is no appeal. The famous ball player passed away . . . his old friends watching every phase of his last uphill fight in the game where defeat is sure . . ."

He would have appealed, given the opportunity. He wasn't ready for death. He had often bragged, while money jingled in one hand as it flowed out the other, that the "Ten-Thousand-Dollar Beauty" would never be a pauper. Yet he was broke often enough even then, and he was broke when he died. Left destitute, his widow was taken in by Honest John Kelly's family.

But if Mike died poor it was only in money. More than 5,000 fans filed through the rooms of the Boston Elks Hall where the King lay in state, and thousands more filled the street outside St. James Church while the religious services were being conducted. It would be baseball's biggest and best-attended funeral until Babe Ruth's body was honored at Yankee Stadium in 1948. Straitlaced, teetotaling Cap Anson, who always claimed he had traded Kelly to Boston because of his bad influence on the younger players, provided a dry sort of epitaph: Kelly had "one enemy . . . himself."

But baseball historian Tom Shea's final tribute comes closer to the heart: "The gods must have loved him. They took him quickly when he could no longer shout—'I'm in the game!'"

Death of Kelly

Boston Daily Globe, November 9, 1894

BASEBALL GIANT GIVES IN TO PNEUMONIA.

**Had Been Ill Since Monday When He Came Here.
His Plans Were to Play at a Boston Theater.
History of "King's" Career on Many Diamonds
Anson Pays a Tribute to His Partner of Old.**

At 9:55 last night "King Kelly" heard the decision of the Great Umpire from which there is no appeal. The famous ball player passed away at that hour at the emergency hospital, with a few of his old friends watching every phase of his last uphill fight in the game where defeat is sure.

So died "Kel" of pneumonia, in the city of his greatest triumphs. He came to Boston, where he has been idolized as few ball players have, and though his latest work has been done far from here yet his deathbed was in this city and among the people he loved so well.

He came here Monday from his home at Paterson, N J, to play an engagement at the Palace theater. He caught a slight cold on the boat from New York, but thought little of it. He went to the Plymouth house, the proprietor of which is an old friend of his and a brother Elk. Mr. Anderson noticed that Mike was not well, and put him to bed at once. The slight cold, aided by the east wind and murky chill of last Monday, were too much for the player, and he grew worse so rapidly that Dr. Galvin, another old and dear friend, took him to the emergency hospital, and gave up his private room to him.

About 3 o'clock yesterday he was very low, and the doctor called in a physician from the city hospital. The patient rallied about 5 o'clock and the last sacraments of the church were administered by Fr. Hickey of St. James' church. After this he rallied a little more, but soon began to sink again, and continued to do so until the hour above stated, when he was called out for the last time.

He has a brother, John, at Troy, N Y, and a wife and child in Paterson, N J. His wife was sent for yesterday, but did not arrive in time to see her husband alive.

There will be many sorrowing and sympathetic friends all over the United States this morning, for Mike Kelly was loved for the unyielding pluck and courage with which he did his work. Among his mates and his profession he left not one enemy. He was a welcome figure on any ball field, and a familiar one from Portland, Me, to San Francisco, Cali. Old men and young, bankers, brokers, statesmen, clergymen, lawyers, physicians have applauded him, with the American small boy.

Mike Kelly, the beau idol of a ball player, shrewd, skillful, and so quick-witted that his word was always a wonder and a delight, will be missed by the baseball public. They will say: "Take him for all in all, we never shall see his like again."

––––––

Michael J. Kelly was born in Troy, N Y, in 1857. His career as a ball player began with the Haymakers of Troy, N Y, in 1873, with whom he played right field until 1875. His first professional engagement was in 1876 and 77 with the Olympics of Paterson, and in 1878 he played with the Buckeyes of Columbus, O, McCormack pitching. In 1879 he was right fielder and change catcher for the Cincinnati league team, and was considered the best catcher in the profession. In the fall of 1879 he went with the Cincinnati-Chicago combination to California, where he was engaged by the Chicagos as change catcher and right fielder. Feb 14, 1887, he was sold to Boston for $10,000 by the president of the Chicago club.

The first trips of the Boston team after Mike Kelly joined it will probably never be forgotten by those who participated in them. The release of the "only" had just been purchased by the Boston club for the magnificent sum of $10,000. The check sent by A.G. Spalding was photographed and used for advertising purposes, and in some of the cities the dead walls and show boards were placarded with pressing invitations to "Come and see the great Kelly," "Don't miss the ten thousand dollar beauty" and other inspiring legends. Kelly himself suggested the "beauty" attachment, inasmuch as he one day announced to the occupants of the bleachers, with whom he was engaged in one of those wordy warfares that are so characteristic of the man: "O, I'm a beaut; you can bank on that—a regular $10,000 beauty. I come high, but they had to have me."

Up to that time, 1887, no player had ever received the advertising and booming given to Mike Kelly. All Boston expected him to win the championship by himself, and were greatly disappointed when he didn't do it. For all that he played great ball for the club.

———

"Kel's" first appearance abroad in a Boston uniform was at Baltimore, in the spring of 1887. The Bostons played four exhibition games there, which were exciting and interesting. Barnie's grounds (not the present park) were taxed to their capacity on the first day. The local papers called the crowd 10,000. It was a tremendous crowd anyway for Baltimore, and every man and boy present wanted the home club to win. They cheered Kelly at first, but after he got to quarreling with Capt. Tom Burns of the Orioles and the umpire, the crowd jeered the "Only," and guyed him terribly for dropping a couple of easy flies. Mr. Barnie "rung in," as Kelly called it, a man named Marshall as umpire, and he robbed the Bostons on every possible occasion. "Kel" wouldn't have him the second day, and he got a man who was quite as bad. Boston got two of the games, and would have had all four, despite the umpires, had the balance of the team shown the nerve that Kelly did.

Kelly's first appearance in Chicago was a memorable one. The papers devoted columns to it. There was a tremendous crush at the Leland hotel to see him. The teams went to the grounds in carriages, and the streets along the route were filled with people, and the "King" got cheers enough to flatter his cap to jump from his head. The crowd at the grounds was an intense one. Kelly played great ball, but his team was beaten, and "Mike" himself was stricken with "charley horse."

He ought not to have played the next day, but Anson persuaded him to do so, promising to let him have a runner, a promise he forgot at the most critical stage of the game.

A business firm sent a silver service to the grounds, which was to be given to the captain of the successful team. The service was moved from players' bench to players' bench, according to the score, until "Kel" alleged it was a Jonah, and refused to have it on his side of the diamond.

It seemed "Kel's" property, sure, with Boston three ahead, but Anson saved his bacon by making a home run with the bases full and two out. Then "Kel," not to be outdone, made a three-base hit, bringing in the run that tied the game, and would have won it but for the bad base running of Madden, who was caught napping at third base. In the last inning "Kel" had a chance to win the silver, and really made a hit that would have done it under ordinary circumstances, but having to run for himself, and being awfully slow, Williamson got the ball in left center, and had time enough to run in and throw the "Only" out at first, and the silver went to Anson.

Kelly was a fine looking athlete, standing 5 feet 11¼ inches in height, and weighing when in condition 180 pounds.

As a batsman, base runner, thrower and a player to take advantage, he never had a superior, and in the four good points never had an equal.

In 1886 Kelly led the league basemen with an average of .370, and though considered one of the finest all-round ball players on the diamond never figured very high in fielding averages, for the reason that he always took too many chances. Mike Kelly's work for the Boston team is familiar to all the lovers of baseball.

When the players broke away from the league in 1890 Kelly was on the side of the players, and remained with them through the season, refusing some very large offers to jump his contract.

In 1891 Kelly preferred the new American association to the league, as they had offered him a very small salary. The Cincinnati club of the association was in need of a captain, and Kelly was transferred to that city. About the middle of August of that season, finding the sledding rough in the queen city, Kelly accepted an offer from the Boston league team for the remainder of the season of 91 and the season of 92. In 1893 Kelly was released to the New

York club, but had some trouble with Capt. Ward, and finally retired from the league to manage the Allentown club of the Pennsylvania state league.

For the last two winters Kelly went on the variety stage, giving songs and recitations, and was fairly successful. Kelly had a fund of natural wit, and was one of the biggest-hearted fellows in the profession and a universal favorite with his fellow players.

ANSON'S TRIBUTE TO KELLY.

Played Ball for the Good of His Team
at Expense of His Own Record.

CHICAGO, Nov 8—While with the Chicagos Kelly was Anson's right hand man. He acted as change catcher and right fielder. Said Anson tonight: "Kelly invariably played ball for the good of his team, and in this way injured his individual batting, fielding, and catching record. It was this self-sacrificing spirit, coupled with a natural quickness of thought and execution, that made him so valuable as a ball player to the clubs he played with. He was a great strategist, well versed in every point of play, and competent to play any position."

PART II

FROM THE COLTS TO THE DYNASTY

Season	Wins	Losses	Winning Percentage	Games Behind	Attendance	Ballpark	Owner
1888	77	58	0.570	9	228,906	West Side Park I	Albert Spalding
1889	67	65	0.508	19	149,175	West Side Park I	Albert Spalding
1890	84	53	0.613	6	102,536	West Side Park I	Albert Spalding
1891	82	53	0.607	3½	201,188	West Side Park I and South Side Park	Albert Spalding
1892	70	76	0.479	30	109,067	South Side Park	Albert Spalding
1893	56	71	0.441	29	223,500	South Side Park and West Side Park II	Albert Spalding
1894	57	75	0.432	34	239,000	West Side Park II	Albert Spalding
1895	72	58	0.554	15	382,300	West Side Park II	Albert Spalding
1896	71	57	0.555	18½	317,500	West Side Park II	Albert Spalding
1897	59	73	0.447	34	327,160	West Side Park II	Albert Spalding
1898	85	65	0.567	17½	424,352	West Side Park II	Albert Spalding
1899	75	73	0.507	26	352,130	West Side Park II	Albert Spalding
1900	65	75	0.464	19	248,577	West Side Park II	Albert Spalding
1901	53	86	0.381	37	205,071	West Side Park II	Albert Spalding
1902	68	69	0.496	34	263,700	West Side Park II	James Hart
1903	82	56	0.594	8	386,205	West Side Park II	James Hart
1904	93	60	0.608	13	439,100	West Side Park II	James Hart
1905	92	61	0.601	13	509,900	West Side Park II	Charles W. Murphy
1906	116	36	0.763	—	654,300	West Side Park II	Charles W. Murphy
1907	107	45	0.704	—	422,550	West Side Park II	Charles W. Murphy
1908	99	55	0.643	—	665,325	West Side Park II	Charles W. Murphy

6. From Teetotaling to Egypt

BASEBALL HISTORIANS LIKE PETER LEVINE, author of *A.G. Spalding and the Rise of Baseball*, consider Albert G. Spalding as the single most important character in establishing baseball as America's pasttime. Not only did Spalding perform mightily as a hurler in baseball's early professional years, posting a mind-boggling 254–46 record from 1871 to 1876, the last season of which he pitched for the world champion Chicago White Stockings, but he served as president of the Chicago club for much of the 1880s. He also founded what became one of the world's most successful sporting goods companies, A.G. Spalding & Brothers. His athletic prowess, business acumen, and daring spirit fit well with the rise of America during this time and the rise of Chicago (the city's population went from 300,000 in 1870 to 1.7 million a mere thirty years later).

While business-wise he seemed full of vim and vigor, Spalding's personal habits seemed, at least outwardly, to reflect the Victorian past more than the rush and boom of an emerging modern America. Little did people know, however, that Spalding carried on an affair for years with Elizabeth Churchill and even had a son with her before he married her two years after his wife Josie's death.[1] He also held prejudices against the Irish.

Nonetheless, publicly Spalding strove to show that he championed the morally upright life, in particular one that avoided alcohol. His temperate ways are evident in the first selection here. The article comes from his A.G. Spalding & Brothers' legendary annual baseball guidebook, and it supports the Spalding-led movement to ship away fast-living, intemperate White Stockings, like Mike "King" Kelly, in exchange for the cleaner-cut young men that became known as the Colts.

In addition to his work with the Cubs, in the late 1880s Spalding organized an ambitious world tour to help spread baseball across the globe, described in the second selection. This tour lasted for six months during the 1888–89

An undated cabinet photo of Albert G. Spalding offers a fine look at the young, aspiring ball-player/businessman. Courtesy Chicago History Museum.

off-season—keeping base-ball in the papers—and involved a series of games between a "Chicago" club, which was comprised of Chicago-based players, and an "American" club, which was comprised of the game's leading play-ers from elsewhere. The touring stars, among them "Cap" Anson and the New York Giants star John Montgomery Ward, played in Hawaii, Australia, Egypt, and Europe before returning for action in America.

All the while, the savvy Spalding worked to spread his business interests. The man who made it a point to firmly establish the myth that baseball was created in Cooperstown by Abner Doubleday even managed to get the Chicago club to play several innings of extra action in Bristol, England, against some of Eng-land's leading cricket players, including Dr. W. G. Grace, which the English press seems to have loved. Historian Mark Lamster, author of the book *Spalding's World Tour* and who has described Spalding as a mix between P. T. Barnum and Michael Jordan, thinks that the world tour quixotically helped entrench baseball's reputation as America's game, partly because so many newspapers carried reports of Spalding's effort to spread baseball to exotic locales.

The tour resonated with the American public. Indeed, on the evening of April 19th, the day on which Spalding, Anson, and the rest of their globetrot-ters made it back to Chicago, they were welcomed with a massive parade. The players sat in open carriages, flanked by prominent businessmen and others, as

1,000 bicyclists led them through the streets of Chicago en route to the Palmer House for a finale banquet. As baseball historian David Fleitz noted, "More than 150,000 people lined the streets for a glimpse of Spalding, Anson, and the players who carried the American national game around the world."[2] Though the tour might not have made baseball paramount in England and Australia, in the United States it not only reflected the rise of baseball but of America itself.

The Lessons of the
League Campaign of 1888

Spalding's Official Baseball Guidebook, 1889

Among the noteworthy results of the League championship campaign of 1888 meriting special comment as affording lessons to be profited by in the future, may be named, first, the success of the Eastern Club of New York, in winning the pennant from the West; secondly, that of the Chicago Club in attaining second place in the race in the face of drawbacks which, under any other management, would have sufficed to have left the Club among the tail-enders; and thirdly, the remarkable failure of the Boston Club to attain even one of the three leading positions in the race, after that club had incurred such a heavy expense in strengthening its team with "star" players. The success of the New York Club in winning the championship, introducing, as it did, a new possessor of the League pennant and its accompanying honors, may justly be regarded as an advantage to the general interests of the National League, inasmuch as it is anything but desirable that one club should, season after season, carry off the honors, as the old Boston Club did in the early history of the professional championship contest; or as the Chicago Club has done in monopolizing the championship of the national League during the past thirteen years of its history. Such monopoly of the honors of each season's campaign, by one or two of the leading clubs of each year, materially lessens the public interest taken in the annual competition. Besides which, it interferes, to a costly extent, with the financial prosperity of a majority of the competing clubs. Now that a club, new to championship honors, has replaced one of the monopolists, the other previously unsuccessful clubs will begin to entertain hopes of being able to "get in at the death," as the fox hunters say, in future pennant races, if not this ensuing year, and thereby a new interest will be impaired to coming campaigns.

A feature of the past campaign of 1888 worthy of remark, too, is the fact of the surprisingly good work on the field accomplished by the so-called "weakened Chicago team." While this work was unquestionably due in a great measure to able management, the assisting element of "temperance in the ranks" had much to do with it. It is equally unquestionable that the very reverse had a great deal to do with the lamentable failure of the Boston team to follow up the success with which that club's team opened the campaign. The contrast these two clubs presented in this special respect calls for the most earnest consideration of the vital question of insisting upon temperate habits in all the club teams during the period of the championship season each year. The evil of drunkenness among the professional teams is one which has grown upon the fraternity until it has become too costly an abuse to be tolerated. Drunken professionals should be driven from service just as the crooks of a dozen years ago were, never to be allowed to return. Drunken players are not only a costly drawback to success individually, but they permeate the whole baseball fraternity with a demoralizing influence. The fact is, professional baseball playing has arrived at that point of excellence, and reached so advanced a position in regard to its financial possibilities, that it will no longer pay, in any solitary respect, to allow players of drinking habits in first-class teams. The demands of the game, as it is now played, are such as to require a player to have all his wits about him to play ball up to the standard it has now reached. He needs the steadiest of nerves, the clearest eyesight, the most unclouded judgment, and the healthiest physique to play the game as it is required to be done by the exacting public patrons of the present day. Another thing, the capitalists who have ventured thousands of dollars in baseball stock companies, can no longer allow their money to be risked in teams which are weakened by the toleration of drinking habits in their ranks. Here is a lesson taught by the campaign of 1888 which points a moral, if it does not adorn a tale.

Another special lesson of the past campaign that was practically illustrated by the Boston Club was that star players do not make a winning team. The fact is, the pennant cannot be won by any costly outlay in securing the services of this, that, or the other "greatest player in the country." It is well managed and harmonious teams, not picked nines led by special stars, which win in the long run. Now and then—as there are exceptions in all cases—a picked nine will attain a certain degree of success. But for steady struggles for permanent success in the professional championship arena, team work of the very best, and admirably managed teams will alone achieve steady victory. The old Boston teams under Harry Wright, and the Chicago teams under Anson, are a standing proof to this fact. Let the National League magnates ponder the truths earnestly.

The Great Baseball Trip
Around the World in 1888-'89

Spalding's Official Baseball Guidebook, 1889

The greatest historical event recorded in the annals of the national game was undoubtedly the journey to Australia, which began in November, 1888, and ended in March, 1889, on a trip around the world. While in 1874 Mr. A.G. Spalding was the *avant courier* of the visiting party of base ball players to England, and also one of the most prominent of the victorious team of players; in 1888 Mr. Spalding was the originator of the trip, the master spirit of the remarkable enterprise, and the leader of the band of base ball missionaries to the antipodes. Of course, in recording the Australian trip in the GUIDE for 1889, only a cursory glance can be taken of the trip, as it would require a volume of itself to do the tour justice. Suffice it to say that the pluck, energy and business enterprise which characterized the unequaled event reflected the highest credit not only on Mr. Albert G. Spalding, as the representative spirit of Western business men, but also on the American name in every respect, and it did for the extension of the popularity of our national game in six short months what as many years of effort under ordinary circumstances would have failed to do.

The party of tourists which started on their journey to Australia on October 20, 1888, met with an enthusiastic welcome on their route to San Francisco, and in that city they were given a reception on their arrival and a send-off on their departure for Australia, unequaled in the history of the game on the Pacific coast . . .

The teams, when they left San Francisco on November 18, 1888, included the following players:

CHICAGO TEAM.	ALL AMERICA TEAM.
A.C. Anson, Capt. And 1st baseman.	J.M. Ward, Capt. And short stop.
N.F. Pfeffer, 2nd baseman.	G.A. Wood, 1st baseman.
Thos. Burns, 3rd baseman.	H.C. Long, 2nd baseman.
E.N. Williamson, short stop.	H. Manning, 3rd baseman.
M. Sullivan, left fielder.	J. Fogarty, left fielder.
Jas. Ryan, center fielder.	E. Hanlon, center fielder.
R. Pettitt, right fielder.	J.C. Earl, right fielder.
Thos. P. Daly catcher.	F.H. Carroll, catcher.
J.K. Tener & M. Baldwin, pitchers.	John Healy & F.N. Crane, pitchers.

Earl also acted as change catcher. The All America team included players from the league clubs of New York, Philadelphia, Detroit, Pittsburgh and Indianapolis, and from the American Association clubs of Cincinnati and Kansas City. Mr. Spalding stood at the head of the tourist party with Mr. Leigh S. Lynch as his business manager, and H.H. Simpson as assistant, Mr. J.K. Tener being the treasurer and cashier. . . .

While en route to Australia the tourists stopped at Honolulu, where they were given a public reception by King Kalakaua, but their first game played after they had left California was at Auckland, where they first realized what a cordial reception the Australians had prepared for them. On their arrival at Sydney, and afterward at Melbourne, the hearty welcome accorded them, not only as ball players but as representatives of the great Western Republic, was such as to surpass all their anticipations, the heartiness of the greeting, the boundless hospitality and the crowded attendance at their games imparting to their visit a brilliancy of success which fully remunerated Mr. Spalding for all the pecuniary risks he had incurred by the trip. It was originally intended to have made the tour of the colonies a more extended one than was afterward found possible, and so the sojourn of the players on the Australian continent ended sooner that anticipated, only four cities being visited, instead of eight or ten, as laid out . . .

After leaving Australia the tourists called at Colombo, Ceylon, and from thence went to Cairo, and while in that city visited the Pyramids, and they managed to get off a game on the sands in front of the Pyramid Cheops on Feb. 9. Their first game in Europe was played at Naples on Feb. 19, and from there they went to Rome, Florence and Nice, the teams reaching Paris on March 3 . . .

In commenting on the physique of the American ball players, the editor of the Melbourne *Argus* says:

"Right worthy of welcome did those visitors appear—stalwarts every man, lumps of muscle showing beneath their tight fitting jersey garments, and a springiness in every movement which denoted grand animal vigor and the perfection of condition. We could not pick eighteen such men from the ranks of all our cricketers, and it is doubtful if we could ever beat them by a draft from the foot ballers. If base ball had anything to do with building up such physique we ought to encourage it, for it must evidently be above and beyond all other exercises in one at least of the essentials of true athletics."

The Melbourne *Sportsman* in its report of the inaugural game in that city, said:

"The best evidence offered that Melbournites were pleased and interested in the exhibition lies in the fact that the crowds of nearly ten thousand people remained through not only nine or twelve innings of play, and then many of them stayed to see a four inning game between the Chicago team and a nine composed mainly of our local cricket players, who made a very credible show, considering the strength of the team they were playing against, and the fact that they were almost utter strangers to base ball. Not only did the spectators remain upon the ground but they heartily applauded the heavy batting, the base running and base sliding and the brilliant fielding executed by our Yankee visitors. Perhaps the truest realization of just how difficult it is to play a finished game of base ball was obtained by the cricketers who went in against the Chicagos. A man may be able to guard a wicket with a degree of skill that would win him wide fame in cricket circles, but when it comes to standing beside the home plate of a base ball diamond, and mastering the terrific delivery of an American professional pitcher, the average cricketer is compelled to acknowledge the wide difference existing between the two positions. Then again, the quick handling of a batted or thrown ball, that it may be returned with all accuracy and lightning like rapidity to the waiting baseman are points which our cricketers are deficient in, when compared with the American professional ball player. It can be seen at a glance that the game is prolific of opportunities for quick and brilliant fielding."

.

7. Hot Time at the Hot Springs

IN MARCH OF 1899 the Chicago Orphans headed west to Hudson Springs, New Mexico (which in 1897 boasted a permanent population of 35 people) for pre-season training that included bronco riding and mountain climbing. They stayed at the renowned Casa de Consuelo (House of Comfort), which Chicago businessman Andrew R. Graham, at the prodding of his friend Albert G. Spalding, had turned into the most sophisticated resort in the territory. At that time, Americans thought highly of the healing powers of hot springs, and Graham had smartly made the springs at the House of Comfort a focal point.[1]

There the Cubs chiseled their bodies in a West that was not quite as wild as it had been just a couple of decades earlier, but one that still produced rugged individuals of the type Frederick Jackson Turner wrote about. And though the frontier may have technically closed by 1890, this article represents how the values associated with it lived on.

This was not the first year that a team sought out a warm climate for "spring training." Some argue that the practice started as early as 1870 when the Chicago White Stockings trained in New Orleans, others credit it with starting in the late 1880s, but regardless the 1899 Orphans did carry out some rather interesting training tactics and they attracted perhaps the wildest group of spectator-revelers.[2] The following *Chicago Daily Tribune* article shows that the Chicago club's training camp that year become an event all its own as it attracted ranchers, herders, townsfolk, and well-known figures such as former Princeton football star Garrett Cochran.

Despite the ballyhoo, the 1899 squad, as with all of the Cubs teams during the 1890s, failed to capture the pennant. Those pennantless squads, which played at the beginning of the decade in West Side Park I, then moved to "South Side Park II" (1891–93) before moving again to "West Side Park II" (1893–1915), did not boast the same seasoned talent as the organization's earlier clubs.[3] But hope lived on and the training continued.

Start Play This Week: Orphans Finish Their Training at Hudson Hot Springs

Chicago Daily Tribune, April 3, 1899

**Go to Kansas City to Open a Series of Games
with Jimmy Manning's Blues—
Although Little Real Baseball Work Is Done
at the New Mexico Resort
the Men Are in First-Class Condition—
Taylor to Be Third Pitcher.**

———

Hudson, N.M., April 2.—[Special.]—The preliminary spring training of the Chicago ball club practically closed today, and in a day or two the club will leave Hudson for Kansas City, where the actual playing will begin.

Five games with Manning's men are scheduled. The first of them will be played on Saturday. The team will remain in Kansas City until April 12, going to Louisville to rest up a day before starting in the pennant race.

The stay at Hudson Hot Springs has given little chance to see the men in baseball or show their form. The few games played offered but little chance for real work, yet the physical condition of the players is well nigh perfect. The free, out-of-door life, bronco riding, mountain climbing, and long hunting trips, have made them hard as rocks. The baths in the waters from the hot spring has driven away all soreness, and the good, plain food of the Casa del Consuelo has kept the men in a state of happy contentment. The Hudson Hot Springs as a resort has drawbacks for real ball playing, but the club has not yet found so good a place for man to get into condition.

On the way to the springs the team stopped between trains at Deming. One of the natives, viewing the crowd, remarked to another: "Big crowd of 'lungers' going up to Hudson." If that same native sees the men as they pass through Deming on the trip to Kansas City burned black by sun and wind and whiskered like a Populist delegation to a State convention he will scarcely recognize them.

PLAYERS ARE CONFIDENT.

The men are full of confidence and expect wonders of themselves. The feeling in the club is better than it has been for many years.

There was a typical frontier ball at the Casa del Consuelo Thursday night given by Mr. Graham, the proprietor, for the club. From ranches, towns, and mines the inhabitants poured down to the "House of Comfort"—cowpunchers from distant ranches far up the Mimbres River galloped in across the plain and, obeying the legend, "Please remove your spurs before entering the ballroom," stripped off their great Mexican spurs, hung up their sombreros, and entered the room, their high-heeled boots cracking on the polished floor.

The belles of Silver City and Deming came twenty-five miles over mountains and across deserts to lend grace to the function, and swung over the polished floors in the arms of sweater-clad ball players and flannel-swathed cowboys. Men from the diggings—the silver and lead mines on Cook's Peak, the mines of the Burro and Black Mountains—threw aside the overalls and candle grease of the mines and returned to the civilization that they had deserted for the delving for riches. Old Indian fighters, rough riders who served with Roosevelt, bear hunters, cowpunchers, ball players, and the citizens and merchants of the towns danced with more spirit than grace.

Bill Lange, Jimmy Callahan, and [Gene] DeMontreville were the stars of the occasion and there were no wall flowers, for the men were in the ratio of three is to one.

GARRETT COCHRAN A VISITOR.

Garrett Cochran, the old Princeton football player and coach, rode down from a ranch near Silver and joined the merrymakers.

The young pitchers of the team are, of course, the main objects of speculation when the players start to figure out the pennant chances of the club. All three, [Bill] Phyle, [Jack] Taylor, and [Jack] Katoll, pitched at the end of last season, and the fans had a chance to observe their work.

The showing of Taylor was remarkable. He not only led the Western League pitchers, but won all five of the games he pitched in the National. This spring he is stronger than ever and will probably be the third pitcher of the club. He is a cool little fellow and full of self-confidence, which nothing can shake, and besides he has an easy, free motion, using great speed without seeming effort, and he uses a slow ball that promises to be the principal source of his success. Speaking of Taylor, a few days ago [Tim] Donahue said:

"I never thought he was much of a pitcher until this spring. He is the most deceptive man I ever caught. A fellow don't really know what a good pitcher he is until after he has studied his style. I believe he is a wonder and one of the coming pitchers of the country."

"A fellow who can pitch the ball Taylor did last fall must be a good pitcher, besides he holds runners close to bases," was Manager [Tom] Burns' only comment.

PHYLE IN GOOD CONDITION.

Phyle is looked upon by many to become a great pitcher. He is strong and is a good student of batters. Last fall he was all out of condition, but since reporting at Hudson has worked hard to get down to proper weight. He is pitching well and is determined to show those who may have got the impression he is a drunkard that it is not true . . . Phyle's stock in trade is speed and a beautiful fast curve ball, but he mixes up the speed and curves with a deceptive slow ball.

The new balk rule will probably trouble Phyle and Katoll more than the others.

Katoll is a big, strong-armed boy with wonderful speed. He is hardly a finished league pitcher, but is a handy man to have on a club and will win many games from weak hitting clubs if given a chance.

The infield looks fast but fragile. It is certainly a speedy crowd of young-sters, and, if McCormick accepts the manager's idea and plays short, the team will be stronger, probably than last year. "Mac" does not want to play in [Bill] Dahlen's old place, and in practice games has stuck to second base or not played at all, while DeMontreville played short. Teams, however, usually shape themselves before the season is a month old, and until after actual play is commenced the positions of the men will be the same.

Some in the club believe the team would present a stronger front with [Barry] McCormick at third and [Jim] Connor at second, although on last year's form neither McCormick nor Connor is a good hitter, and [Harry] Wolverton, unless all signs fail, is a hard, clean hitter and a winning, hustling ball player.

Easter services were held in Alkall Park this afternoon, the principal attraction being a farcical game between the Chicago club and a team made up of pitchers and cowboys. The game was played for the amusement of a crowd of excursionists from El Paso and Deming and the cowboy ranchers and miners of the district. A sandstorm turned the game into a farce, and Burns called a halt in the sixth inning, with the score 22 to 11 in favor of the regulars.

The game was a weird exhibition, but some brilliant accidental catching and lively base running injected enough joy to satisfy the excursionists, who came more to see the players than the play. Twenty-six errors were made by the two teams, Callahan alone making nine at short, after which he grew disgusted and pitched out the game. Katoll, Phyle, and Taylor took turns in pitching, [Clark] Griffith [legendary pitcher and future owner of the Washington Senators—Ed.] playing third, where he made half a dozen impossible stops and catches.

8. Chi-town Fandemonium

BASEBALL MADE CHICAGOANS MAD IN 1906. That year the city's two professional baseball teams qualified for the World Series, making Chicago the first city to accomplish this feat. As baseball journalist Hugh S. Fullerton explained at the time, "Chicago is the baseball center of the earth."[1] Indicating the heady times, when it became clear that both squads had locked up their respective pennants, Chicagoans could be seen cheering on street corners and standing in jubilation in "elevated trains."[2] The first article here, from the *Chicago Tribune*, captured the "mad" thrill for baseball that permeated the city as its two professional teams closed in on their pennants.

Seeing these two teams pitted against each other was novel enough in 1906— the annual "City Series" between the two, which took place after the regular season, had only been occurring since 1903—but seeing them matched up for Major League Baseball's outright championship was truly unique. Indeed, the 1906 World Series remains a fixture in both Cubbie and White Sox lore. Street ticket-prices to the games reached $20 ($456 in today's dollars), and the controversial Alderman, "Bathhouse" John Coughlin, even shut down City Hall to enable his cityworker cronies to attend.[3]

The series didn't just generate cash on the street. New owner Charles "Webb" Murphy had bought a controlling interest in the Cubs in 1905 from the retiring James Hart (a baseball innovator credited with changing the shape of home plate, among other things) for $105,000, one-hundred-thousand of which came from a loan that Murphy was given by his friend Charles P. Taft—half-brother of and advisor to future president William Howard Taft. Thanks to the amazing 1906 season—some say Murphy cleared $165,000 in year one—Murphy was able to pay Taft back in full immediately.

Now, you might think the only owner in Cubs history to have won a World Series—actually two of them—would've been a beloved figure in Chicago. But

"Best Part of the Cubs' Eastern Invasion Is Still to Come." Editorial cartoon detailing the Cubs' fast start to the 1907 season. *Chicago Daily Tribune*, May 16, 1907.

Murphy, who owned the team from 1905 to 1913, wasn't. Some say Murphy, a former writer for the *Cincinnati Enquirer*, got a bad rap because he didn't cow-tow to his former brethren in the newspaper business, or to the whims of baseball stars, or to the rich. That's what Murphy thought. Explaining his lack of popularity by the end of his reign as Cubs owner he wrote, "It is some task to run a championship ball club and cater to 25 'prima donna' ball players. When night comes you are all in and don't care for wine parties or bacchanalian revels—at least I did not."[4]

Others say Murphy was cantankerous and that he alienated fans by alienating beloved Cubbies like Frank Chance, whom he fired as manager in 1912, and Johnny Evers, whom he fired in 1914. Plus, Murphy did things like choosing not to build a visitor's clubhouse at the West Side Park, though the league expected him to, and making journalists at the 1908 World Series sit in the back row of the grandstand, which didn't help on the public relations front.[5]

After the 1913 season, having fired Chance the year before and facing financial pressure from the up-start Federal League as well as peer-pressure from National League president John Tener and fellow owners, many of whom wanted him out of baseball, Murphy sold his interest in the Cubs to his original financier, Taft, for half-a-million dollars. Later in life, when asked if he'd been pushed out of the game, Murphy said, "I sold out to Mr. Charles P. Taft and without force, but for what every other thing of value is obtained—a price. Imagine a man being forced to take $500,000 for a baseball franchise, with a war on and money being sunk by everybody concerned in large gobs." Murphy took a good chunk of that half a million to build the larger-than-life Murphy Theater in Wilmington, Ohio. To be sure, the 1906 World Series brought Murphy plenty of high moments, but watching children revel in a show at his hometown theater was among his life's greatest joys.[6]

The second selection presented here, from the *Tribune* as well, covers the night of the 1906 Series' sixth and final game, which ended in a White Sox victory. In this article we learn of players' reactions to the outcome, and we learn about Sox fans who stormed the playing field and then later roved the South Side in search of players with whom they could celebrate. We also learn about a bizarre bet that led to an unfortunate injury that occurred while the barefoot losers of the wager, two Cubs fans, pulled two Sox fans on a buggy through the

Fans catch 1907 World Series action between the Cubs and Detroit Tigers at the West Side grounds. Surrounded by Taylor, Wood, Polk, and Lincoln (now Wolcott) Streets, this was the Cubs' second West Side Park. The Cubs played in this park until 1915, at which point they moved to what is now known as Wrigley Field.

streets of Chicago. The selection highlights the two clubs' presidents as well, Charles Murphy and Charles Comiskey. The excitement that ripped through Chicago seems palpable in the *Tribune*'s coverage.

Nearly Everybody in Chicago Is Crazy About Baseball
Chicago Daily Tribune, September 9, 1906

Chicago has gone stark, raving mad on baseball. The city never has witnessed a similar phenomenon, even in those dear dead days when the Chicago Colts, captained by the redoubtable A.C. Anson, were the most talked of baseball team in the world. The madness of Chicago of today is to those days as a raving cataract is to a placid mill pond.

More money now is being spent in Chicago upon baseball than it ever was before. Baseball is talked about more than it ever was before. More people are interested in it. More people are acquainted with the minutiae of the game, the biographies of the players, and the fortunes of war, as they are exemplified in the activities of the two baseball teams upon the uniforms of which appear "C-H-I-C-A-G-O."

Crowds larger than those record breaking assemblages that witnessed the post-season games last year already have seen games in Chicago. The crowd the size of which was a record breaker last year is the ordinary crowd of this season, while the big crowds of this year are multitudes so vast that their counterparts never have been gathered together in baseball parks in this city.

RECORD BREAKING CROWDS AT THE BALL PARKS.

Each Saturday and Sunday and holiday that the Cubs, the leaders of the National league, or the White Sox, the midsummer leaders of the American league, play in Chicago the game is seen by more people than are contained in the city limits of thousands of flourishing cities in the United States. It now looks as if the Cubs and the White Sox will play a post-season series of games for the championship of the country, for the Sox are due to win the American league pennant, notwithstanding they lost Tuesday's games and fell to second place temporarily. If they do, the wise men say that the seats will be held and sold for the post-season series at a premium never before exacted for any tickets ever sold for any event in the city.

There is so much interest in baseball here and now that at a game played by either of the two big teams more money is taken in at the gate than any race meeting, theatrical performance, or circus ever played to. The baseball teams make more money on an average day than the average theatrical entertainment plays to in a week.

But not all the frenzy is confined to the baseball park on the west side, where the Cubs play, or to the park on the south side, where the White Sox devour their victims. More amateur games are played in Chicago each Saturday and Sunday than ever have been played in this city before. The Gunthers, the West Ends, and Logan Squares, the Artesians, the Normals, the Oak Leafs, the River Forests, the Leland Giants, and scores of other amateur teams, play to big crowds each week. Some of them have regular parks of their own, where admission fees are charged, where scorecards are sold, and where the general organization is that of the big teams, although upon a smaller scale.

Never before have so many baseball games been played in Chicago in one summer. Many of the theaters have baseball teams. There are teams representing different business houses. Other teams are made up of members of different theatrical organizations. The democratic alderman have played with the republican alderman. Almost every public office in the service of the county or the city is represented by a baseball team. The newspapers have a league.

There are teams representing the suburbs, and each Saturday and Sunday baseball teams from cities in Illinois, Indiana, and Wisconsin are brought to Chicago, here to play one of the hundreds of baseball teams that are made up of Chicago players.

So much for the extent of the game itself. It is now patent to anybody who patronizes baseball at all that it is now easier to see more and better games in Chicago than it ever has been before. It also is evident that more money is being spent directly and indirectly upon the sport than ever was spent before.

Now for the people that have made this possible.

PROFESSIONAL AND BUSINESS MEN HAVE THE CRAZE.

Take a big day at either of the parks. The grandstand and the bleachers and the roped off lawn and the stands outside the fence are occupied by thousands and thousands of men and women that temporarily go insane as soon as the umpire calls "Play ball," and that do not regain their mental equilibrium until the last man is out in the ninth inning. In this crowd there are many representatives of that enviable class that toils not, but that always has the price to see an entertainment that it likes. But in that crowd, too, there are sure to be distinguished representatives of the learned professions, business men whose businesses are the greatest in town, society people who have taken up baseball as they never took it up before, and many others whose names and faces are familiar to everybody who knows his Chicago.

Out of the crowds at any big baseball game could be pressed a delegation that could try a most intricate lawsuit, perform the most delicate operation, build the highest skyscraper, sell the largest bill of goods, and swing the biggest deal on the market.

BOARD OF TRADE DAY ON THE WEST SIDE.

Foremost in this multitude of devotees of baseball are the brokers from the board of trade. It was they who made the most elaborate demonstration that has been made on a Chicago baseball field this season. This occurred a few weeks ago upon the return to Chicago of the Cubs from the series in New York. While in New York Muggsy McGraw, he of the iron jaw and the exhaustless vocabulary, caused to be excluded from the Polo grounds Umpire Johnstone, whose decisions had not fallen in with McGraw's ideas as to balls and strikes. The board of trade crowd had a dislike for McGraw that amounted almost to a monomania. They paid their respects to him in a manner the foreknowledge of which sent the price of box seats to the game up $10 a seat.

They rode to the grounds in automobiles and tallyhos. They had with them rooters whose leathern lungs and quick wit and scorching invective had endeared them to their fellow rooters throughout the season. They brought megaphones and other musical instruments. They carried countless yellow banners upon which the honored name of McGraw was inscribed. These they waved furiously. They lifted their voices in yells that split the skies and they made more noise that afternoon than the west side grounds ever had echoed to.

PARKS JAMMED TO THEIR FULL CAPACITY.

Which is saying a great deal, because those grounds hold 20,000 persons when they are packed and a few more on Sundays, and this season there have been in attendance there crowds so vast that the games have been closed and locked an hour before the game. The park at these times has been crammed to its capacity and just as many more people have been lined up outside waiting to get in.

Loyal as thousands and thousands are to the Cubs, this allegiance is equaled by that paid to the White Sox. These probable pennant winners in the American league have not been in first place so long at a stretch since the halcyon days of 1901. They won the pennant that year as they won it the year before. This year they didn't catch their stride until the dog days of July. Then they began to come like quarter horses and as they came there fell in behind them with cheers and the wildest enthusiasm thousands and thousands of baseball fans who had plugged for them when they had been on top or who were won afresh by their gallant fight.

EVERY MAN IS AN INTENSE PARTISAN.

Men who are neighbors, who may be in business together and in their private lives may like and respect many qualities that they find in the other, become something entirely different when one finds that the other's favorite team is the White Sox, while his is the Cubs. Although everybody in Chicago wants to see both Chicago teams win all the time, the line is drawn sharply between the supporters of the White Sox and the advocates of the Cubs. Each of the men who go to the baseball games steadily has his favorite team. Naturally he likes that team so well that he cannot find in the other team that represents Chicago any virtues that can compare with those which he ascribes to his own band.

That is one reason why, if the White Sox and the Cubs play a post-season series of games in Chicago, that series in all probability will be more noteworthy for enthusiasm and interest than any other series that has been played in the history of baseball.

A Cub fan or a White Sox fan has in his possession more erudition upon which he can't get anything at the bank but that is priceless to him just the same than has even the hardened follower of race horses. The "past performances" that the lover of horses figures on and the "dope" he makes up are as nothing when compared with the intimate knowledge of the baseball fan.

Chicago being baseball crazy, talk about the game and the players goes on everywhere. The barber that shaves you has a eulogy of Frank Chance of the

Cubs that he must get rid of. The boy that blacks your shoes "sure wonders" why Lajoie of Cleveland can hit almost any pitcher that the White Sox can put in against him. The baseball talk is incessant in the stores, the factories, and the office buildings.

Along in the afternoon the only question that needs no preliminary explanation is: "What's the score now?"

The baseball craze was responsible for one musical remedy, as least three vaudeville sketches, and nobody knows how many topical songs and extra or encore verses in current ballads. In one of the musical comedies now running in Chicago the leading comedian gets eleven and twelve encores a night with one verse in a song he has called "Thursday Always Was My Jonah Day." The verse that wins the applause is the verse about the Chicago baseball teams. In another play there is an interpolated scene that now gets more laughs than it ever did and gets them simply because one of the characters smokes a cigar that it so large that it prompts another character to ask him if it is one of the White Sox's baseball bats.

BASEBALL SOUVENIRS AND POSTCARDS.

There are on sale in Chicago just now more souvenirs of baseball than it ever has been possible to buy before. Thousands of ribbons bearing the words: "World Championship Series—Cubs vs. White Sox" have been sold. Thousands of tin representations of a cub's head or a white stocking's have been sold. Men wear them pinned to their seats. Souvenir postal cards bearing pictures of either of the two baseball teams that represent Chicago may be bought at the newsstands and many of them are bought each day and sent away.

The newspaper correspondents that come to Chicago with the other teams say that in no city in the country is there so much and such sincere madness about baseball as there is in Chicago. New York has it pretty strong and one Saturday a few weeks ago 32,000 people turned out at the Polo grounds to see the New Yorkers play.

"It was a pretty good crowd, the Chicago fan says, "but you know what brought it out, don't you?" The Giants were playing the Cubs."

It is a fact that although some of the other teams in both leagues are playing mighty fast baseball, the fans in the other cities turn out in larger numbers to see the White Sox or the Cubs play their home team than they do when any of the other clubs is the opponent.

BOSS AND OFFICE BOY GO TOGETHER.

In Chicago it has got so that the old grandmother's funeral excuse is no longer needed by the office boy. The chances are ten to one that his boss is going out to the game himself and is willing that Willie come along too. This frankness that is born of the real baseball prose shows itself with the employer as well as with the employee. Many a business man leaves his office in the afternoon now and leaves a card on his door reading: "Come to the ball game." A few years ago, or even last season, he would have said: "Out of town for the day," or something like that. This year he knows that in all probability the man that will call at his office in his absence will be a fan too, and, finding him out will say: "Well, I can get out there in time for the second inning myself," and that he will also go.

FRANK BETS ARE MADE UPON THE GAMES.

Baseball scores are displayed in more places than they ever were seen before and more people go out to see them.

Officially there is supposed to be no gambling in Chicago. There are really no poolrooms, as there used to be when races flourished in and near Chicago. In those poolrooms bets were taken upon baseball games. Bets are made on baseball games today. Much of the betting is done at the grounds and some of the propositions that are bet upon show the extreme interest that is taken in the game. Bets are made as to whether the man at bat will make a hit, whether he will be struck out, upon the number of bases that will be stolen during the afternoon, whether such and such a player will make an error and upon almost every conceivable development of which the game is capable.

It is one of the most difficult things there is to get anybody to bet against either of the Chicago teams except at great odds. The amount of money that is bet at each annual football game between the University of Chicago eleven and the wearers of the maize and blue from the University of Michigan is exceeded many times during the baseball season by the amount of money bet upon either of the Chicago baseball teams.

BASEBALL TALK IS EVERYWHERE.

Never before—and Chicago has had before this opportunities for losing itself in an excess of emotion about baseball—never before has this little big town gone so daft over the national game. Everybody seems to be interested in it. Knowledge of it is the passport to many a conversation.

"What's the score?" is the open sesame to many an afternoon gathering.

Knowledge of batting and fielding averages has come to be looked upon as a part of a liberal education. The man that knows nothing about baseball is lonesome. He could be no more lonesome if without knowing anything about land or sea he found himself at a meeting of the geographical society.

But if he knows baseball, if he has broiled on the bleachers or sat jammed in the grand stand, if he has yelled himself hoarse and broken his hat in applause, if he has jeered at the umpire and hissed—well, let us say Muggsy McGraw—then the gates of the earthly paradise have been opened to him. He is baseball mad. He knows it. He glories in it. Like the man in the song he asks, "Gee, ain't it great to be crazy?"

Frantic Rooters Crowd the Field

Chicago Daily Tribune, October 15, 1906

Like Charge of Soldiers, They Swarm to Diamond After the Contest.

PLAYERS FLEE ATTACK

Seek Shelter, Leaving Murphy and Other Officials to Accept Applause.

Thrilling almost as a battle scene was the invasion of the bleacherites upon the field at the close of the game—the charge of the white brigade.

The instant Donohue's foot touched first base, retiring the last batter of the world series, they swarmed over the short fences in center, right, and left and joined the already large army that had ringed the field during the game; then the united forces tore up the field at breakneck speed toward the grand stand, a maddened army o' White Sox supporters whose hopes of years had just been realized. . . .

PLAYERS DASH FOR FREEDOM.

In the meantime the players, knowing what was in store for them, made a dash for the exits beneath the stands. The outfielders had started as soon as the infield hit which ended the contest left Schulte's bat, and they never stopped running until the enthusiasts grouped in front of the grand stand impeded their way, while men tried to grasp their hands, pecked their sleeves, patted them on the back, and shouted bravos into their ears. All of them succeeded in making their escape—from their friends—before the main army was upon them, notwithstanding the charge made by the latter was phenomenally quick. Spectators [were] fascinated by the scene as the big army swarmed across the field, and it was minutes before the crowd began to leave the structure.

In the meanwhile the invading army, foiled in its efforts to surround and capture the player heroes, formed a compact throng in front of the stands and began concerted cheering. Finally it spotted President Murphy of the west side team in one of the boxes directly in front of the center of the crowd. Even had Mr. Murphy desired to escape he could not have done so. He was hemmed in by a congested mass of people who were watching the proceedings on the field. As soon as the rooters recognized the west side official they turned their shafts upon him, shouting in unison, "One, two, three, four, five, six, seven, eight," and making him the target of other remarks, winding up by good naturedly demanding a speech.

MURPHY SPEAKS; MORE CHEERS.

Mr. Murphy then stood up and said: "The White Sox played better ball and deserved to win. (Cheers.) I am for Chicago, and will say that Chicago has the two best ball teams in the world. (More cheers.) The contests have been well contested, and Chicago people should be proud of both their clubs. (Add to cheers.) If we had to lose I would rather lose to Comiskey's club than any other club in the world." (Lots of cheering and shouts of 'That's right.')

Then Mr. Murphy sat down and a woman spectator in an adjoining box, where several of the wives of White Sox players were seated, handed him a White Sox banner, asking him to wave it. Mr. Murphy complied, which led to boisterous applause and three cheers for Murphy, which were given with a will. In response to this Mr. Murphy proposed three cheers for the White Sox, which were given, and then the west side leader said: "Chicago now has the world champions and also the club which has won the largest number of wins on record," which led to three cheers for the Cubs. Mr. Murphy then added:

"These contests have been made possible by the excellent patronage which Chicago has for its two ball clubs, thus enabling the management to go out and secure good players. The games of this series have been fought fairly and squarely, and we accept defeat gracefully," which led to further cheering and shouts of "Murphy, you're all right."

CUBS HAVE MANY FRIENDS.

Former Sheriff Magerstadt, who with Charles Schmalstlz of Cincinnati, one of the stockholders of the Chicago National league club, was in the box with President Murphy, then made a short address and started a round of cheers for the individual players of both clubs, beginning with the victorious White Sox. The crowd joined in the shouting heartily and everybody got a round of applause.

In the meantime, most of the players of both teams had left the grounds, their carriages being surrounded by the enthusiasts outside the grounds, making it difficult for the drivers to get away.

The defeated Spuds were not without plenty of friends, many of their supporters crowding about them and offering words of cheer. "Never mind, you'll get back at 'em next year," was a frequent comment. The west siders were the objects of some taunting remarks from some of the south side fanatics, but in the main were treated considerately. "You're all right, boys, but you're not quite good enough for the Sox," said one.

RIVAL PRESIDENTS MEET.

As soon as President Murphy could get through the crowd in the stand he made his way back to President Comiskey's private office, into which the White Sox president had fled as soon as the game was over. Walking up to the gray haired leader, Murphy shook his hand and said:

"Commy, I want to shake hands and congratulate you. If I had to lose, there's no one I would rather lose to than you."

To which Comiskey replied: "Well, Charley, I'd rather beat any other club in the country than yours. Maybe we'll get another whack at each other next year. I've only evened up for last fall, you know."

"That's right," said Murphy. "I hope both clubs win again next year, and that we'll have another meeting next fall."

EARLY BIRDS BRING LUNCHES

While the gates had not been opened until noon, spectators anxious to secure seats had begun to arrive at the park as early as 9 o'clock in the morning. Many of them came with lunch baskets and took their place in the long line that gradually formed at the gates in order to take their place at the ticket windows.

Many policemen were on hand to see that spectators did not attempt to climb fences. "It's the biggest baseball day in the history of the city," declared one of the bluecoats who had been on duty for hours seeing that the lines were kept intact and stopping embryo quarrels. . . .

FANS FRANTIC IN STREETS.

Wild Demonstration of Joy Made Over the Winning of World's Pennant by White Sox.

"What's de matter wid de White Sox? Dey're all right. Who's all right? De White Sox-x!"

This triumphant cry, in many variations rang throughout the downtown street until early this morning. It was a glorious victory, and was celebrated enthusiastically by the stalwart supporters of the American league champions and victors in the world's championship series.

Charley Comiskey, owner of the White Sox, was joy unrestrained, and in the Pompeian room at the Auditorium Annex wine flowed like the water in the fountain. With a roll of bills big enough to choke a herd of cattle, and consisting of some $2,000 or more, Comiskey announced there would be no sleep for him for the next twenty-four hours.

"All I can say, boys," he hesitatingly remarked when the cries for a speech became insistent, "is that I'd rather beaten any team on earth than Chance's. He's got a fine lot of fellows, and I wish I could find him tonight, for he's game enough to help me celebrate."

Mr. Comiskey announced that his players had won $25,000 on the series, and incidentally remarked that, to show them he was a good fellow, he'd given Manager Jones $15,000, which is to be added to that $25,00, so that an additional $40,000 is to be distributed among the fortunate White Sox.

SOX SUPPORTERS JUBILATE.

A gigantic demonstration was under way early in the evening on the south side below Thirst-first street.

Nearly 2,000 White Sox rooters, led by Clem Keeney and a party of south side business men, made the rounds of the homes of those of the world's champions who live in this section of the city. The first stop was made at the residence of Dr. Harry White, but the star twirler was absent. With unearthly noises of enthusiasm, the fans headed for the house of Manager Fielder Jones.

While en route along Cottage Grove avenue one eagle eyed "rooter" spied Shortstop George Davis seated at a table in a restaurant. With a yell of glee the ringleaders hustled Davis to the sidewalk, demanding that he "Tell us all about it." Davis thanked the fans for their compliments and said the credit for the phenomenal climb of the Sox from sixth position in the American league race to the champions of the world was due to the splendid management of Fielder Jones.

March on Manager Jones.

Davis was carried on the shoulders of his admirers to the home of Manager Jones, 3521 Ellis avenue, where Mr. Jones, with his family, was entertaining Pitcher White. The deliriously happy throng yelled for a speech and Jones smilingly responded:

"Boys, it goes deep with me to see the demonstrations our friends are making. Every man on the White Stockings team is as proud of Chicago as you are of them, and I want to say to you that it has been the individual work and hearty cooperation of every man that has landed the championship for us. That's a big title—'World's Champions'—but you need never fear our club will not live up to it."

Jones then took from his pocket a slip of paper, held it up to the crowd, saying:

"Look at this, a certified check for $15,000 handed me by President Comiskey at the close of the game. That's one sample of appreciation. That money is to be divided equally among the club, share and share alike. I thank you and all the other friends whose hearty support has been as vital as good ball playing."

STORM ROHE NEXT.

The fans cheered wildly, and "Doc" White suggested that they call on Third Baseman George Rohe at Hotel Hayden, 152 East Thirty-sixth street. A stampede was made down Thirty-sixth street, and when the Hayden was reached nearly every resident in that otherwise quiet neighborhood had joined the ranks. They simply would not stir one foot until Rohe complimented the management, and paid a glowing tribute to the fans and fandom. When last seen the huge "White Sox" and a joyous crowd were headed for the White city.

A huge bonfire, started by baseball enthusiasts, blocked the traffic in front of 3554 Cottage Grove avenue until firemen extinguished the blaze.

CROWD SEES FREAK BETTORS HURT.

After attracting a crowd of more than 1,000 persons and impeding street car traffic on Milwaukee avenue, two men who had made a freak wager on the Cubs and two men who had been supporters of the White Sox were injured severely. The winners were in a buggy, which was being drawn by the losers, when the buggy wheels dropped into a cable slot, throwing the buggy's occupants to the street.

The Cubs' supporters were Thomas Ryan, 731 West Ohio street, and Benjamin Jacobs, 208 North May street. The Sox adherents were Patrick Ryan and Henry Holland, 406 West Division street. By the terms of the bet the losers were to pull the winners in a buggy on Milwaukee avenue from Chicago avenue to North avenue and back again, the losers to wear neither shoes nor socks.

As soon as they learned the south side team had won the series, Patrick Ryan and Holland demanded that the wager be executed. A buggy was obtained and the journey was begun, friends of the winners forming an escort. Two pairs of white socks were hung from the sides of the buggy and the way was lighted with Roman candles and torches. As they proceeded the crowd increased and soon the street was packed.

BOTH WINNERS AND LOSERS SUFFER.

On the return trip just before they reached Division street the losers jumped on a car that had crawled through the crowd, keeping hold of the buggy shafts. They had gone in this way but a few feet when a buggy wheel caught in the slot. Ryan and Jacobs were dragged off the car and Patrick Ryan and Holland were thrown from the buggy. All suffered severe injuries.

The crowd in a north bound Halsted street car all but mobbed a dopey fan who was a Cub fanatic and hadn't heard of the Sox victory. He had come to town on a late train, and by some miraculous chance failed to hear the news. In blissful ignorance, he was explaining to a friend how the Cubs would be sure to win, as they had the batting record, etc., etc. About that time a bunch of husky Sox enthusiasts woke him up and it was so warm in that car that two blocks farther on he alighted, vowing he'd go home. . . .

"FAIRLY WON," SAYS CHANCE.

Nevertheless Cub Leader Believes He Has Best Team—
Other Opinions on the Result.

Manager Frank Chance gives the White Sox all the credit in the world for their victory over his team.

"It was the greatest series ever played," said Chance, "and we have got to give it to Comiskey's champions. The Sox played grand, game baseball, and outclassed us in this series just ended. But there is one thing I never will believe, and that is that the White Sox are a better ball club than the Cubs. We did not play our game, and that's all there is to it. The Sox, on the contrary, were fighting us in the gamest kind of way. They fought so hard that they made us like it and like it well. We played our hardest to win, but in this series we did not show we were the best club. But we are just the same. Next year you will see the Cubs come back again for another battle, for I think we will again win the pennant. As for me, well, Frank Chance will be fishing pretty soon at Ocean Springs, Cal. but we are coming back next year, remember."

Johnny Evers said: "I can't understand it, but probably I will in two or three days."

Johnny Kling—"They outplayed us and we have to give it to them."

Joe Tinker—"They beat us all right, by great ball playing, too."

In the evening President Murphy issued the following statement to the press:

"On behalf of the Chicago National league club I desire to thank the public for its liberal support. The series which closed today was the most remarkable ever known and was made possible by the liberal patronage which the national game has enjoyed in the greatest baseball city in the world—Chicago. It is now demonstrated beyond doubt that this city has the best two baseball clubs in the world. We were defeated fairly and have no excuse to offer. The White Sox outplayed us in the short series and are entitled to all the honors and usufruct which goes with victory. The games were conducted admirably under the supervision of the national commission—the supreme court of baseball—and not one word of fault can be honestly found with the work of the umpires—Messrs. Johnstone and O'Loughlin. Our team had won more games of ball this year than any club ever did and I naturally thought it would win, but it is a consolation to myself as well as to the baseball enthusiasts of Chicago to know that the greatest honor in organized professional baseball—the championship of the world—remains in this city. I extend the hand of congratulations to the victors as much as the vanquished can gracefully do that."

"Charles W. Murphy."

"President Chicago National League Baseball Club."

President Pulliam sent the following telegram to President Comiskey: "You won the championship fairly and squarely and you have my heartiest congratulations."

To Manager Jones, Pulliam wired the following:

"I congratulate you and every one of your players on your great victory."

National League Secretary John Heydler said: "The series was fairly contested. The team that we expected to bat well did not do so, and the team we expected not to bat well did the slugging. That's baseball for you."

NATIONALS HAVE MADE $100,000

Report That President Murphy Is to Be Given Club as a Christmas Present.

Barney Dreyfuss is given as the authority for the statement that Charles P. Taft, the Cincinnati backer of Charles W. Murphy in the purchase of the Chicago National league club, intends to make Murphy a present of the club at Christmas. Murphy invested some of his own money at the time the club was purchased, and the price paid is said to have been $105,000. The club, under Murphy's control, is said to have cleared $100,000 this year.

9. Evers on the Glory Years

ON SEPTEMBER 15, 1902, the official scorer for the Chicago–Cincinnati game penned the words "Double Plays: Tinker-Evers-Chance." It was the first time the words were entered into a major league box score, although there was nothing unusual about double plays. But there was magic in the words, at least for the *New York Mail* columnist and baseball poet Franklin P. Adams. He was a New York Giants fan who dreaded the linking together of these three names, in that awful combination, because usually these names strung together meant the end of an inning that had shown possibilities, and as often as not another defeat at the hands of the Cubs. Adams ended up immortalizing these names in "Baseball's Sad Lexicon," writing:

"Tinker to Evers to Chance."
Trio of Bear Cubs, and fleeter than birds.
Tinker to Evers to Chance.
Ruthlessly pricking out gonfalon bubble.
Making a Giant hit into a double—
Words that are heavy with nothing but trouble.
"Tinker to Evers to Chance."

Poetry. During the Cubs' greatest decade, shortstop Joe Tinker, second baseman Johnny "the Crab" Evers, and first baseman Frank Chance struck fear in opponent clubhouses and created disharmony in their own. As harmonious as they were on the field, they were thoroughly discordant off it. Tinker and Evers fell out over something or other during the 1907 season and seldom spoke except in anger for decades after. (For what it's worth, in 1937 Evers gave his version of events, claiming that Tinker had thrown a hard ball his way in '07 that broke a finger and when Evers called Tinker a "so and so" Tinker just laughed. After that, "We didn't even say hello for at least two years. We went through two World Series without a single word," he maintained.)[1] In the clubhouse,

Joe Tinker and Frank Chance, two members of the famed "Tinker to Evers to Chance" trio.

after a tough loss or for almost any other reason, the two would have words (if they even took the time to) and begin fist-fighting. Sometimes a teammate would break up the fight, other times they would join in, but still they played brilliantly and on brilliant teams.

In 1910 Evers wrote a book with famed baseball journalist Hugh S. Fullerton about Evers' career and the game he loved. Well, he apparently mainly edited the book, whereas Fullerton wrote it. Nonetheless, *Touching Second: The Science of Baseball* is an interesting analysis of baseball's development into an "exact mathematical sport" and yet a sport that also needed "more dash, less mechanical work."[2] *Touching Second* considers the history of the sport, key players and seasons, and offers insight into what it took to win at the big league level. This excerpt from it covers the authors' analysis of the many years and the many steps that it took to build the juggernaut Cubs squads of the first decade of the twentieth century—the team that won back-to-back World Series titles in 1907 and 1908. According to Evers and Fullerton, a key part of the team's development occurred because of Frank Chance's superb leadership and eye for baseball talent, coupled with owner Charles Murphy's willingness to give Chance thorough control—at least for the time being. Though Chance did earn a reputation as a taskmaster, in *Touching Second* Evers certainly does not seem bothered by the "Peerless" one's style. Instead the authors stress Chance's ability to land pitcher Ed Reulbach, a physical wonder, as well as the unconventional Mordecai "Three-Finger" Brown. They also emphasize Chance's skillful trades for Harry Steinfeldt and Orval Overall, as well as others. In addition, Evers and

Fullerton promote the idea that it takes patience, brains, money, and luck to win a pennant, though not necessarily in equal measure: they ranked patience and luck as most important.[3] Nowadays most Cubs fans would probably rearrange those rankings—how patient can you be?

Excerpt from *Touching Second: The Science of Baseball*

John J. Evers and Hugh S. Fullerton, 1910

The real beginning of the Chicago Cubs was in March, 1898, when a big, bow-legged, rather awkward young player came from the Pacific coast to be tried as a catcher. Quiet, good-natured, rather retiring off the field, serious, and in deadly earnest while playing, honest and sincere in everything, Frank Leroy Chance reported at training quarters at West Baden, Ind., carrying a bunch of gnarled and wrecked fingers at the end of each hand. Anyone who at that time had predicted that Chance was to become the leader of the greatest club ever organized would have earned a laugh. He had no experience except the little gained in amateur games in California. He played with the Fresno High School team in 1893, for two years with Washington University at Irvington, Cal., and he participated in the great amateur tournament played between all the school teams of California, catching for Fresno, which team finished close to Oakland and Stockton. Bill Lange, then with the Chicago club, saw Chance and recommended him for trial.

While awkward and unfinished, pitchers who worked with him declare that Chance from the first showed his genius for leadership and great skill in handling pitchers and watching batters. His fearless recklessness brought him many injuries as a catcher and twice he was nearly killed.

There was not much sign of promise of a championship team in Chicago then, for [Cubs owner Jim] Hart, in spite of his theories, still had his old stars; and it was not until 1900 that the club, with all its scouts, its purchases and trades, made another rich strike. This lucky find was John Kling, who was born knowing baseball in Kansas City. He was manager, pitcher and first batter of the Schmeltzers from 1893 to 1895, when he went to Rockford, Ill., as a catcher and lasted one pay day, being released as a failure. Returning to Kansas City, he led the Schmeltzers three more years. In 1898 he joined Houston, Tex., under the name Klein, and quit because the team would not pay him his salary. He again caught for the Schmeltzers until 1900, when he went to St. Joseph, Mo.

Ted Sullivan, the veteran scout, went on a secret visit to St. Joseph to buy Sam Strang, later of Chicago and New York, and was so impressed with Kling that he also was purchased, Chicago securing the greatest catcher the game ever has known.

The season of 1901 passed without permanent improvement of the club, which was disrupted by the war between the American and National Leagues. A host of players were purchased, but not one was of championship caliber; and it was not until the coming of [Frank] Selee that the prospects of a winning team brightened. Selee and Hart reached an agreement as to the management in the fall of 1901, and Selee immediately laid plans to strengthen Chicago. His first step was a bit of strategy to secure [Jimmy] Slagle, who was wanted to lead the batting list.

Slagle was a quiet, cool, left-handed batter with much patience and judgment. His career in baseball had been full of vicissitudes. He started playing with Clarion, Pa., in 1889, and afterward went to Ohio Wesleyan University at Delaware, where he played the outfield two seasons. In 1894 he signed with Franklin, in the Iron and Oil league, then played with Omaha for one season; next went to Houston, Tex., where a scout discovered him and took him to Boston in the fall of 1896. Boston banished him to Grand Rapids, from which place he went to Kansas City. Pittsburgh bought him, but before he played there he was traded to Washington, and when the National League was reduced to eight clubs in 1898 Slagle was sent to Philadelphia, where, in the greatest aggregation of batters ever organized, the little fellow led the list. He was sold to Boston in 1901 and near the end of the season broke a finger. Selee, having a scheme, sold him to Baltimore. The release to Baltimore was part of the plot to get him to Chicago, for as soon as Selee became manager of Chicago he brought Slagle back.

That same spring Selee found the man to stop the gap at short stop which had existed for years. The man was Joe Tinker, who began playing ball with the John Taylors in Kansas City in 1896. He was so good even then that the next year Hagen's Tailors paid $2 for him, and he helped that team win the city championship in 1898. Then he went to the Bruce Lumbers, with which team he met and conquered Kling's Schmeltzers. The next season Kling traded two uniforms and a bat for Tinker and brought him to the Schmeltzers, but in June he went to Parsons, Kans., and later in the summer to Coffeyville. Denver purchased him and tried him at second base, but he was so bad that he was quickly sold to John McCloskey, who was managing the Great Falls team. It happened that Great Falls was in financial straits, and needing money, McCloskey sold Tinker to Helena for $200 and Joe Marshall, saving the team and the league from bankruptcy. He was taken to Portland, Ore., in 1901, by Jack Grim. Playing third base, he helped win the pennant of the Northwest League. He played so well that scouts for both Cincinnati and Chicago bid for him. Jack McCarthy, who had been ill-treated by Cincinnati, advised Tinker to try Chicago and he joined the team as a third baseman. Selee insisted upon making a short stop of him, and after a long dispute Tinker agreed to try—and became one of the greatest in the league.

Perhaps the greatest luck the Chicago club ever had was in forming an alliance with George Huff, athletic director of the University of Illinois, for the association of Huff with the club as scout marked an era in the making of the championship team. Huff's first contribution to the team was Carl Lundgren, the University of Illinois pitcher who had twice won the Intercollegiate championship for the school. Lundgren was quiet, studious, and the "Human Icicle," one of the most careful observers of batters ever found. He was of the type that studies three aces and a pair of tens for two minutes before calling—and studies a pair of deuces just as hard. When he calls, he wins, and he pitched wonderful ball for Chicago.

(The following is by Fullerton.)

Late that same season [Bobby] Lowe, the famous second baseman, injured his leg and the team was left without any man for the place. A scout was in Troy, N.Y., to get Hardy, a pitcher, and in despair Selee wired him to get a second baseman, and forwarded him C.O.D. When the scout returned bringing John J. Evers almost everyone laughed. Evers was then not nineteen years of age. No one suspected that he was destined to become the greatest second baseman that ever lived and the foremost exponent and developer of the "inside game," for neither his appearance nor his experience indicated any great promise. He began playing ball when eight years of age, with the Cheer Ups at Troy. After playing on school and amateur teams, he was signed, in 1902, to play short stop for Troy, the opportunity with Chicago coming before he had played a season in the minor league.

All there is to Evers is a bundle of nerves, a lot of woven wire muscles, and the quickest brain in baseball. He has invented and thought out more plays than any man of recent years. He went to second base to fill Lowe's place the first day he reached Chicago, played twenty-two games to the end of the season without an error, and became the baseball idol of Chicago.

(Evers wanted that left out.)

Prospects for getting a winning team improved, but luck deserted Selee's banner in 1903. However, a change was made which was of as much importance, possibly more, than anything else before or since. Selee persuaded Chance after long resistance to play first base and transformed him into a great first baseman.

With Chance, Evers, and Tinker in position, the team began to be formidable, but Selee was sick, and really unable to perform the duties of manager. His sickness forced him to rely more and more upon the judgment of Chance, who suddenly developed a genius for handling men. Lowe was out of the game and a captain was needed. Selee decided to try something unheard of; to submit the election of a captain to the vote of the players themselves. There were three candidates, none especially active. Selee's choice was [Doc] Casey; Kling and Chance both had admirers among the men. The election was held in the club house, Selee actively exerting his influence for Casey, while some of the players were urging Chance as the veteran of the squad. The result of the vote was Chance, 11; Casey 4; Kling, 2. Selee was dumbfounded and for a time annoyed, but events proved the players had made the wisest selection and the vote was the turning point in the career of Chance and in the development of the club.

Chance, although only advisor to Selee, at once assumed the task of building up the team. He seemed to know just what men he wanted, and how to get them, as well as the weaknesses of his own team. His first move was to get Mordecai Brown. The Omaha management, desiring to keep Brown, told Selee his arm was bad, but Chance declined to believe it. Chance had been watching Brown and wanted him, but was overruled and St. Louis filed prior claim and secured him—but only temporarily. Chance was persistent, and when Jack Taylor fell into disgrace after the loss of the city championship, a deal was arranged whereby Taylor and [Larry] McLean were given to St. Louis for Brown, who had not pitched well there.

Late of the same season Scout Huff discovered three more men of championship caliber. The story of Huff's work that season reads like a Sherlock

Holmes adventure, especially the tale of his pursuit of three ghostly pitchers. The story properly begins three years earlier, when Ed Reulbach, a giant youngster, was pitching for Notre Dame, Indiana, University. Reulbach is as near a physically perfect man as possible. Huff had seen his terrific speed and wonderful curves in college games and set watch on him. That next year, while beating the underbrush for young players, Huff began to receive reports from Sedalia, Mo., of a pitcher named Lawson and finally went there to see him pitch. The day before he reached Sedalia, Lawson disappeared, leaving no trace or clue. Huff wanted a pitcher, needed him, and hurried to find Reulbach, but imagine his surprise when, immediately after the close of school, Reulbach disappeared as utterly as Lawson had done, leaving no trace.

Then Huff began to receive reports from Montpelier, Vermont, of a young pitcher who was winning everything in the Green Mountain League and whose name was Sheldon. Huff disguised himself as an alderman and went to Montpelier to see the new prodigy perform. The mystery was solved— Sheldon, Lawson and Reulbach were all pitching and they were one man; all Reulbach under assorted names. Huff straightened out the tangle and returned to Chicago with one of the greatest modern pitchers.

Hart had heard that McChesney of Des Moines was worth having and sent Huff to observe. Huff reported McChesney only a fair ball player, but that [Artie] Hofman, short stop, was one of the greatest players in the country. Both were purchased and Chicago thus accidentally secured the best utility man of modern times. Hofman played every infield and outfield position for Chicago during three pennant-winning seasons, being so good a substitute that Chance could not afford to use him as a regular until 1909 when he went to center field. Two seasons he saved the pennant for Chicago by understudying every man on the team who was injured, playing almost to the standard of every man he replaced. In one week he played six positions on the infield and outfield.

Hofman came into baseball from the amateurs of St. Louis. He played with Smith Academy team for a time, then with semi-professional teams in St. Louis and finally got into the Trolley league, where he became a contract jumper. His contract with East St. Louis guaranteed him $8 a game when weather conditions permitted play. One day the sun was shining, the weather warm, and everything favorable, but the Mississippi River had risen and flooded the grounds. Hofman contended that weather did not prevent the game and claimed his money. The management refused to pay and Hofman jumped to Belleville, where Barney Dreyfuss found him in 1903, and took to Pittsburgh, but immediately released him to Des Moines where Huff discovered him.

Huff made one more important discovery that season. McCarthy's legs were giving way, and an outfielder was needed. Huff went to Syracuse to see Magee. He telegraphed Selee to get [Frank] Schulte, a quiet, droll New York state boy, and Mike Mitchell. Both were secured, but Chicago offered Mitchell less money than he was getting at Syracuse. He was forced to accept the offer, but openly stated he would not give his best efforts to the club, and so was lost to Chicago, Cincinnati securing a great player. Schulte quickly developed into one of the best players in the National League.

If anyone could have found Schulte up to 1898 a more detailed map would be needed. He was born in Cochecton, New York, and started playing ball with Glen Aubrey. From there he went to Poseyville, from Poseyville to Poseytuck, to Hickory Grove, to Blossburg, and finally in 1897 got upon the edge of a map at Waverly, playing there two years. Then he went to Lestershire, and reached Syracuse in 1902.

Schulte proved to be the man needed. In him Chance had found one of the rarest baseball treasures, a "third batter." The third batter in any team is the most important. He must hit long flies, hit hard, bunt and run, because ahead of him in a well constructed team are two batters who are on the team for their ability to "get on," and the third man must be able either to move them up or hit them home.

The team, after eighteen years of effort, was growing strong, but not steady. It fought hard for the pennant in 1905, but was beaten. Chicago at last had a contender in the pennant race. Selee was sick, and he did things he would not have done had he been well. Having a team almost complete, he was kept from wrecking it only by Chance. Selee wanted to release Slagle; he wanted to let Evers go; he was so anxious to get rid of Hofman that he refused to permit him to practice on the diamond with the other players. In the middle of the season Selee's illness forced him to surrender and Chance was chosen as manager. The big, awkward youngster who had joined the team at West Baden seven years earlier, suddenly showed himself a great baseball leader. The day he took charge of the team he said: "We need pitchers, we must have a new third baseman, and a hitting outfielder before we can win the pennant."

Casey was playing a fair third base and Maloney was a sensational, if erratic, outfielder, and was the idol of the crowd. That winter the team was sold by Hart, who had spent many years trying to create a winner, to C. Webb Murphy, who gave Chance absolute power as far as playing and getting players was concerned.

Chance knew the men he wanted. He wanted four; and three of them he got. To get the first one he made one of the most spectacular deals ever recoded in baseball history. This man was James Sheckard, a brilliant, clever and much wanted outfielder who had disturbed the Brooklyn club by playing hop scotch with the American League during the war. Here the gossip of the club proved valuable. Sheckard was dissatisfied with Brooklyn, and Chance knew it. The Brooklyn management did not think Sheckard was giving his best services, but feared to trade a man who was popular with the spectators. The trade Chance made to get Sheckard stunned Chicago followers of the game. He gave Outfielders McCarthy and Maloney, Third Baseman Casey and Pitcher Briggs, with $2,000 added. Chance was satisfied. His outfield was complete at last. He swung Schulte to right field, his natural position, put Sheckard at left, and with Slagle in center regarded the work as finished.

Chance realized third base must be filled or his pennant hopes would filter away at that corner. He knew the man he wanted, Harry Steinfeldt, who was playing indifferent ball with Cincinnati. He was slow, a heavy hitter, a good fielder and a wonderful thrower. Again inside gossip directed Chance to a man while older managers, not closely in touch with players, listened to other stories. Chance knew Steinfeldt, had played with him two winters, in California, and knew also that internal dissentions were causing the trouble in the Cincinnati ranks. The Cincinnati club was anxious to trade Steinfeldt, but gossip among its enemies in Cincinnati had kept other clubs from bidding for the player. Chance asked Murphy to make a trade. Murphy went to Cincinnati, but the stories whispered to him sent him flying back to Chicago without the player. A few days later Murphy asked Chance: "What third baseman can we get?"

"Steinfeldt," said Chance.

Murphy argued, but went to Cincinnati and again returned without the player, but with even more startling stories to tell Chance. "Who shall we get?" he asked.

"Steinfeldt," replied Chance, unmoved.

So Murphy, still unconvinced, went to Cincinnati and traded [Jake] Weimer, a left-handed pitcher, for Steinfeldt.

The team was complete at last. The day Steinfeldt signed Chance remarked that if he could add a little pitching strength the team would win the pennant.

Huff was sent in frantic search of the additional strength and recommended Jack Pfiester, a big left-hander who, after a career extending all over America, was pitching well for Omaha; well and often. Pfiester had a non-reserve contract with Omaha, so he owned himself, and when Huff and Chance tried to get him they dealt with him direct and purchased him for $2,500. Still Chance was not content. He wanted another strong catcher to assist Kling and he traded for Pat Moran, who had for five years hit well and caught steady ball for Boston. Then he profited again by his knowledge of players and the inside gossip of teams. He knew Overall was a fine pitcher, and he knew that the reason Overall was not pitching well for Cincinnati was that he was being overworked and was weak. Chance had played with Overall in California, had attempted to buy him from Tacoma, when Cincinnati secured him, and had kept constant watch on the giant young pitcher. He knew better than Manager [Ned] Hanlon of Cincinnati how to handle the man—and believed he could win. A deal was made—Chance giving [Bob] Wicker for Overall and $2,000, a deal which proved the joke of the season.

The team was complete; finished in every detail and with the pitching staff working like machinery, it swept through the season of 1906 breaking all records, winning 116 games and losing only 36. Two more years it won the National League championship and twice the World Championship, before it was beaten out by Pittsburgh in 1909.

The experience of Chicago in making a club is the experience of all winning teams; the details of the finding, developing, buying and trading show those who complain because their home team fails to win, why the management cannot follow their advice and "buy some good players."

10. Bartman's Got Nothin' on Merkle

FRED MERKLE'S "BONEHEAD" PLAY remains one of baseball's best-known gaffes. The circumstances surrounding it could not have been more dramatic. In an important late September game in 1908, the Chicago Cubs and New York Giants, locked in a fierce battle for the pennant, found themselves tied with two outs in the bottom of the ninth. The Gothamites' Fred Merkle stood on first and Moose McCormick on third. Next, the Giants' Al Bridwell ripped a single and McCormick crossed home plate, delivering what appeared to be the game-winning run. However, as jubilant New York fans stormed the field,

Frederick Charles Merkle. Few would have predicted in 1906 that "bonehead" Merkle would help get the Cubs to the 1918 World Series as a member of the North Side squad.

CHICAGO DAY.

Oct. 9, 1871—When the cow kicked over the lamp.

Oct. 9, 1908—When the Cubs kicked over the Giants.

"Chicago Day." Editorial cartoon celebrating the Cubs' victory over the New York Giants for the National League pennant. *Chicago Daily Tribune*, Oct. 9, 1908.

Johnny Evers, with a ball in-hand—whether it actually was the game ball is still up for debate—went over to second base to register a force-out of Fred Merkle, who had not advanced from first base to touch second base.

A similar scenario had occurred earlier in the season, but on that occasion Evers' attempted appeal was futile. This time, though, umpire Hank O'Day, who grew up within a few miles of the Cubs field and would later *manage* the Cubs, ultimately decided that Merkle was out on the force play, negating the run. Adding to the drama, O'Day's decision on Evers' appeal did not come until the game had reached the point of needing to be called off due to the fans coming onto the field and because of darkness. Therefore the contest was rendered a tie, which led to a one game re-do on October 8th that ended up deciding the National League pennant. The Cubs, of course, claimed that pennant.

Within days of Merkle's "boner" the *Chicago Tribune*'s I. E. Sanborn delivered a scathing assessment of those New Yorkers who wanted O'Day's decision overturned—even though National League President Harry Clay Pulliam had upheld O'Day's call. Four years after Merkle's gaffe, Sanborn re-hashed the circumstances surrounding it to set the record straight and to help fans overcome a "surprising vagueness" regarding what really happened.

Compounding the uncertainties that still surround that evening's events, in 1914 the by-then former umpire O'Day, as seen here, spoke out about it for the first time, claiming that Evers actually shouldn't have gotten credit for making the appeal for the force out. Instead, O'Day, who was then the Cubs manager, maintained that centerfielder Artie Hofman deserved the bulk of it. Interestingly enough, four years after this statement from O'Day, Merkle suited up for the Cubs.

Bluff of Giants Typical

I. E. Sanborn, *Chicago Daily Tribune*, Sept 27, 1908

PROTEST IS WITHOUT BASIS.

INJURY TO BASEBALL MAY RESULT

IF THE CLUB "GETS AWAY WITH IT."

The New York National league club is engaged in one of its familiar fourflushes in an endeavor to convince the baseball public of Gotham that the Giants were robbed of a hard earned victory on a mere technicality when that game of last Wednesday was declared a tie by Umpire O'Day, whose verdict later was sustained by President Pullam.

And because Broadway, from Times square to Battery, is the native heath of the fourflush; because New Yorkers have become so accustomed to it that they take their hats off to a good one; because the average Gotham fan's knowledge of baseball is confined to the standing of the Giants in the pennant race, to the number of games Mathewson has won, and to guessing at the size of Freedman's bankroll; because in baseball, as in everything else, anything from across the Hudson, the Harlem, or the East river is regarded as barbarian and a rank outsider to be repulsed at any cost, the officials of the New York Nationals are likely to get away with this latest bluff in New York.

ALL BUT NEW YORKERS KNOW.

Outside of Manhattan island, however, where baseball is considered a national pastime and not a form of paying tribute to New York, it is a recognized fact that the Giants lost that victory over the Cubs by a blunder more stupid than the rankest of fielding errors ever perpetrated by a ball player. To fans who know their baseball it was worse than that. Supposing the bases had been full of Cubs in the last inning with two out and New York a run ahead. If an easy pop fly had been batted to Merkle and that player had muffed it, letting two Cubs score and win the game, instead of retiring the side by catching the fly, even New York fans would have understood it was Merkle's fault.

If Merkle had done that there might have been some excuse for him, but there was none for what he did. This minor league graduate was on first base, with McCormick on third and two out in the last half of the ninth inning, with the score tied 1 to 1. Bridwell, at bat, drove a single into center field, and Merkle thought that was all that was necessary to win the game.

WOULD THEY HAVE ADMITTED THAT?

New York officials are trying to convince their public that Merkle was right. In the same situation, with the same runners on the same bases, if Bridwell had hit a grounder to Tinker and the shortstop had stepped on second base or thrown the ball to Evers before Merkle reached there, even Gotham fans would have admitted McCormick's run could not count, and, therefore, that the score was a tie. Even if Bridwell had hit the ball over second so far that he could not possibly be thrown out at first himself, thereby being entitled to a safe hit as surely as if he had hit through to the outfield, and yet Tinker or Evers had knocked down the hit in time to make a snap throw forcing Merkle out before he could get to second, there would have been no question of what the score was. New Yorkers have seen that play so often that they know it. Even if Bridwell had hit a fly to Hofman and Artie had muffed it sadly, thereby entitling McCormick to score the winning run, but because of Merkle's slowness he had failed to reach second before Hofman could pick up the ball and throw it there for a force out, that play would have been simple enough for Gotham fans to grasp.

PRINCIPLE IS THE SAME.

What did happen was no different in principle. The same rule governs the play which the Cubs did pull off on Merkle as governs every play mentioned here. When Bridwell made his hit to Hofman along the ground the same possibility for a force play existed as if the ball had been handled by Tinker. All Merkle had to do to prevent such a play was to run down and touch second base, then, McCormick's run would have counted and nothing could have wiped it off.

There is not argument as to whether or not Merkle did touch the base before he was forced out. Even the New York club does not claim Merkle touched the base as he should have done, but it does claim the Chicago club is taking advantage of a "technicality" in claiming a tie game, whereas it is merely a plainly worded rule on which the Cubs base their contention.

Exactly the same play came up in Pittsburgh a short time before when the same thing was pulled off on First Baseman Gill of the Pirates, also a minor leaguer. At that time Umpire O'Day was not looking for the play and did not see it, consequently the Cubs could not establish their claim, because in baseball the umpire's word is final as to such matters and the testimony of players and fans alike is considered biased, hence not admissible.

O'DAY SEES THE PLAY.

But in New York Umpire O'Day again was in charge of the game, and, recollecting the former protest of the Chicago club, was looking for a possible repetition of the play, consequently saw what came off. For that reason President Pulliam and the National league are in possession of all the facts from an unbiased and official source.

If New York papers printed baseball news pertaining to anything outside Manhattan and Brooklyn, the Gotham fans might have understood from the Pittsburgh tangle what came off before their own eyes last Wednesday. Possibly, too, Merkle might have read of that play and have remembered it long enough to avoid duplicating Gill's bush league blunder. In that case the

Giants would have another victory to their credit and would not be fourflush-ing about the technicalities to cover the ignorance of the rules displayed by one of their own players. But the only mention in New York of the play that came off in Pittsburgh was in slurring references to President Murphy's lack of sportsmanship in protesting that game, although that protest was based upon the official code of playing rules.

MAY INJURE THE SPORT.

Because of their ignoring that Pittsburgh mess Merkle now is the cause of one of the worst tangles ever produced in a pennant race and one which threatens the good name of the National league and of the sport itself. The events of the next few days may make that blunder of Merkle's extremely costly. Upon the eventual decision of that tangle by the National league board of directors may hinge the winner of the National league pennant, and until that is known the hands of the national commission are tied absolutely in the matter of making arrangements for a world's series. The slow unwinding of the necessary red tape and the certainty that the New York club will ap-peal to the limit, if the verdict is against it, may delay the world's series until weather prevents it altogether or makes it necessary to play under conditions impossible to good baseball, rendering the series a joke.

The only escape from the tangle is for one club to win enough games so that the possible award of the disputed game to either Chicago or New York cannot make any difference. In that case the old leaguers can fight their battle out at their leisure, and for that the fans are devoutly hoping.

GIANTS CLAIM IS GROUNDLESS.

An award of that game to the Giants would mean the National league still is forced to truckle to the New York club owners. In the face of Hank O'Day's testimony the Giants have not a shadow of a claim to that game, but instead should be glad to escape a forfeit. There was only one thing to do last Wednesday after Merkle had been forced out. The decision should have been made known at once, the field should have been cleared, and the game finished in extra innings if possible. There was plenty of light to go on with the battle, and there were less than 13,000 people at the game, according to liberal estimates. Consequently with any kind of management the field could have been cleared. In fact, there should have been no fans on the field, as the stands seat more than 18,000.

But there are no screens or barriers to prevent Polo grounds fans from pouring out on to the diamond as soon as they think a game is over, or nearly over, and there had been no real police protection there all season. The danger existing in this absence of regular policemen has been pointed out repeatedly, and the old league warned on all sides that it was courting not only serious trouble but actual scandal in permitting such conditions to go on unchanged. Now that the scandal has arrived there is no occasion for handing out sympathy.

NO PROTECTION FOR UMPIRES.

If it had happened at any other grounds than New York's there is no question but that the umpire would have forfeited the game to the visiting club on account of the crowd's interference. Anywhere else an umpire would have been assured sufficient police protection to enable him to do his duty as prescribed by the rules, without endangering the wholeness of his scalp. One hates to think what would have happened to O'Day in New York if he had remained and tried to make the Giants resume that game.

In the first game of the world's series with Detroit last fall O'Day was called upon to make a much tougher decision, when he called Jimmy Slagle out at the plate for Steinfeldt's interference with a play which in itself could not possibly have prevented Chicago's winning the first game on the west side. There were more than 24,000 people jammed into the west side grounds, and every one of them thought Slagle's run gave the Cubs a victory, so started to swarm over the field. But O'Day called Slagle out, wiping out the winning run, and not only was that big crowd held back in its place so that the game could continue, but there was hardly a murmur of dissent and no demonstration whatever against O'Day when the game finally ended in a draw at the end of twelve innings. And the stakes the Cubs were playing for that day were much higher than the Giants and Cubs were playing for on Wednesday.

SHOWS DIFFERENCE IN CROWDS.

That illustrates the difference between the temper of a baseball crowd in Chicago and one in New York, where the fans have been taught by years of tolerating Freedmanism (former Yankee owner) and McGrawism (Yankee manager) that New York is a law unto itself in baseball.

Story of the Merkle Game

I. E. Sanborn, *Chicago Daily Tribune*, Nov 10, 1912

SANBORN RECALLS CONTEST WHICH DECIDED 1908 PENNANT.

UMPIRE STICKS TO HIS POST

AND GIVES DECISION COSTLY TO GIANTS.

How Fred Merkle, then one of the New York Giants' recruits, saved Chicago's Cubs from otherwise certain defeat in the National league pennant race of 1908 will be remembered for the rest of their lives by all who saw the most costly bonehead play yet perpetrated in baseball.

It cost New York the league championship, cost the owners of the Gotham club around $50,000, and cost the individual players of the team between $3,000 and $4,000 apiece. Everybody thought it would cost Merkle his job and his career, but it didn't. The Giants managers simply figured it out that Merkle never would do it again.

Wherever baseball is spoken of hears frequent references today to that famous play, and until some one beats it the name of Merkle will be used to indicate the apotheosis of ivory. Even the Snodgrass muff, which cost the Giants a world's pennant and $1,500 a piece this year, will not eclipse Merkle's failure to touch second. Snodgrass ended a sensational world's series, but Merkle began a train of events which were almost epoch making and raised a wrangle that could be heard around the world.

WHAT REALLY HAPPENED.

Everybody knows Merkle failed to touch second base on that memorable Sept. 23, 1908, but we have found a surprising vagueness in the minds of baseball's fans regarding the whys and wherefores of that act. Nearly every explanation that could be imagined has been used as the reason why Merkle robbed Bridwell of a base hit and McCormick of the tally that would have won a ball game and eventually a league pennant.

Merkle has been accused of running out of line before the winning run scored; of turning to the right after passing first base on his own hit, which, the fan said, made it necessary for him to advance to second immediately to avoid being put out, and for several other impossible baseball crimes of which he was innocent.

Here is what did happen and why: Cubs and Giants went into the last half of the ninth inning (New York's half) with the score knotted at 1 to 1. Seymour went out on a grounder via Evers. Devlin hit to center for a single. McCormick grounded out to Evers forcing Devlin at second, then Merkle singled into right so far that McCormick went to third on it. That set the stage for the play with Giants on third and first, two out and one run needed to terminate the game in New York's favor.

FATAL ERROR BY MERKLE.

Bridwell whaled the first ball pitched to him safely into center and ran to first base, while McCormick crossed the pan with what ought to have been the winning run, but wasn't. Merkle was the answer. This young man, who was subbing for Fred Tenney on first that day, started toward second on Bridwell's hit, but, when half way there ducked his head and ran for the clubhouse back of right field to beat the crowd, which already was swarming on the arena in the belief the game was over.

But the Cubs and at least one of the umpires, Hank O'Day, knew that game was not over until Merkle touched second base. Only three weeks before this identical situation had arisen in Pittsburgh. Warren Gill, another recruit from the bushes like Merkle, forgot to touch second under exactly the same circumstances. But on that day the umpire was hurrying under the grandstand and did not see the play, which Johnny Evers made. The Cubs protested, but there was no way to establish by nonpartisan testimony that Gill did not touch second, so nothing but talk came of it at the time.

O'DAY ANTICIPATES MISTAKE.

On the 23rd day of September at the Polo grounds, when O'Day saw this opportunity for the same play to be pulled, he remembered the protest and the things the Cubs had said because he did not stay to see the finish of a game. So he waited to see whether or not Merkle touched second, although it really was Bob Emslie's business to see to that. But Bob had not been among those present at Pittsburgh, and he was on the way to the shower bath when the play came off in New York, just as Hank O'Day had been in Pittsburgh.

When Merkle started for the clubhouse Evers set up a yell, demanding the ball from Hofman, who had stopped it. That wised up several Giants to what was going to happen. Cap Donlin started on the run after Merkle. McGinnity, who was crossing the field near second, butted in, catching the ball as it was thrown to Evers. Three or four Cubs pounced on the Iron Man, and to keep them from taking the ball away McGinnity threw it among the spectators crossing the lot. Floyd Kroh dashed among the bugs and rescued the ball and while Floyd was trying to thrash half a dozen Gotham fans, Steinfeldt and Tinker conveyed the ball jointly to Evers, who touched second. At the time Donlin had Merkle by the neck and was towing him as fast as possible toward the keystone sack, but it was too late.

Ever since New Yorkers have referred to that play as a technical robbery and for a whole season they referred to the Cubs as "technical champions." Always have they refused to see that it was just as if when Birdwell hit that ball over second base, Evers had gone back, knocked it down and—without a possible chance to retire Bridwell at first—had managed to toss the ball to Tinker before Merkle could touch second.

Chaos reigned for a while and it was not until the matter reached the National league's board of directors that a definite decision was made. The board finally declared the game a draw at 1 to 1, produced a tie between Cubs and Giants for the league pennant and ordered the Cubs to go to New York and play it off, producing another historical battle.

JOE TINKER A HERO.

Jack Pfiester and Christy Mathewson were the opposing slabmen in the Merkle game and the Giant had all the better of the argument. He struck out nine Cubs and allowed only five scattered hits. To Joe Tinker who had seventeen chances in the field that day, must be given credit for making the famous play possible at the finish. Without Joe's home run in the fifth inning Chicago never would have scored at all off Big Six. With one down in that fifth Tinker hit a low rakish liner to right. It shot past Donlin on the ground and before the Giant captain could overtake the ball and return it Joe was over the plate with time to spare. That was the first run of the game.

Pfiester would have blanked the Giants until the ninth, but for an error by Steinfeldt. Herzog in the sixth hit a nasty bounder to Steiny and reached first in safety ahead of the poor throw which hit the grandstand and let the runner go along to second. A sacrifice by Bresnahan and a single by Donlin scored Herzog with the tying run.

Manager O'Day Takes from Evers Credit for Famous Merkle Play.

Chicago Daily Tribune, Oct 18, 1914

Has John Evers "Keystone King" and author of "Touching Second," been enjoying for six years the fame that rightfully belongs to some other member of Frank Chance's famous old Cub machine? When Fred Merkle forever branded himself an ivory king by neglecting to touch the middle bag in that historic battle at the Polo grounds in the fall of 1908, was it Evers who discovered Merkle's horrible mistake?

Hank O'Day was chief umpire in that game of games, and yesterday Hank in the first statement he has ever given out concerning that famous play at second declared Evers had nothing to do with the discovery of Merkle's slip.

Angered at various "roasts" credited to Evers regarding O'Day's alleged assertion that the Boston Braves would not win a single game from the Athletics in the world's series, O'Day spoke thus of the Merkle play:

"Evers was made famous by that Merkle play in 1908 and was not in on it at all. We did not make the decision at New York because Evers is supposed to have touched second base when Merkle started for the clubhouse, but because Joe McGinnity, when the ball was thrown back to the infield by Artie Hofman, interfered with one of the Cub players who got the ball. I think it was Joe Tinker. Evers stood at second base and did not know what was coming off until Tinker ran over and grabbed Emslie [the other umpire working the game—Ed.] to call his attention to the fact that Merkle had not touched second base.

"Artie Hofman deserves credit for the play. He was the one who used his head. When the ball was hit to center field he did not grab it and dash for the clubhouse, thinking the game was over, but instead shot it to the infield. That play saved the day for the Cubs. If Joe McGinnity had not run from the coacher's box and interfered with the players Hofman would have been given all the credit for the play, and he deserved most of it."

Joe Tinker, who played shortstop for the Cubs in that game, says O'Day is wrong in at least one particular.

"It was Pfiester with whom McGinnity wrestled. Jack picked up the ball after Hofman's throw hit me in the back of the neck. I was running over to inform Emslie that Merkle had not touched second. McGinnity got the ball away from Pflester and threw it in the back of third base. The crowd was out on the field by that time and a spectator got the ball. Harry Steinfeldt ran over and fought for the ball, but did not get it until Pitcher Kroh ran over and punched the man who had it. Steinfeldt then ran over to second base, and, instead of touching second himself, handed the ball to Evers, who stood there while all the wrangling was taking place.

11. Cubs, Champions!

THE CUBS LAST WON A WORLD SERIES in 1908. For perspective, at that time the airplane did not include wheels and no crossword puzzles, bras, or zippers as we know them existed, let alone a commercial refrigerator or television. The automobile was still largely a plaything for the rich, though that soon changed because it was in 1908 that Henry Ford first offered his Model T. Baseball games commonly featured just one umpire, and he was armed with only three new baseballs. If he ran out of balls, the home team had to supply them, and if the home team was winning it just so happened that the balls offered up were oftentimes well-worn and popless—darn near "dead." The average

"It is To Laugh!" Editorial cartoon continues to poke fun at New York fans over "Merkle's Boner." *Chicago Daily Tribune*, May 11, 1909.

major league ballplayer made $2,500 per year (inflation adjusted, that amounts to roughly $57,000 dollars).[1]

Nonetheless, the 1908 campaign not only ended in a Cubbie title, but it's considered perhaps the greatest season in baseball history, and not just because of the "bonehead" play by Merkle. With only two days left in the regular season, six teams remained in pennant contention.[2] In the National League, the Cubs overcame the Pittsburgh Pirates and, of course, the New York Giants for the pennant, and then defeated the Detroit Tigers in the World Series four games to one.

Surely few reckoned then that another title would not come for more than 100 years, especially since the Cubs had won the 1907 World Series, had gone to the Series in 1906, and still had shortstop Joe Tinker, second baseman Johnny Evers, and first baseman Frank Chance. As seen here in classic I. E. Sanborn prose, the 1908 team was an outstanding squad, and it gave Cubs fans ample reasons to look forward to the next year, well before the refrain, "Well, there's always next year" became so common and so dreaded.

Cubs Supreme in Baseball World

I. E. Sanborn, *Chicago Daily Tribune*, October 15, 1908

Final Victory Over Detroit Gives Chicago Team Greatest Record in History of the Game.

———

TIGERS ARE BEATEN, 2–0.

———

Overall Holds the Jungle Men to Three Hits, While the Little Bears Pound "Wild Bill" Donovan.

———

Detroit, Mich. Oct. 14—[Special]—When Overall shut out the Detroit Tigers 2 to 0 today in the fifth and final game of the 1908 world's series he drove the final nail into the greatest honors that ever fell to one baseball club—two straight world's championship pennants on top of three straight league championship emblems.

There have been other clubs which wore the title of three times champions, but Chicago has worn it twice, only when Cap Anson's old White Stockings were at their best in the middle of the '80s and once again when Cap Chance developed and led an even-greater team in the young years of the twentieth century.

Boston, Baltimore, and Pittsburgh share with Chicago the honor of having won three consecutive National league pennants. Never has any club been able to add to those laurels the winning of two world's pennants. Nor is that the end of Chicago's laurels, for Chance's men today gave the great metropolis of baseball its third consecutive world's championship, including that won by the White Sox in 1906.

ALL GLORY TO THE CUBS.

Not in the memory of this generation of fans has any team ever won its honors with greater credit than that which belongs to Frank Chance's warriors. Not in a thousand years has a team been compelled to fight as hard for its titles as the Chicago team, which won the National league pennant twice inside of five days under the most trying circumstances. But, once assured of the National league's banner, the rest proved comparatively easy, just as Chance's men and their admirers have contended. For the same reason undoubtedly today's final crowd of the year was the smallest that has watched a world series battle under modern conditions, the official count showing only a little over 6,000 fans present despite ideal conditions.

Overall was the final selection for the game that was to end the series, and Overall was extremely right. That was shown in the first inning, when he struck out four men, thereby establishing a new strikeout record for the majors. Before he was through whiffing for the day Big Jeff (Overall) had the scalps of ten batsmen dangling at his belt and seven of these strikeouts were put over when there were men on bases. Three hits were all the Tigers could get off Overall, yet two of these coming together in a single round made the outcome of the game doubtful for the actual space of five minutes. In that time the tall Californian disposed of the two batsmen who stood between him and victory.

OVERALL VS. DONOVAN.

Against Overall was pitted "Wild Bill" Donovan, who came back for a second pitched battle with Jeff in an effort to win one more game in the series. The spectators settled back to watch a contest such as electrified the west side crowd for seven innings last Sunday, but it was only a minute or two before it was shown that "Wild Bill" was not nearly as fit as in his previous battle, for the Cubs batted him hard in the first inning and actually settled the game right there.

One Cub run was made with three hits in the opener, and with that Overall could have won his spurs, for with his grand pitching the Tigers had no real chance to score, although on two occasions they threatened rather seriously. After the fifth inning, when the Cubs scored their second run off Donovan and the Tigers failed in their bitterest rally because Overall struck out the slugger Crawford in the pinch, it was an easy task for Overall. He finished the string out as strongly as he began and registered his second victory over Donovan in the series.

CUB ROOTERS JUBILANT.

As Kling camped under a high foul from Schmidt's bat in the ninth inning and caught it for the twenty-seventh out the band of Cub rooters gathered in the grand stand let out a wild and prolonged yell, while the Tiger adherents folded their banners and hid their megaphones under their coats in the double distress of having watched their idols humiliated for the second year in succession after passing out the American league pennant.

Gamely Jennings' men trotted over to the Cub bench and congratulated Chance and his men on their triumph and the two-time world champions hurried away to their camp to dodge the wildly enthusiastic fans who tried to hand them off and make them a feature of a parade down town.

What those gray clad modest young warriors have accomplished will be remembered longer than any one of them lives. For in this series, as never before, they have demonstrated the perfection of their machinery. Flawless, save for Kling's failure to make an almost impossible play when Rossman struck out in the first inning on a ball so low that it hit the ground, was the work of that machine today, and even the dismally disappointed Detroit fans were compelled by sheer force of its excellence to acknowledge they never have seen anything like the airtight baseball of which the Cubs have given them two demonstrations in as many days.

OUR STONEWALL INFIELD.

That stonewall has never been better, and Chance and Evers have written their names above those of Anson, Pfeffer, Williamson, and Burns, Chicago's original and long famous stonewall defenders. That lightning fast outfield, Schulte, Hofman, and Sheckard, has nothing to ask or learn from the fastest that ever won three pennants before. And in the batteries there is nothing in stonewall history in Chicago or elsewhere to equal the gameness and cunning that have been exhibited by those Cub twirlers who have borne the severest burdens of the battle, Brown, Overall, and Reulbach, with the help of John Kling and Patsy Moran.

Today brought out the defensive excellence of Chance's magnificent machine in greater prominence than ever before, for the Tigers were desperate and were battling desperately to stave off the final defeat for yet another day if possible. They wore at Overall's delivery with all their might and strength and when they did not strike out breaking their backs after his phenomenally fast drop curve, they hit the ball on the nose occasionally, giving the Cubs' fielders some difficult chances.

EVERS GOBBLES 'EM UP.

To Evers fell the lot of accepting the hardest of the opportunities offered, and twice he helped Overall keep the hits down to three by reeling off his copyrighted stabs and throws on sharp grounders which were tabbed for hits. Once Hofman barely missed a sensational diving catch which would have kept the hits down to a measly two.

In their attack the Cubs did not shine as brilliantly as they have, but that was through no fault or slip of theirs. It was due to the perfect work behind Donovan and the determined efforts of his feline supporters to give him the best they had in stock. The Cubs played their usual dashing, tearing game on bases, but were checked up repeatedly in brilliant fashion by their beaten but game opponents.

Schmidt steadied his throwing arm and kept the Cubs from stealing anything, even when strapped to the ground, and when an attempt was made to pull off a double hit and run play and steal combined in the eighth, a double play resulted, Donovan striking out the batsman and Schaefer and Schmidt nailing one of the stealers at the plate in gallant fashion. Another effort by Evers to run the Tigers off their feet in the ninth inning was foiled by a neat double play to first and third bases.

TIGERS BATTLE BRILLIANTLY.

The Tigers were battling brilliantly all the way, but found themselves up against a tribe of warriors equally game and determined and far better equipped both offensively and defensively.

It was a furious assault the Cubs made right at the start, and it drove the Tigers into their dens for a moment in swift retreat, but they emerged again later on. Sheckard popped out before the Trojan Evers led the assault that won with a swift poke into center field out of all reach.

A minute later McIntyre was tearing in after Schulte's single to left, and one more trip of the second hand around its tiny circle brought a ripping single from Chance's bat into center field. That scored Evers with the only run Chicago needed to earn the lion's share of the diamond laurels of the twentieth century.

12. Centennial Brown

DURING THE YEARS WHEN the Chicago Cubs ruled baseball, barely a hundred years ago or a mere blink of the eye in geological time, Mordecai Peter Centennial "Three Finger" Brown was the ace of the pitching staff. The right-handed Indiana native won 20 or more games every year from 1906 to 1911, and during his career he won 239 games and had a remarkable 2.06 earned run average, one of the lowest in major league history. He retired from the major leagues after the 1916 season and returned to Indiana, where he ran a filling station and pitched for a number of years more in the minor leagues. He died in 1948, the year before he was elected to the Baseball Hall of Fame in Cooperstown.

As great as he was on the mound, Brown's lasting fame centered on his mangled pitching hand. Perhaps if Brown had known he had a Hall of Fame future in baseball, he would have been more careful in his youth with his pitching hand, or maybe even given up farm life. He lost most of his right index finger in a run-in with a threshing machine, and then a short time later reinjured the finger, as well as breaking the two middle fingers and hurting the pinkie finger, in a bad fall while chasing a pig. The accidents left him with a right hand that looked like it had tried to catch a live hand grenade, but his arm was fine and what grip he had left allowed him to throw a ball that dropped and moved like a Bruce Sutter split-fingered fastball would decades later.

In the following article from 1953, Ed Burkholder details the career of "Three Finger" Brown, highlighting how he developed his most famous pitch and a surprising friendship with the great Christy Mathewson, even before they commenced their legendary major league rivalry.

Mordecai Peter Centennial "Three Finger" Brown. Note the gnarled digits on his right hand.

Three-Fingered Immortal

Ed Burkholder, *Sport*, November 1953

It's one of those arguments that will never be settled. Forty years ago it raised blood pressures, caused fist fights, and broke up lifelong friendships. Even today it can set off a loud and vociferous explosion when old-time sportswriters and fans get together. Recently, at a dinner held by ten of the veteran scribes at a New York restaurant, the management had to request the elderly gentlemen to either calm down or go outside to settle their argument.

The rumpus started when somebody mentioned the names of Christy Mathewson and Three-Fingered Brown, the two great pitchers of the first decade of this century. To the starry-eyed worshippers of Mathewson—and they are still legion—the mention of Three-Fingered Brown is like waving a red flag in front of an infuriated bull. Three-Fingered Brown to them is the usurper, the villain, the one thorn in the side of the immortality of the great Matty.

These supporters have seen to it that Matty fared well in the brick colonial house that stands at the end of the main street in Cooperstown, New York, wherein is housed the Baseball Hall of Fame. At the bottom of Mathewson's plaque are the words: "Matty was the master of them all."

There were heretics in 1908, just as there are today, who questioned that. Among the sportswriters at the abovementioned dinner there were six of them. The argument ended, as most arguments do, by the taking of a poll. The vote was 6–4 in favor of Three-Fingered Brown.

The next day Jimmy Powers, in his New York *Daily News* column, added fuel to the fire by taking up the cudgels for Brown, going much further than did Mordecai's supporters at the dinner. Powers classed Brown as the greatest pitcher of all time, barring none. This sparked a nationwide controversy on the sports pages reminiscent of the violent arguments of 40 years ago. On one point, however, friend and foe agreed, Three-Fingered Brown, whether the greatest or not, was a wizard of the curve, and his deformed fingers did much to revolutionize pitching. The legend built up around him, like most legends, has certain inaccuracies. For one thing, he wasn't three-fingered. He had four and a half fingers. And while the deformity had much to do with his amazing career, it wasn't the whole story.

The records show that Brown was born on the night of October 19, 1876, in the little mining town of Nyesville, Indiana. His parents were English and Welsh, deeply religious and fervently patriotic. They gave the new-born son the resounding name of Mordecai Peter Centennial Brown, the Centennial being in honor of his birth on the anniversary of the founding of our country.

When he was five years old, young Mordecai, a chubby-faced and jovial boy, had an unassailable curiosity about everything around him. Baseball in general, and pitching in particular, owe a great debt to this trait. Visiting a farm one day, the future mound hero was watching a threshing machine. His young mind couldn't quite grasp how it worked, so he proceeded to stick his index finger inside and find out. Half the finger remained there. The country doctor who treated the severed member didn't do a very good job and the stump healed with a large knot on the end of it. But the curiosity of the youth hadn't as yet completed its full contribution to baseball. The next year he was again on the farm. He saw two hogs in a stubble field and took after them, running as fast as his little legs could carry him. Halfway across the field, he stumbled and plunged head first to the ground. Instinctively, he put out his right hand to stop the fall.

It did that, but two of his fingers were broken in the act. The country doctor again was called. He set the fingers, but they remained stiff and twisted. So young Mordecai grew up with three deformed fingers. At 15, he entered the mines. He hated coal mining and he had only one ambition. He wanted to be a baseball player. The deformity of his fingers made this seemingly impossible. He was barely able to grip a ball with his right hand.

It was at this time that a man who was to be more responsible for his amazing career than anyone else stepped into his life. "Legs" O'Connell, a lanky and rawboned Irishman, a pro baseball player of some minor-league fame, was a timekeeper at the mine. He took a liking to young Brown and undertook the job of tutoring him in baseball. His home was near the mine, and each day after work he would take Brown to his home and have him practice throwing the ball. If posterity has been singularly [neglectful] in giving credit to "Legs" O'Connell for his work with Brown, his protégé never missed a chance to do so himself.

"If it hadn't been for 'Legs,'" Brown said many years later, "I would never have been anything more than a water-boy or a mascot for a ball club. He was a hard teacher but he taught me how to overcome the handicap of my fingers and even to put them to great advantage."

It wasn't an easy or quick job for "Legs" O'Connell. For three years he worked with young Brown, showing him how to grip the ball to make the best use of his four-and-a-half fingers. Brown could throw with terrific speed, but the knot on the stub of the index finger caused the ball to jump in weird and unpredictable ways.

"Don't let that jump bother you," "Legs" would tell him. "That stump of a finger may be worth a million dollars to you."

Unfortunately, the managers of the small-town teams around Nyesville didn't have the same idea. Brown didn't prove to be a wonder child in baseball. At 22, when most big-league players are hitting their stride, he was only a substitute third-baseman for the Coxsville team at a salary of two dollars a day when his team played. He was fast and alert, a sparkplug for his team. His weakness was fielding. He got the ball fast enough, and his throw would reach first far ahead of the runner. The only trouble was the first baseman never knew what kind of a jump it would take.

O'Connell, still his loyal instructor, pleaded with the manager of the team to give Brown a chance on the mound. The idea seemed a joke to the manager. If a man couldn't throw to first base without making the ball jump around, how could he hope to get it over the plate for a strike? Curves were little known then, the pitchers depending on the fast ball clipping the corner of the plate for their success.

On July 17, 1898, Coxsville was playing the town of Brazil. The score was 2–2 in the fifth inning. Speed Lathrop, the Coxsville pitcher, fielding a bunt, fell on his right arm, breaking it. The Coxsville manager was in a quandary. His only pitcher had a bad arm and had pitched the day before.

Give Brown a chance O'Connell pleaded. "He'll win the game for you."

The manager shrugged. "Makes no difference now," he grumbled. "We've lost the game, anyway. Maybe this will shut you up about the kid."

What happened next is baseball history. Young Mordecai Brown sauntered out to the mound, grinned at O'Connell and then, without bothering to warm up, went into his wind-up. The ball left his deformed fingers in a slow lob. Chuck O'Brien, the batter and veteran hitter, took a lusty cut at it. All he hit was air. The ball jumped as it neared the plate, going higher than his head. O'Brien waved at two more pitches and struck out. The next two hitters did the same thing.

For five innings the Brazil batters and the crowd were treated to an amazing, unbelievable sight—a pitcher who could make the ball jump as it neared the plate. Only one batter was able to hit the ball, and that a slow grounder to first for an easy out. Coxsville won, 9–2. The manager was stunned, unable to believe what he had seen. By the time he got his bearings, the Brazil club had surrounded Brown and had signed him up to pitch for the unheard-of sum of ten dollars a game.

Overnight young Mordecai became famous. In those first days of his baseball playing he was nicknamed "The Miner" because of his work in the coal pits. He wasn't called Three-Fingered Brown until later.

In 1900, the Three-Eye League, made up of small cities in Indiana, Illinois, and Iowa, was formed. Terre Haute signed up Brown. And in the same year a 19-year-old youth, born in Factoryville, New York, named Christopher Mathewson, started his career with the New York Giants. Matty's first year in the big leagues was a dismal failure. He pitched five games, and lost three. His National League career probably would have ended then and there had it not been that his pitching was on a par with the performance of the rest of the club, which ended the season deep in the cellar. George Stacey Davis, manager of the Giants, figured the kid was entitled to another chance, a decision that was to bring great profit to the Giants.

In September, Christy was in Chicago with the Giants. He had heard rumors about a pitcher for Terre Haute who could throw a weird curve and Matty knew he needed something like that. So he journeyed to Terre Haute to watch Brown pitch. After the game he and Brown spent some time on the field where Brown showed him how his deformed fingers enabled him to throw the jumping ball. Out of this meeting was born Christy's famous "fadeaway" curve, which enabled him the next year to win 20 games for the Giants and to go on to become one of the great pitchers of baseball.

Also at this meeting was born one of the great friendships of the game. In those nerve-chilling races between the Cubs and Giants in 1906, '07, and '08, when the pennant seemed to hang on every pitch by these two great hurlers—and when their supporters were fighting and screaming at each other—Mathewson and Brown remained totally oblivious to the turmoil they were causing. After each game they would discuss their curves and their pitches, arguing like two little boys over what the other should have done.

On that chill October day in 1925, when the last earthly remains of Christy Mathewson, [mourned by millions] and the man grumpy John McGraw once called the "most lovable bad boy of baseball," were lowered in the family plot at Factoryville, the man who stood alone beside the newly-filled grave long after all others had left was Three-Fingered Brown.

Brown's rise to fame was not as meteoric as Christy's. In later years Brown wrote, "Much has been written about the part my deformed fingers played in my career. Undoubtedly, they did have much to do with curves. I couldn't throw any other kind of ball. Yet those fingers were a tremendous handicap. Few know the excruciating pain I suffered when I had to grip the ball in certain ways. I always felt if I had had a normal hand, I would have been a great pitcher. It took me several years to finally perfect my best ball, the down-curve. Yet if it hadn't been for those fingers I might never have even thought of such a curve."

In the fall of 1902, Patsy Donovan, manager of the St. Louis Cardinals, decided that Brown and his freak ball were just what his club needed to get out of the second division. So Brown signed with St. Louis. The experiment was not a great success. St. Louis landed in the cellar in 1903. Brown's first season with the big league wasn't quite as mournful a failure. He won 9 and lost 13. The bouncing curve, which he used with such deadly effect in the bush leagues, wasn't so deadly against the National Leaguers.

"That was a real awakening for me," he later said. "Up to that time I thought I was something of a freak. The truth is, I knew very little about pitching. So I started to learn."

Good fortune smiled on him and gave him one of the finest teachers of the day. Frank Chance, the shrewd maker of players, asked Frank Selee, who was managing the Chicago Cubs, to get Brown, no matter the cost. The trade with St. Louis wasn't expensive. Patsy Donovan wasn't too much impressed with the rookie and quickly agreed to the trade.

Chance had this to say about the deal: "Even in that year, his first in the big-time, Brown had all the earmarks of a great pitcher. His curve left a lot [of players baffled. His ability to] handle the ball that way indicated there were great possibilities with his deformed fingers. Brown had a lot more than a curve. He was fast as lightning, weighed around 170 pounds, and was five feet ten. I never saw a man, rookie or veteran, who had as perfect command of the infield as Brown. Time showed me I was right. Brown was beyond any question the greatest fielding pitcher the game ever had."

Franklin P. Adams, in the old New York *Evening Mail*, wrote his famous ballad, "Tinker to Evers to Chance." He could have written another, "From

Brown to Chance." This combination proved just as deadly to opponents as the Tinker-to-Evers-to-Chance double-play combination. Chance and Brown worked long hours perfecting Mordecai's down-breaking curve that was later to prove such a nemesis for hitters in both the National and American Leagues. The knob on the stump of the right index finger gave Brown support to grip the ball and it gave him more spin on his curve.

All this sounds simple as you read it. It wasn't. Few persons ever knew what pain this caused Brown. His forefinger, stiff and twisted, had to be bent back almost to the breaking point to get a firm grip on the ball. After several years, the constant bending of the finger limbered it up a little, but to the end he was never able to throw the ball without some twinge of pain.

Just how good was that down-curve? Let Ty Cobb give his opinion. He should know. In the 1907 World Series he faced Brown three times.

"It was a great ball, that down-curve of his," Cobb said. "I can't talk about all of baseball, but I can say this: It was the most deceiving, the most devastating pitch I ever faced. Christy Mathewson's fadeaway was good, but it was nothing like that curve Three-Fingered Brown threw at you."

McGraw had taken over the Giants and Christy Mathewson and his fadeaway were playing havoc with the other teams in the National League. In 1903 he won 33 games and in 1904 won a total of 31. Then, in 1906, something happened. It took Christy's loyal fans some time to realize that the answer was the gentleman with the deformed hand—Mordecai Brown. Brown had coasted along the two previous years, winning 15 and 18 games, respectively, working overtime to get those stiff fingers in shape to handle the down-curve.

They were ready when 1906 rolled around. The Mathewson fans had a forewarning of what might happen when the Cubs and the Giants met in their first game of the season in Chicago. Brown's curve dazzled the Giant batters and they managed to get only two hits, while the Cubs were pounding Christy for nine.

In that year Brown won 26 games, and his pitching did much to hold Christy's win total to just 22. It was simply a case of the teacher surpassing the pupil, but the Mathewson fans didn't seem to like it. The Cubs won the pennant, setting an all-time winning percentage record, winning 116 out of 152 games.

But in the World Series, against the White Sox, they sustained a humiliating defeat when the White Sox, dubbed the "Hitless Wonders," staged one of the great upsets in baseball. Brown did his best, winning a two-hit shutout, but that wasn't quite good enough.

The next year the Mathewson fans, still seething over the defeat handed their hero by Brown in 1906, saw Matty nose out Brown, 24 wins to 20. The Cubs faced the Detroit Tigers—and Ty Cobb—in the World Series. There was no upset this time, the Cubs winning in four games, with one tie.

The year 1908 will long be remembered in the National League. Things were seen that year that will in all probability never be witnessed again. In Philadelphia a lanky rookie from the bush leagues, dubbed the Giant-Killer Coveleski, beat the highly-touted Giants three times in five days. It was the year of the Merkle boner. And the great Christy Mathewson lost nine games straight to Three-Fingered Brown between June and October. This feat was about the only glimmer of hope the Cubs had when they started East in September. Frank Chance, it was reported, said he would sell his pennant chances for one thin dime. Only Brown was hopeful and he tried to keep up the failing spirits of the team. He gave them a real shot in the arm on September 22 when he won both games of a doubleheader with the Giants. Orval Overall started the first game and was knocked out of the box in the sixth. Brown took over, beating Leon Ames, 4–3. In the nightcap he started against Otis Crandall and beat him, 3–1.

The next day saw the famous Merkle boner and the Giants and Cubs eventually tied for the flag. Mathewson was rested for the playoff game but Brown had pitched in 11 of the last 14 games.

Some idea of the feeling over Brown and Mathewson can be seen in the 20 phone calls Brown received the night before the game and the 20 letters that came in the morning mail. The calls and letters were blunt warnings that if he pitched against Mathewson he would meet a sudden and unpleasant end before the game was over. Brown pleaded with Chance to let him start the game. Chance vetoed it and started Jack Pfiester. The Giants, mad as hornets over the Merkle boner and their hard luck during the season, made quick work of Pfiester. The first three men up got hits and Pfiester then allowed two walks. The Giants were quickly ahead, 3–0.

Orval Overall and other Cubs pitchers were warming up in the bullpen. Brown was on the bench. He looked at Chance, didn't wait to get the manager's answer, got up quickly and walked out to the mound. The cheers of his supporters weren't quite as loud as the jeers from Mathewson's admirers.

Brown didn't bother to warm up. He faced Art Devlin, one of the most dangerous Giant hitters. Brown went into his windup, and when the ball left his deformed fingers, it was the old lobbing one he had used in Terre

Haute. Devlin swung and missed. He swung and missed on the next two pitches. Brown retired the other two batters on four pitches. For seven innings he gave a demonstration of pitching skill seldom seen in a big-league park. Mathewson wasn't as lucky. The Cubs got two runs in the third, one in the fourth, and a fourth one in the sixth. But in the seventh inning—well, everybody including Chance expected it. Twelve games out of 15 was too much for any human to handle. Brown seemed to break, and his curve was gone. The first three men got on base. Chance ran out to the mound, waving Brown to the bench.

Brown didn't go. He said: "Take it easy, Frank. I'm just getting my second wind."

Chance later said he never knew why he walked away from the mound, leaving the tiring Brown in at that critical moment. Every instinct told him to take Brown out, but he didn't. Larry Doyle was sent in to pinch-hit for Christy Mathewson. Brown's wind-up was slow, more deliberate than usual. The ball nipped the corner of the plate in a down-curve that seemed to drip a foot. Doyle swung, his bat grazing the ball. He was out on an easy foul. Fred Tenney was next. The count went to three and two. Tenney forced a man at the plate. Merkle walked up to the plate, with cheers and boos greeting him. He fanned on the first three pitches. In the ninth inning, Brown retired the Giants with three pitches.

This was Christy Mathewson's most bitter defeat in his many duels with Three-Fingered Brown, but the next day the New York *Times* quoted him as saying: "Brown is great—perhaps the greatest pitcher today."

The Cubs made short work of the Detroit Tigers in the World Series, winning four games to one. Brown's contribution consisted of two games pitched and two won, one a shutout.

Summarizing the statistics for that hectic year for both pitchers, the fans of each had plenty to boast about. Mathewson pitched 56 games and won 37—his best record—and lost 11. Brown had 44 games, won 29 and lost nine. Brown's supporters like to call attention to certain details about these figures that don't show on the surface. Of the 11 games the great Christy lost, ten were to Brown, nine of them successive defeats.

In 1909, the rivalry between Brown and Mathewson reached new heights. The Mathewson worshippers, smarting under the stinging defeats their hero had suffered the years before, jeered and booed Three-Fingered Brown whenever he took the mound. The easiest way to start a fight was to taunt one of the Mathewson fans about Three-Fingered Brown. In that year Brown surged ahead of Christy, winning 27 games and losing nine, while Mathewson won 25 and lost six. For the first time in four years the Cubs failed to win the pennant, Pittsburgh being the lucky team.

In 1910, Christy evened the score with Brown. He won 27, Brown 25. But the Cubs won the pennant, ran into Connie Mack's load of dynamite in the form of a bunch of young players, and lost the Series. Brown won his game, but no other Cub pitcher did.

That winter Brown was in Havana, Cuba, pitching exhibition games. His foot slipped off a bag and some ligaments in his leg were wrenched. Treatment failed to correct the injury, and he had to wear a brace on his right leg. None of the jeering—and cheering—fans in 1911 knew there was a brace on his right leg or that excessive movement caused Mordecai excruciating pain. But even with his handicap, he won 21 games to Mathewson's 26.

This was Brown's last big season. After some years the ligaments partly healed, but the injury was too big a handicap. He was traded to the Cincinnati Reds and won 11 games for them, then joined the insurrection against the National League and went to the St. Louis Federals.

In 1916, he was back with the Cubs. Things were different. Chance was managing in Boston. Brown was now an old man, as baseball ages go. But for one brief hour the great rivalry between Three-Fingered Brown and Christy Mathewson was renewed again. Christy was with the Cincinnati Reds. He, too, had passed his peak and was an old man for baseball.

The two old friends and bitter rivals met in one game. The Reds got 19 hits off Brown, and the Cubs 15 off Christy.

Mathewson won the game, 10–8.

This was Brown's last game. During his short career he won 239 games and lost 130. He pitched 52 shutouts in the National League, three in the World Series.

Returning to Terre Haute, he purchased a filling station which he operated until his death in 1948. The next year he was elected to the Hall of Fame in Cooperstown.

His plaque hangs beside that of Christy Mathewson, his great friend and rival.[1]

13. Politics at the Park

ON SEPTEMBER 16, 1909, President William H. Taft, along with some 30,000 other baseball fans, watched the Chicago Cubs play their legendary rival the New York Giants. It was a fitting team for him to watch because in 1906 the president's half-brother, Charles, had financed Cubs owner Charles Murphy's purchase of the team.[1] The game also marked an important moment in the long history that U.S. presidents, Taft in particular, share with baseball. Though he did not throw out the first pitch at this 1909 game, on opening day in 1910, at Washington D.C.'s Griffith Stadium, he became the first president to do so.

Some even give Taft credit for starting the tradition of the seventh-inning stretch, when, on that same opening day game in Washington, he stood up to stretch, only to see everybody else rise out of respect because they thought he was leaving. As legend has it, once people realized he was just getting the blood flowing, they did the same and the tradition was born. There is evidence, however, that the tradition stretches back to at least the very beginnings of professional baseball—to the 1869 Cincinnati Red Stockings. In the following selection, in fact, we learn that, at the 1909 Cubs game that Taft attended, the president rose to his feet in the last half of the seventh as other Cubs fans were doing so, "for luck."

Regardless of how much credit he deserves for the seventh-inning stretch, President Taft catalyzed the relationship between our nation's highest office and baseball. Previous presidents did not ignore the game: to pass time, George Washington's troops at Valley Forge played rounders; Abraham Lincoln played baseball; and Lincoln's successor, Andrew Johnson, was the first to invite ballplayers to the White House and to declare baseball "the national game." But Taft took it to a new level.

After Taft the tradition continued. Dwight Eisenhower played semi-pro

President William Howard Taft, baseball fan, at a major league game in Washington in 1912.

ball at West Point under a phony name. George H. W. Bush played first base at Yale. Ronald Reagan, of course, announced Cubs games. And few can forget the October strike that George Bush threw after 9/11 at Yankee Stadium during the Subway Series or the cheers and boos that he attracted throwing out the first pitch at a Washington Nationals game in 2005.[2]

President's Day at Chicago

Spalding's Official Baseball Guide, 1910

"Let me sit with the fans," said President William H. Taft, Thursday afternoon, September 16, 1909, when he walked into the Base Ball park of the Chicago National League Base Ball club, the guest of Charles W. Murphy, the owner of the club.

And he did.

Though a special box had been provided for him, the President preferred that he might join the real "rooters," and, among them and one of them, he enjoyed one of the brilliant games of the year in company with more than 30,000 other enthusiasts, who witnessed the defeat of the Chicago team by New York by score of 2 to 1.

A good game? Indeed it was, for not only were those two warm rivals, Chicago and New York contesting against one another, but Mathewson and Brown, the kings of the National League in the pitcher's position, were "on the mound"—the technical vernacular for pitching—and animated by the strongest desire to win before their distinguished guest.

It was the first time in the history of the National game that there has been a real "President's Day." It was the first time that the executive head of the nation had accepted a special invitation, extended to him early in the year, to be present at one of the historic contests which have made Base Ball famous, not only in the land of its birth and development, but in most of the countries of the globe.

Long before the game began thousands of the citizens of Chicago and hundreds from nearby cities and towns, who had been attracted to the contest because the President of the United States was to be present, filled street cars, motor cars and other means of conveyance on their way to the park, and when the Presidential party arrived at the main entrance to the grounds every seat was filled, standing room was at a premium, and the crowd was divided between admiration for the players as they went through their preliminary practice and the expected arrival of the President.

Shouts of "Here he comes" greeted the President as he slowly made his way down an aisle of the densely-packed grand stand, and when he appeared in the front of the structure and was visible to the waiting throng, a volume of cheers rolled up, such as Americans bestow when they are excitedly pleased and vigorously demonstrative.

He walked through the crowd, greeted on every side by cries of welcome, and was escorted to the field, where the players of both teams were quickly assembled and introduced to him, one by one, in person. There was a handshake for every man who was to take part in the game, and for the men on the bench as well, and now and then, as well known players, such as Mathewson, Brown, Tenney, Evers, Devlin, or Tinker, were introduced to the head of the nation, a word of congratulation as well. When Chance and McGraw, the famous managers of their equally famous clubs, met the President, he congratulated them briefly on their skill in their calling.

Anson, hero of battles for years on the diamond, was introduced to the President, who shook him warmly by the hand. He was introduced to August Herrmann, the Chairman of the National Commission, one of the "chief justices of the supreme court of Base Ball"; to John A. Heydler, President of the National League and also a member of the National Commission, and to others who are famous by their connection with the national game. Mr. Heydler was invited to join the President's party, and was frequently consulted by the President on plays and decisions of the umpire. Charles W. Murphy of the Chicago club also joined the President for part of the game.

In the first inning of the contest Doyle led off for New York with a two-base hit. Seymour sacrificed and McCormick was safe at first. Murray and Devlin followed for New York with singles and Doyle and McCormick scored. Those were the only runs made by the Giants in the game, but they were enough to win.

In the second inning a two-bagger made by Tinker and a single by Archer scored the only run made by Chicago in the game.

Through the third, fourth, fifth and sixth innings the teams fought gallantly, and in the first half of the "lucky seventh" the Giants failed to make a run. When the last half of the seventh began and the local enthusiasts arose to their feet "for luck," President Taft also stood up, and when the crowd saw him on his feet there was a mighty cheer from the "bleacherites," who attested their appreciation of the good efforts of the head of the Nation in behalf of Chicago. Although the inning brought forth only a blank for the home team the crowd did not forget that the President had "joined the fans" and been with them in the hope that the tide of battle might turn.

Once during the game Mr. Taft was asked by one of his party: "Mr. President, whom are you for, Chicago or New York?"

"I am for Cincinnati," was the quick and unexpected reply, which brought forth a shout of laughter. He gave an anxious look toward the score-board, which showed that Cincinnati had two and Pittsburgh had two in the seventh inning. A moment later the score-board boy marked up four for Pittsburgh in the eighth and two more in the ninth, and the President sadly shook his head amid a roar of laughter, and said that he was dumbfounded.

As he left the park at the conclusion of the game the cheers followed him for miles into the city. It was a great day for Chicago and a great day for Base Ball.

"Let me sit with the fans." Truly a historic remark. One that will not be forgotten for years to come. How aptly it showed the true democracy of the man and the game! Base Ball welcomes all. Be they high in estate or low, they are one when they meet on a common footing to witness a contest for supremacy of a type such as that which professional Base Ball has established throughout the Republic.

The "fan" is a great, big, true-hearted, staunch American citizen. Loyal to the core, all that he asks is fair play and true sportsmanship, and none knows better than President William H. Taft of the United States, who preferred to be one of them rather than an occupant of a private box, isolated by even so trifling a matter as a mere bit of pine scantling. It was a great tribute to the "fans" as well as to Base Ball, when President Taft saw New York and Chicago play in Chicago on September 16, 1909.

PART III

FROM THE HANGOVER THROUGH THE ROARING TWENTIES

Season	Wins	Losses	Winning Percentage	Games Behind	Attendance	Ballpark	Owner
1909	104	49	0.680	6½	633,480	West Side Park	Charles W. Murphy
1910	104	50	0.675	—	526,152	West Side Park	Charles W. Murphy
1911	92	62	0.597	7½	576,000	West Side Park	Charles W. Murphy
1912	91	59	0.607	11½	514,000	West Side Park	Charles W. Murphy
1913	88	65	0.575	13½	419,000	West Side Park	Charles W. Murphy
1914	78	76	0.506	16½	202,516	West Side Park	Charles P. Taft
1915	73	80	0.477	17½	217,058	West Side Park	Charles P. Taft
1916	67	86	0.438	26½	453,685	Weeghman Park*	Charles H. Weeghman
1917	74	80	0.481	24	360,218	Weeghman Park	Charles H. Weeghman
1918	84	45	0.651	—	337,256	Weeghman Park	Charles H. Weeghman
1919	75	65	0.536	21	424,430	Weeghman Park	Charles H. Weeghman
1920	75	79	0.487	18	480,783	Cubs Park*	Partnership†
1921	64	89	0.418	30	410,107	Cubs Park	Partnership†
1922	80	74	0.519	13	542,283	Cubs Park	William Wrigley, Jr.
1923	83	71	0.539	12½	703,705	Cubs Park	William Wrigley, Jr.
1924	81	72	0.529	12	716,922	Cubs Park	William Wrigley, Jr.
1925	68	86	0.442	27½	622,610	Cubs Park	William Wrigley, Jr.
1926	82	72	0.532	7	885,063	Cubs Park	William Wrigley, Jr.
1927	85	68	0.556	8½	1,159,168	Wrigley Field	William Wrigley, Jr.
1928	91	63	0.591	4	1,143,740	Wrigley Field	William Wrigley, Jr.
1929	98	54	0.645	—	1,485,166	Wrigley Field	William Wrigley, Jr.

*Weeghman Park and Cubs Park are earlier names for Wrigley Field.

†Partnership included William Wrigley, Jr., A. D. Lasker, and Charles H. Weeghman.

14. Oh My! It's O'Day!

AS ALREADY NOTED, between 1906 and 1910 the Cubs went to four World Series, winning two of them. Additionally, in each of the next three seasons the team registered roughly ninety wins. However, in 1914 a run of less success started. And, as it happened, on the eve of the disappointing 1914 season the team let go of the immensely popular manager and second baseman Johnny Evers (in 1921 he returned to the Cubs to manage for one more year). It was a surprising move to many. Yet with hindsight the fact that the Cubs hired Hank O'Day to replace Evers, as the following selection notes, is perhaps even more startling. The long-time umpire who had grown-up near the Cubs' home field was, of course, the same O'Day who had helped get the Cubs that famous 1908 National League pennant when he called Fred Merkle out for not touching second base.

When the Cubs announced Evers's 1914 firing, it marked the second time in as many years that the organization cut ties with a member of the famous trio immortalized in the poem "Tinker to Evers to Chance." First baseman and manager Frank "Peerless Leader" Chance was let go in 1912. The Cubs won ninety-one games that season, but owner Charles Murphy and Chance squabbled over contract terms during the campaign and Murphy accused the team and its manager of carousing and drinking too much. As for Evers, his pink slip arrived partly because boss Murphy did not agree with some of Evers's decisions during the Cubs 1913 loss to the Chicago White Sox in the city series.

In the four seasons following the firing of Evers (1914 through 1917), the Cubs placed no higher than fourth in the eight-team National League, and in the fifteen seasons after Evers' firing the Cubs won just one pennant. In contrast, in 1914 Johnny Evers signed on at second base with the National League's Boston Braves and not only led his new team to a miraculous season that ended with a World Series title, but he won the National League batting title—which the Chalmers Automobile Company celebrated by giving Evers a brand new Chalmers Model 30. This 1914 article from the *Chicago Daily Tribune* ran the day after Evers' North Side sacking and sheds light on the relationships between Murphy and the two fired former players who had given him and Chicago so much joy for so many years.

Evers Deposed As Cubs Leader; O'Day Gets Job

Sam Weller, *Chicago Daily Tribune*, February 11, 1914

SECRETARY THOMAS GIVES OUT STORY
IN THE ABSENCE OF MURPHY.

———

ACTION BIG SURPRISE

———

STATEMENT ISSUED BY CLUB APPEARS
AS INTERVIEW FROM NEW YORK CITY.

———

STATEMENT BY EVERS.

NEW YORK, Feb. 10.—"I will never play for Murphy again under any condition," declared John J. Evers, deposed manager of the Chicago Cubs, when the news that he had been dropped as manager became known at the uptown hotel where the National league's schedule meeting was in progress. "I have been approached by the Federals and have held conferences with some of them, but I would rather be with the 'old boy.'"

This was accepted by every one as a reference to Frank Chance, and immediately there were rumors of Evers going to the New York Americans, who are badly in need of a second baseman.

Johnny Evers has been deposed as manager of the Cubs. After serving one year of a five year contract as leader of the Chicago National league baseball team, the little Trojan, an idol of the west side fans and considered one of the greatest second basemen of all time, has been replaced by the veteran umpire, Henry "Hank" O'Day, who, according to an indirect statement by President Charles W. Murphy, will lead the Cubs through the season of 1914.

The news of Evers' discharge will be almost as great a shock to the fans of Chicago as was the announcement of the discharge of Frank Chance in the fall of 1912. Evers was considered a success in his first year as manager because he took a dismantled ball team and after a tough struggle succeeded in finishing third in the National league race. The Chicagoans played the best baseball in the league from Aug. 1 to the finish.

ANNOUNCES CHANGE BY PROXY.

The announcement of the change in management came in a peculiar way and showed that in reality Evers had been discharged several days ago. President Murphy left on Sunday, supposedly at noon, for New York to attend the annual schedule meeting of the National League. Yesterday afternoon, while several baseball scribes were in the Cubs' office in the Corn Exchange bank building, it was learned a telegram had been received for Secretary Charles Thomas and was being held by Assistant Secretary Al Campton in the absence of Thomas.

Thomas was located finally be telephone and the message was read to him, whereupon he appeared at the office within the next few minutes and said to the scribes that a telegram from President Murphy announced that Henry O'Day was to succeed Johnny Evers as manager of the west side team. Immediately after exposing the telegram, Secretary Thomas asked the scribes to wait a minute. He walked into his office, opened his desk, and took out several copies of a typewritten statement distributing them to the reporters.

STATEMENT PREPARED IN ADVANCE.

The statement was one of Murphy's well known interviews with himself, but apparently was being made public a bit prematurely. It read as if the whole world already knew that Evers had been deposed, while, as a matter of fact, no one dreamed of such action. The interview, although handed out in Murphy's office here by one of his officials, carried a New York date line and was dated Feb. 11, although at the time it was only Feb. 10, and the interview must have been left here by the Cub boss last Saturday or Sunday, which would be Feb. 7 or 8.

HERE IS THE "TELEGRAM."

The paper read as follows:

"New York, Feb. 11, 1914.—The announcement made today that Henry O'Day is to manage the Chicago Cubs came as a great surprise, but it was well received in baseball circles. O'Day is one of the most popular men identified with the national game, to which he has practically devoted his entire life. He was born on the west side of Chicago within six blocks of the Cubs' metropolis.

"While we are sorry Evers will not be with us," said President Murphy of the Chicago Club, "we feel mighty good over securing O'Day, the former battery partner of Connie Mack. I have known O'Day for many years and I do not know any man who knows more practical baseball. He is very popular and his admirers are going to give him a monster banquet on the night of April 22 when the 'Cubs' play their first home game of the 1914 season.

"Every man, woman, and child of the great west side of Chicago—and that means two-thirds of that wonderful city—knows O'Day by reputation. Gov. Tener placed Henry on the National league rules committee and thus recognized him in a proper way. O'Day is the author of the foul strike rule and many other in our code, and he will be a success as manager of the 'Cubs' without a doubt. Incidentally I hope to see him in charge of the 'Cubs' for many years to come.

"Without wishing to criticize anybody I think the Cincinnati club made a mistake in not retaining O'Day as manager. He did wonders with that club until his regular players got crippled and he did not have the reserve strength to help out, and his pitching staff was none too strong. Despite that fact he finished in the first division and all his men liked him. We are very happy over securing O'Day and you watch the condition our boys are in when they open the season at Cincinnati."

O'DAY VETERAN IN BASEBALL.

Henry O'Day needs no introduction to baseball fans. He is one of the greatest umpires the game ever had, and many years ago was a player himself. In 1912 he broke away from the arbitrating end of the game and took the job of managing the Cincinnati Reds. For a few weeks at the start of the season his team led the league, and the Cincinnati fans enjoyed thrills for the first time in years. However, the team finished badly, and when the season was over O'Day was "in bad" with the public, the press, and the Reds' directors. He was discharged at the close of the season and Joe Tinker taken for the position. O'Day went back to the old job of umpiring.

So far as could be learned, there had been no recent quarrel between Murphy and Evers. However, it was known by those who were in touch with Cub affairs last season that the west side magnate had had several "run ins" with his manager, and it was believed that only the success of the Cubs for the last six weeks or two months of the season prevented the discharge of Evers at the end or even before the end of the regular season.

EVERS NOT SURE OF JOB.

Long before the season was over Evers had confided to some of his friends that he didn't feel sure of his job and in reality was manager in name only, because he dared make no move of any consequence without the sanction of Murphy. He explained that his financial condition compelled him to stick to the job no matter how unpleasant it might be.

The first intimation that Murphy intended to depose Evers came last Friday afternoon when he discussed at some length the advisability of having a bench manager instead of one playing in the game, and closed his discussion by declaring Evers' bad judgment had enabled the White Sox to defeat the Cubs in the fall series of 1913.

MURPHY CRITICIZES EVERS.

At that time President Murphy's talk was about as follows:

"There are three types of managers—the man who manages and plays in the game as Chance did in his best days, the man who manages from coaching lines as McGraw and Callahan do, and the man who manages from the bench like Connie Mack and George Stallings. Chance was a great man of the first type, McGraw and Callahan are great in the second, and Connie Mack and Stallings are leaders in their line. Evers is a great ball player, but too impulsive to be a manager and a player at the same time.

"We ought to have beaten the White Sox easily last fall and would have licked them if the team had been properly handled. Evers' bad judgment cost us the series. The worst case of bad judgment was in the fifth game, the one that Benz pitched against us and won in eleven innings by a score of

2 and o. Cheney was pitching for us and neither side had scored when we went to bat in the last half of the ninth. We had made just one hit off Benz, but Archer opened the last of the ninth with a base hit, the second off Benz. Right there is where Johnny erred. He should have put a fast man in to run for Archer and a pinch hitter for Cheney.

HOW THE CUBS "LOST" A RUN.

"Archer turned and looked at the bench after reaching first base, expecting a runner would relieve him. But Evers paid no attention to him. Cheney went to bat for himself and struck out, after trying to bunt, leaving Archer on first base, with one out. Still if a fast man had been substituted at that point the Cubs would have won. Leach followed with a base hit to right field, and Archer, being a slow runner, went only to second base, while a fast man such as Miller or Stewart would have raced to third. Evers followed with a long fly to right field which would have permitted a man to score from third, but, of course, Archer wasn't there. That made two out, and the inning ended when Schulte fouled out.

"We never should have been licked by the White Sox, and better handling of the team in the games would have won that series. Callahan and "Kid" Gleason both said after the series was over that Evers could be thanked by the south siders for giving them the big end of the purse."

EVERS SIGNS UP PLAYERS.

It is doubtful if Evers knew of his impending discharge any more than did Frank Chance last year. During the fall Johnny lived in Chicago and gave most of his time to the Cubs. When the Federal league became active late in December Evers was dispatched about the country signing the Cubs before the "outlaws" could nab them. He journeyed beyond Fort Worth, Tex., and down to Tampa, Fla. He was successful in signing Vaughn, Leach, Phelan, Pierce, and perhaps two or three others. While he was on this trip Murphy employed Hank O'Day to go to Chattanooga to sign Jimmy Johnston, the young outfielder.

It is unlikely that Evers will remain with the Cubs. In his statement Murphy says, "although he is sorry Evers will not be here," indicating that Evers will be traded as well as deposed as manager.

There is not a club in the National league which would not welcome the Trojan as a player, but few of them would care to pay a manager's salary to one simply to play second base. It is supposed that Evers' contract calls for something like $7,500 per year. If he is traded and his salary cut it might be construed as breaking the contract, thus giving Evers a chance to jump to the Federal league. Undoubtedly the Trojan could get a job with the new league at a salary as high as was paid him by the Cubs.

SKETCH OF HANK O'DAY.

Hank O'Day, old time pitcher and umpire and now manager of the Cubs, is a native Chicagoan. He was born about fifty years ago on a farm "way out on the west side," located at what would now be the intersection of Jackson boulevard and Campbell avenue.

Dan O'Day, father of Hank, was employed by the city as a plumber and later became engineer of the Hayes school at Walnut street and Oakley avenue. O'Day pere conducted his farm with the help of his four sons, employing extra help when necessary.

Hank attended the Hayes school until he thought he had sufficient education, then prevailed upon his father to allow him to work as a steamfitter's apprentice. Fond of outdoor sports, he had played baseball from the time he was old enough to handle a ball and bat. Therefore, his job as a steamfitter's apprentice was terminated when he was about 16 years old and Hank became a professional baseball player while the National league still was in its infancy.

According to some chronicles, O'Day's first job was with a club in Toledo, O., but other reports credit him with holding a position in Savannah, Ga., even before his Toledo experience.

PLAYS WITH THE GIANTS.

In 1888 O'Day got into the big leagues as a member of the Washington club. Connie Mack, present manager of the Athletics, was his battery partner. The following year O'Day joined the New York Giants, where he made his reputation. New York won the pennant in 1889 and played a four game post season series against Brooklyn. O'Day pitched and won the first game. New York lost the second. Hank was called upon to pitch the third and fourth games in the series. New York won them both.

Later O'Day drifted west and spent a year or two in Nebraska and Iowa, after which he returned to the national game as an umpire in the early '90s. He filled the role of National league arbitrator for about twenty years and was considered one of the best in the business. He resigned his position as an umpire to become manager of the Cincinnati Reds in 1912.

MANAGER OF REDS IN 1912.

Cincinnati got off to a running start in the early weeks of the season and the hopes of the fans ran high. The team was the surprise of the league, although critics who understood baseball thought the Reds were going above its true form, because O'Day did not have the pitcher strength for a pennant contender. Late in May the New York Giants played a series in Cincinnati and took the lead. The Reds slumped and went into the second division. Toward the end of the season the pitchers improved in their slab work and the team finished in the first division, just ahead of the hard luck Philadelphias.

Despite what was regarded as a favorable showing for a new manager with the material at his disposal O'Day was released by the Cincinnati club directors and was superseded by Joe Tinker, who also lasted only one year. O'Day was reappointed to the umpire staff by President Lynch and took up his old duties last season.

SKETCH OF JOHN EVERS.

John Evers, deposed manager of the Cubs, joined the west side team in the fall of 1902 from the Troy club of the New York State league. In 1903 he jumped into a regular berth at second base, where he has played ever since. He became manager last year following the release of Frank Chance.

While Evers did not gain the sympathy and support of all members of the club, which became more or less demoralized by the dismissal of Chance, he finished in third position in the pennant race. This was the position picked for the team by I. E. Sanborn in an article in THE TRIBUNE, written in advance of the season's opening. Many critics pegged the Cubs for a second division berth.

Evers also was handicapped by the suspicion held by players and fans alike, that he was not allowed full sway in the management of the team by President Murphy. Although trying to fill the shoes of the popular Chance, Evers was highly regarded by the fans.

The Sox victory in the city series last fall was a great disappointment to Evers and President Murphy. The latter criticized his manager's tactics severely in conversation with his friends.

Evers was born July 21, 1883, in Troy, N.Y., which he regarded as his home until he became manager of the Cubs, when he established his residence in North Edgewater. He is married and has two children.

———

F. CHANCE HAS A WORD TO SAY.

———

Only One Is Needed to Express Sentiment of Peerless Leader When He Hears Evers is Discharged.

———

Los Angeles, Cal., Feb. 10.—"Well, h--l, is that so?" ejaculated Frank Chance, when told tonight that Boss Murphy had fired Johnny Evers from the Cub's management. But just when the reporter thought he was going to get a howling slam from the Peerless Leader against his old employer Chance smiled and quietly remarked: "Well, I haven't a thing to say. I have no interest in anything Murphy does," and shut up tight as a clam.

15. Grover's Highs and Lows

GROVER CLEVELAND ALEXANDER, born in the first Grover Cleveland administration, seemed uncomfortable as a twentieth-century athlete. Throughout his brilliant pitching career he never looked very athletic. His run looked more like a controlled stumble, and he appeared singularly uncomfortable in his perennially ill-fitted uniform. But his pitching motion—the only thing in life that seemed to come naturally to him—was the essence of economy and ease. With barely a windup and an abbreviated stride, he looked like he was throwing darts. During his pitching career between 1911 and 1930, he amassed 2,198 strikeouts, a 2.56 earned run average, and 373 wins. Playing for the Cubs between 1918 and 1926, he performed solidly, though a bit below his pre-1918 years with the Philadelphia Phillies, where in a three-year run he won 94 games.

As great as he was on the field, off the diamond he battled a host of demons, and a certain quality of sadness dominated his life. Troubled throughout his career by epilepsy—an affliction that was then little understood and all-to-often regarded as a moral stain—he seemed to fear fits and, as a result, was painfully uncomfortable in public. His epilepsy was probably aggravated during his military service on the Western Front in 1918. After the Great War he suffered from a partial loss of hearing, shell shock, and more frequent seizures. He also drank more, developing into a severe alcoholic. After his major league career ended in 1930, he continued to pitch for barnstorming teams until 1938. After leaving baseball his lows became lower and his highs mostly alcohol induced. As seen in the following article by Andrea I. Paul, he died in November 1950, alone in a run-down rooming house.

Paul provides an overview of Alexander's remarkable career and a sense of the tragedy of his life. As Paul notes, Alexander's greatest moment came when he struck out New York Yankee Tony Lazzeri with the bases loaded in the sev-

Grover Cleveland Alexander at spring training on Catalina Island, California, 1926. Courtesy Chicago History Museum.

enth inning of game seven to help the St. Louis Cardinals win the 1926 World Series. Alexander recalled that moments before the pitch that ended Lazzeri's at-bat, the Yankee great hit a hard foul ball that just missed being a grand slam by a foot or so. "A few feet made the difference between a hero and a bum," he said. It was a line the pitcher walked all his life.

His Own Worst Enemy

Andrea I. Paul, *Nebraska History,* Spring 1990

The life of Grover Cleveland Alexander, a Nebraska farm boy who scaled the heights of baseball greatness and died poverty-stricken and virtually friendless in his hometown, was marked by great successes professionally and miserable personal failures. As the third winningest pitcher in major league history, the legend known as "Alexander the Great" holds national league records for victories, career shutouts, and complete games; the rookie record for victories; and the season record for shutouts. In one three-year span, he won ninety-four games for the Philadelphia Phillies. The height of his success came in 1926 when he pitched the St. Louis Cardinals to a world championship, in the process striking out Tony Lazzeri with the bases loaded, in what many consider to be the game's most famous strikeout.

In contrast to his baseball career, Alexander's personal life was marred by physical and emotional problems. Deafened by artillery shells during World War I, he also suffered from epilepsy.[1] It is unclear whether these afflictions contributed to his alcoholism, a problem that reached legendary proportions. After a twenty-year major league career, Alexander was removed from the lineup by the Cardinals after a drinking binge and ended his career with a barnstorming House of David team. After his retirement from organized baseball, Alexander joined a New York flea circus and appeared in a penny arcade, earning pocket money by answering questions about his glory days. Only a few months after his 1939 induction into baseball's Hall of Fame, Alexander summed up his financial condition by complaining, "They gave me a tablet up at the Cooperstown Hall of Fame, but I can't eat any tablet."[2] Twice married and divorced from the same woman, Grover Cleveland Alexander died alone in a St. Paul, Nebraska, rooming house on November 4, 1950.

The son of William Alexander, an Elba (Nebraska) farmer, and his wife, Martha, Grover Cleveland Alexander was born on February 26, 1887, and was named after the president of the Unites States. Baseball's influence was strong in rural areas during the early years of this century, and it's likely that Grover and his twelve brothers were involved in the sport during their childhood. In reviewing his local career, the *St. Paul Phonograph* reported in 1926 that Grover Alexander played with the Elba team, as well as with other local teams that needed a good pitcher. In the fall of 1907, he attracted outside attention when he pitched a game for Ord at the Valley County Fair, winning 8–0 while striking out thirteen batters. During a game the next day, he held Ord's opponent scoreless for four innings, earning another victory and a reputation in central Nebraska.[3]

In 1908 Alexander was working for the Howard County Telephone Company, doing field construction work and earning $1.75 a day. His Sundays were spent playing baseball for the St. Paul team. In June he was recruited by the Central City team, and on June 30 he recorded his first victory for his new team by downing Aurora 7–2. The local newspaper referred to their new pitcher as *George* Alexander, a mistake the reporter would not make again, and claimed that his pitching "proved to be a mystery to the South Platte warriors."[4] During that season with Central City, Alexander's pitching remained a mystery to the opposition as he won twenty-one games, including a no-hitter, while losing only four contests.

From Central City, Alexander went to Burwell, where he pitched during September and early October 1908, compiling a winning record. Among his victories were two against the celebrated Green's Nebraska Indians, one of the best semi-pro teams in the Midwest.[5]

Word of Alexander's success reached semi-professional teams outside Nebraska. In 1909 his professional career began when Alexander signed a contract with Galesburg of the Illinois-Missouri League. Alexander's physical attributes—over six feet in height with red hair and freckles—were immediately reported by a Galesburg newspaperman, who described him as:

> A blonde of the ruddy type . . . (with) the build of a switch engine. Manager Jap (Wagner) figures he can see the big strawberry slinger floating up puzzles to the opposing batsmen already and is much taken with his looks.[6]

The Galesburg Boosters' first test was an exhibition game against hometown Knox College, a 6–4 win. Alexander ended the game as a relief pitcher, keeping the collegians "guessing all the time." His legendary pinpoint control was not yet evident as he walked three batters during this brief appearance.[7] He was back in form for the season opener against Monmouth, striking out nine men but losing the game 5–4 because of three errors committed by his teammates. After two victories over Pekin in mid-May—a one-hitter in which Alexander himself got three hits and a shutout in which Alexander struck out sixteen—the Galesburg press nicknamed him "Alexander the Great."[8]

The St. Paul newspapers followed Alexander's success with unabashed glee, although the nickname attached to him in the local press was "Dode." After his victory over Pekin, the *St. Paul Phonograph-Press* reported, "It is evident that 'Dode' has won a home in Galesburg. May he continue to strike them out at every game."[9]

There were many highlights in Alexander's first season of organized baseball. In one game, Alexander hit a ball out of the park, over a Regal shoe sign in left field. He received a bonus of ten dollars after the players passed a hat among the fans and presented the collection to Alexander after the game. In addition, he was awarded a pair of Regal shoes.[10] In another game, Alexander led the Boosters to a 1–0 eleven inning victory over Pekin, allowing only five hits by the opposition and driving in the winning run himself.[11]

As his fame grew, Alexander was given still another nickname, "O.U. Alexander" (to be read as "Oh, you Alexander") and was sometimes referred to as "O.U. Alex."[12] After Alexander pitched a no-hitter against Canton on July 22, the Galesburg newspaperman took dramatic license to describe the game and the front page news of a local fire: "Emulating the example of Nero who fiddled while Rome was consumed by the flames, Alexander the Great fiddled with Canton while the Methodist religious edifice went up in smoke."[13] Alexander's next game was even more spectacular, as he made league history by pitching an eighteen inning 1–0 victory. He allowed only eight hits, not giving up any hits during the first nine innings of the game and striking out nineteen batters overall.[14]

Alexander's extraordinary season came to an end just a few days later in a freak accident, which occurred while he was running the bases. Alexander was on first base when the ball was hit to the second baseman, who tossed the ball to the shortstop, forcing out Alexander. In attempting to throw out the runner at first for a double play, the shortstop struck Alexander in the head with the ball, knocking him unconscious.[15]

For the next three weeks, Alexander remained in bed. When he tried to stand up, he complained of dizziness and problems with his eyes.[16] In an effort to help Alexander receive the treatment he needed (and to dump a perhaps permanently injured player), the Galesburg franchise sold him to Indianapolis of the American Association. In Indianapolis Alexander was placed under the care of an eye specialist for the remainder of the season.[17] The best wishes of his St. Paul neighbors went with Alexander as the *St. Paul Phonograph-Press* wrote, "We hope to be able to tell our readers, within a short time, of his complete recovery, and that he is back in the game once more and doing his usual effective work."[18]

Although Alexander didn't pitch for Indianapolis that season, he did return to St. Paul to pitch for the locals against Scotia on October 1, against Greeley on October 3, and against North Loup two days layer. His blurred vision gone, Alexander won all three games, causing the local press to brag, "With Dode on the hill for the locals . . . we can take care of any team in this section of the country."[19]

Alexander never got a chance to pitch for Indianapolis, because the manager felt his injury was a career-ending one. In what was considered by Indianapolis management to be a shrewd move, Alexander was "unloaded" to the Syracuse Stars of the New York State League in a cash deal. Ultimately, it was Syracuse that benefited from this transaction, as Alexander won twenty-nine games for the Stars in 1910, pitching thirteen shutouts over the season and holding the opposition scoreless over the last fifty-two innings that he worked. After pitching and winning both games of a double-header against Wilkes-Barre on July 20, Alexander also won a new nickname, "Iron Man."[20]

Until then, the Stars were mired in sixth place. Alexander soon began a streak in which he would win his last twelve games. By August 27 with league-leading Wilkes-Barre in Syracuse to face the Stars in a double-header, Syracuse had moved into second place. After shutting out Wilkes-Barre 4–0, the *Syracuse Journal* claimed that Alexander had:

> Accomplished what no other player has even come close to doing and he has substantial cause to feel proud, although he isn't. Alexander is one of those unassuming chaps that takes things as they come, good, bad or indifferent. He is the same quiet individual at all times. However, his friends, and he has an army of them, did the gloating for him.[21]

His army of friends in St. Paul met him at the depot after the 1910 season ended to congratulate him on his accomplishments and to claim that "the big 'Sorrel Top' is the king of them all when it comes to pitching."[22] The local fans were anxious to see Alexander pitch before he joined the major league Philadelphia Phillies the next season. They got their opportunity in September and October as he beat Ravenna and Ord easily, carrying his shutout streak through sixty-two successive innings.[23]

Despite his exceptional seasons with Galesburg and Syracuse, Alexander was not a shoo-in to make the Phillies roster. The Philadelphia sportswriters were withholding judgment until they could see Alexander tested against a worthy opponent. Alexander got his chance in an exhibition game against cross-town rival and reigning world champions, the Philadelphia Athletics. To everyone's surprise, he held Connie Mack's team hitless during his five-inning appearance. The St. Paul newspaper picked up the story from Philadelphia and reported, "Five mixed veterans and busher curvers scaled the pitching peak and all did high class work, but honors easily belonged to Emperor Alexander, the great pitcher from Syracuse."[24]

By June 1 Alexander's record stood at eight and two, tops in the National League. The Philadelphia press concluded that he was a consistent winner because of his "torpedo speed and an unhittable curve."[25] By the end of his rookie season, Alexander led the league in victories (28), shutouts (7), complete games (31), and innings pitched (367). Alexander's praises were sung by Phillies fans, particularly in his hometown of St. Paul, where praises were sung in rhymed verse.[26]

On his return to St. Paul at the end of his first major league season, he was greeted by hundreds of fans. After winning twenty-eight games for the Phillies, Alexander's St. Paul fans were upset with a salary of $3,200 offered by the team for the next season. Calling Alexander unappreciated, the *St. Paul Phonograph* adopted the local favorite's cause by stating:

> If it hadn't been for the St. Paul ball player this year, the Phillies would never have been heard of. During the time they were making history on the ball field it was the 'big fellow' from here done the work.[27]

Alexander returned to the Phillies in 1912 and although his win-loss ratio, 19–17, was somewhat disappointing, he again led the league in innings pitched. His earned run average (ERA) at 2.81 was also well below the 3.00 mark, the number considered the dividing line between an average pitcher and a superior one. Over the next five years Alexander compiled a stunning record of 143 wins and fifty losses for the Phillies, nearly three times as many victories as defeats. During the seasons of 1914, 1915, 1916, and 1917, he led the league in victories and innings pitched. Three of those years he led the league in ERA.

According to his contemporaries, Alexander's most amazing feat was pitching sixteen shutouts in 1916, four in a row coming in Baker Bowl, a "cracker box" of a stadium that was the Phillies' home park. The right field wall, only 280 feet from home plate, invited left-handed hitters to pull the ball that way. Rube Bressler, who batted against Alexander while playing for the Cincinnati Reds, said:

> I always felt that perhaps Grover Cleveland Alexander was the greatest of them all, because of the conditions under which he played. Sixteen shutouts in 1916 in Baker Bowl, where there was practically only a running track between first base and the right field wall. Only a giant could do a thing like that.[28]

Certainly the Phillies' greatest achievement during Alexander's peak years was their first pennant and subsequent appearance in the 1915 World Series.

In the series, Alexander pitched one victory over the Boston Red Sox, the Phillies' only victory in the five-game series. (Although the Phillies also appeared in the World Series in 1950, it wasn't until their 1980 appearance that another Phillies pitcher notched a World Series win.) In his second game, Alexander allowed the Red Sox only two runs, but his teammates could not solve the opposing pitcher and the Phillies went down to defeat.

After the 1917 season, Alexander and catcher Bill Killefer were traded to the Chicago Cubs for pitcher Mike Prendergast, catcher "Pickles" Dillhoefer, and $55,000. The Phillies were known for running a tight-fisted operation and Alexander's steadily increasing salary—up to $7,000 in 1915—and the $55,000 cash incentive led to completion of the deal.

World War I disrupted the baseball careers of many, and Alexander spent most of 1918 serving in France with the 342nd Field Artillery. Controversy surrounded Alexander's arrival in the army as some newspapers had pinned the label of "draft dodger" upon the thirty-one-year-old star. The *St. Paul Phonograph*, always Alexander's staunch supporter, came to his defense by detailing his "perfect willingness to go to war" and his "biggest single piece of patriotism . . . when he invested $500 in Third Liberty Loan Bonds."[29]

Alexander was married to Aimee Arrants, a St. Paul neighbor, before being sent to Europe. He went overseas with the Eighty-ninth Division and saw service in the Argonne, rising to rank of sergeant. He endured what appeared to be a minor shrapnel wound to his right ear. This injury would require medical attention years later.

On his return to major league baseball in 1919, Alexander became the mainstay of the Cubs pitching staff, recording sixteen wins and leading the league with a 1.72 ERA. After the 1920 season, he was proclaimed the league's leading pitcher after notching twenty-seven wins and, for the second year in a row, allowing the fewest runs per game.

During his years with the Cubs, Alexander's reputation for drinking came into public view. According to his wife, his drinking became a problem after his return from Europe. The nation's prohibition law did not stand in the way of Alexander, who, as a professional ballplayer, found it easy to gain admittance into speakeasies wherever the Cubs played.

In 1926 Joe McCarthy became the new Cubs manager. According to Aimee, problems started when Alexander broke his ankle and McCarthy, who had to pass the hospital every day, did not choose to visit the ailing superstar.[30] Early in the season, Alexander had to be sent back to Chicago after a drinking binge, and he was placed on indefinite suspension.

The Cubs placed Alexander on waivers, and the Cardinals' player-manager, Rogers Hornsby, picked up the veteran pitcher for $6,000. At the age of thirty-nine, the man called "Old Pete"[31] by his teammates, made his first start for the Cardinals and beat McCarthy's Cubs, 3–2. He went on to win nine of his sixteen starts for his new team and helped to propel the Cardinals to their first pennant.

It is ironic that Alexander's most remembered achievement is a game that he saved, rather than won, in the 1926 World Series against the Yankees. Alexander easily beat the heavily favored Yankees of Ruth and Gehrig in games two and six by scores of 6–2 and 10–2. The world championship was to be determined by game seven.

The stories of Alexander's appearance in that final game are many. According to some, Alexander knew that he might be called upon to pitch in that game so he held off on a victory celebration after his game six win. Others claimed that Alexander celebrated so thoroughly the night before that "he practically needed a seeing-eye dog to guide him in from the bull pen" when he was called upon to protect the Cardinals' 3–2 lead in the bottom of the seventh inning.[32]

When Alexander arrived at the pitcher's mound, the Yankees had the bases loaded and Tony Lazzeri at the plate. Lazzeri, a rookie who had played in the Pacific Coast League the year before, had acquired the nickname "Poosh 'Em Up" by batting in 222 runs for his minor league team. During his first year for the Yankees, Lazzeri had knocked in 114 runs, second only to Ruth.

After starting Lazzeri out with a ball, Alexander delivered a called strike. On the next pitch, Lazzeri lashed at an inside fastball that whistled down the left field line and curved foul at the last moment. Alexander later recalled, "A few feet more and he'd have been a hero and I'd have been a bum."[33] On the next pitch, Alexander broke off a sharp curve, low and away, that Lazzeri missed. To many, this was the most famous strikeout in World Series history. It should not be forgotten, however, that Alexander came back to hold the Yankees hitless for the final two innings, preserving the Cardinals' victory.

Although Alexander asserted that Cardinal starting pitcher Bill Sherdel was the hero of the series,[34] the St. Paul press would have none of it. Never prone to understatement, the *St. Paul Phonograph* viewed Alexander's performance as:

> A wonderful exhibition of nerve and good judgment. That is why we verily believe Alexander was a superman when he faced the Yanks on last Sunday afternoon and pulled the game from the yawning abyss of defeat and safely stowed it away in the archives of the baseball commission where it will remain for all time as one of the greatest beats in world's series conflicts. And again we claim Alexander as the hero of the series and entitled to all the credit for winning the world's series.[35]

Alexander's homecoming celebration attracted some 20,000 people on October 27, 1926. The *St. Paul Phonograph* detailed the day's events, which included a baseball game between Ord and Howard County players, speeches in honor of Alexander, the presentation of a watch charm to the hero, a barbecue in which some 12,000 sandwiches were served, and a street dance that lasted until midnight. . . .[36]

After a colossal drinking binge [as a member of the Cardinals in 1929] in Philadelphia, where he disappeared for three days, he was placed on vacation at full pay, rather than suspended, for the rest of the season. That winter he was traded to the Phillies, the team with which he had first gained stardom. He lost three decisions with the Phillies in 1930 and was released early in the season.

Alexander retired, believing that he had captured the National League mark for total career victories, third in the major leagues behind Cy Young and Walter Johnson. Ironically in the late 1940s, a statistician discovered that Christy Mathewson had won a game in 1902 for which he had not been given credit, thus placing Mathewson and Alexander in a tie for National League career victories. By that time, it was much too late for Alexander to break the record.

The remaining years of Alexander's life were marred by frustration, illness, and poverty. Aimee had divorced him in 1929 after stating in court that Alexander had tried to take "the cure" six times but had reverted to his old habits shortly after each attempt.[37] From 1931 to 1936, he played with the traveling House of David team.[38] Unlike his religiously influenced teammates, Alexander was permitted to shave every day. He tried to land a job as a major league pitching coach or manager, but his reputation insured that he would not be considered. The $250,000 that Alexander was thought to have earned during his career had long since been spent on high living.[39]

He was in and out of both jail and court, once being sued for $25,000 for alienation of affection by a St. Paul husband of Alexander's childhood sweetheart. He faced a variety of charges in Omaha in 1930, most relating to violation of liquor laws.[40] Although he and Aimee were remarried in 1931, his promise to her that he would quit drinking was soon broken. However, Alexander's remarriage apparently served to convince the wronged St. Paul husband to drop his suit.

In 1936 Alexander was thrown out of his Evansville, Indiana, hotel room for nonpayment of rent. He awoke in a local hospital, unable to explain how he had received a large lump on his head.[41] By 1939 he could be found sharing billing with a trained flea in New York. He was able to support himself by answering baseball questions and by serving as a greeter at a local tavern.

Under the title "One of the Greatest Pitchers of All Time Now Walks the Streets, Looking for a Job and a Bite to Eat," a St. Louis newspaper chronicled Alexander's situation in 1944. At that time, he was living in Cincinnati. He had gone there as part of a lecture tour and had awakened alone after the other members of the tour group left. He then worked as a guard at Wright Aeronautical Corporation and as a café floor manager. Both jobs were too hard on his legs, and at the time the article was written, Alexander was unemployed and wondering if he would be expelled from his current hotel room. He was also worried about his right ear, which had been nearly eaten away by an infection related to his World War I shrapnel wound.[42]

Turning up in Long Beach, California, four years later, Alexander had lost his right ear and the hearing in his left ear was impaired. The local newspaper there reported that he had recently fallen down the stairs of an Albuquerque hotel.[43] Later that year, Alexander was arrested in East St. Louis when he was found wandering through the streets in his pajamas. Wherever he went during his last years, a story would appear in the local press detailing his pathetic condition.

Alexander returned to St. Paul in 1950 with a new lease on life after being hired by the American Legion to serve as an advisor to their junior baseball program. Alexander's assignment was to tour Nebraska during the summer, teaching good sportsmanship and providing coaching tips. His first tour stop was St. Paul, and the town set May 24 as Grover Cleveland Alexander Day. Unlike his 1926 homecoming, the people of St. Paul chose to ignore their native son and largely avoided the parade, baseball game, banquet, and Nebraska Navy admiralship presentation. The *St. Paul Phonograph* chastised its readers by stating that the celebration "would have been a much bigger one if more folks would have bothered to attend and pay respect to a man who has brought fame and recognition to 'their home town' even though he HAS had his 'ups and downs.'"[44]

That same year, the Phillies won their first pennant since 1915, when Alexander had led them with thirty-one victories. After associates had made arrangements, Alexander attended the last two games of the World Series in New York, unrecognized in the crowd and by the press. Back in St. Paul, he found himself unable to get a drink in town as the local bartenders refused to serve him. In a letter to Aimee (from whom he was divorced again in 1941), Alexander expressed his discontent with life in St. Paul, writing, "I can't figure out why I was such a fool to come here to be treated as I am and after the days when I had been heard of."[45] Less than a month after penning that line, Grover Cleveland Alexander, at age sixty-three, was found dead in his rooming house. His old team, the St. Louis Cardinals, paid for Alexander's steel casket and his funeral service. He was buried in St. Paul's Elmwood Cemetery in the Alexander family plot.

At the time of Alexander's death, nationally syndicated columnist Grantland Rice recalled Alexander to be the most cunning, the smartest, and the best control pitcher that baseball had ever seen. He wrote:

> Above everything else, Alex had one terrific feature to his pitching—he knew just what the batter didn't want—and he put it there to the half-inch. I would say that Alex was top man among hurlers. He knew more about the true art or science of pitching.[46]

It was Alexander's tragedy that although he could control a baseball, he could not control his life or his destiny.

16. Share Squabble at the Series

THE 1918 WORLD SERIES gets overlooked by a lot of Cubs fans. Many seem to know that the Cubs last won a National League pennant in 1945 only to lose that year's World Series, but few recognize that the Cubs played for a title in 1918. Maybe it's too painful for Cubs fans to remember too many World Series defeats.

The owner of the club for this World Series loss was Charles H. "Lucky Charlie" Weeghman. Born to a homemaker mom and blacksmith dad amid humble surroundings in Richmond, Indiana, the baseball-loving Charlie moved to Chicago as a young man. There he became a "coffee boy" in Charles King's famed loop eatery on what is now Wells Street, and in short order—thanks to his quick smile, willingness to put in a full day's work, and generous nature—made head waiter.

Having saved a few grand, he eventually started his own Chicago restaurant, a kind of precursor to modern-day fast-food joints that served up sandwiches any way you liked them as long as you liked them cold. Mr. Weeghman also put one-armed schoolroom desks in his restaurant to maximize his use of space. The concept worked. Before long he owned fifteen lunchrooms, and by the mid-1910s he was reportedly worth $8,000,000 (about $170 million today adjusted for inflation).[1]

He poured a lot of that dough into baseball. He founded the professional Chicago Whales, who played from 1914 to 1915 in the short-lived Federal League, and built the team a steel and concrete home on the Northside of town that years later would become known the world over as Wrigley Field. When the Federal League went under in 1915, Weeghman, who had previously tried to buy the St. Louis Cardinals, set his sights on the Cubs, which were put up for sale by Charles P. Taft in 1916. In a legendary power-move, aided by backers like William Wrigley Jr., fifteen minutes before the bid deadline Weeghman offered $500,000 in cash to get the Cubbies. He then moved the squad to Weeghman Field (now Wrigley Field).

By the end of the 1910s, though, what with an economic downturn, World War I, and the waning popularity of his pack-'em-in lunchroom concept, Weeghman's cash flow started to decrease. A couple of nightspot ventures and theater investments didn't deliver as hoped either. In 1919, to stave off bankruptcy, he sold his Cubs stake. Three years later he had nothing to do with his original lunchrooms, and his Horatio Alger–like biography turned into one of financial woe.

In 1938 Mr. Weeghman, by then a resident of New York, died in Chicago en route from Hot Springs, Arkansas, back home to New York City.[2] His legacy lives on, though, through that steel ballpark he originally built for his Whales.

The late 1910s weren't just a tough time for Mr. Weeghman. In September 1918 the United States was participating in the Allies' massive Grand Offensive, which would ultimately end World War I a couple months after the World Series. And by the end of the 1918 baseball season a flu pandemic, which caused scores of millions of deaths worldwide, was already ravaging thousands of Americans, with worse to come in the ensuing months.

It was because of World War I, in fact, that the 1918 Series remains the only one to have taken place entirely within the month of September. In July the government had decreed that men of age either "work or fight" to help with the war effort, and therefore Major League Baseball was given until September 15th to wrap things up.[3] By the time the Series started, both the National and American Leagues had lost loads of talent to military service or "essential" wartime work (including the Cubs' standout pitcher, Pete Alexander), which in turn contributed to the championship's low gate—even with slashed ticket prices and with the Cubs' home games taking place in the more spacious Comiskey Park rather than Weeghman Field.[4]

In the buildup to the 1918 World Series, *Chicago Tribune* reporter I. E. Sanborn claimed that, because of the roster turnover that season, "the coming world's series offers a superhazardous proposition to the dopesmiths."[5] While Sanborn equivocated, however, the *Boston Globe*'s Edward F. Martin wrote rather confidently that his home-side would win. Among the players on the Red Sox roster that gave Martin such optimism, was the young, colorful, and ultra-talented George Herman "Babe" Ruth, Jr., who was only just beginning his transition from a super-hurler to a prodigious home run basher.[6] Martin predicted that Ruth would do fine against the Cubs in the field; his only concern about the Babe, and the rest of the Red Sox for that matter, was how he would fare against the Cubs' lefties. But this didn't prove worth worrying about too much, particularly when Ruth pitched, because the Cubs couldn't hit him—he finished the Series with a 2–0 record and a 1.06 ERA.

Not only World War I hurt this Series' gate. So too did the threat of a mid-Series strike by the players, who, already facing a smaller-than-usual cut of Series' proceeds given the attendance shortfall, were upset that the owners had chosen to lessen the players' shares. So on September 10, 1918, in Boston's Fenway Park, a showdown looked imminent as the big leaguers balked at coming out onto the field to start game five. Only after a group of wounded soldiers arrived, causing fans to cheer for them and a band that was on-hand to play "Over There" for them, did the players decide to take the field, for the sake of the game, the fans, and the wounded soldiers, they claimed, "Not because we think we are getting a fair deal."[7]

Though game five did end up taking place, the row between management and the players had already done its damage. Only about 15,000 fans turned out for the Red Sox' championship-clinching win the next day—a drop of about 10,000 fans from game five.[8] Here the 1918 *Boston Daily Globe* explains in detail some of the nuances that led to the odd scene that arose as game five was supposed to begin.

Adjustment Today, Players' Demand

Melville E Webb Jr., *Boston Daily Globe*, Sept 11, 1918

There came very nearly being no ball game yesterday in the World's Series between the Red Sox and the Cubs.

The Boston and Chicago players, dissatisfied with the arrangement laid down by their respective leagues and the conditions the leagues put up to the National Commission to enforce, declared themselves yesterday morning against the same for their own financial welfare, and for a time virtually were on strike.

The ball game, at which almost 25,000 had gathered, was delayed an hour, the fans, not knowing what was up, showing unusual fortitude and lack of uneasiness; while under the grandstand there was a lot doing.

Last Winter, basing the 1918 receipts on past records, the leagues decided that the share proceeds of the World's Series to be given to the players should be split eight ways—that is, that the second, third and fourth clubs in each league should share in the players' rakeoff with the championship clubs.

PLAYERS GET TOGETHER

War conditions were not figured but it was estimated that if the receipts of the World's Series and intercity series should net the sum of about $150,000, the winners of the big major league post-season pennant would receive $2000 each, and the losers $1400 each.

The Boston and Chicago players only a few days ago realized that proceeds of this year's game would not be sufficient to net the maximum amount, and that if the division was made as planned the major league club players share would be far below the sum anticipated. Accordingly, the members of both teams sought to come to an understanding with the National Commission so they would be assured the $2000 and $1400 respectively, and this regardless of the plans for the apportionment of profits among the other first division clubs.

CONFERENCE HASTILY ARRANGED

Since Sunday night the players, represented by Harry Hooper and Everett Scott of the Red Sox and Leslie Mann and Bill Killifer of the Cubs, had been trying to get a conference with the National Commission. Yesterday morning there was a brief meeting, but there was nothing doing, the members stating that the commission had nothing to do with the apportionment, and that the matter in question was not a commission but a National and American League affair.

The commission suggested that the discussion be postponed until after the ball game yesterday, and urged that the right thing would be done; and there the matter ended.

At the ball park, however, the players got together again and decided not to start the ball game until they had been assured of what they believed to be their rightful share of the World's Series profits. None of the members of either club was dressed for play at the time the game was scheduled to begin.

Shortly before game time the members of the National Commission arrived and a conference was hastily arranged.

Harry Hopper, representing the Sox, and Leslie Mann, the Cubs, went to the umpires' room, where Pres Ban Johnson of the American League, Acting Pres, John Heydler of the National League, Garry Herrmann, owner of the Cincinnati club and chairman of the commission, soon made entrance together with the umpires, some newspapermen and not a few fans.

Harry Hooper was spokesman for the players. He pointed out that he was not a ringleader in the trouble but that he had been selected to present the case of the ball players, who, he said, believed they were not being fairly treated.

The commission, through Messrs Johnson and Herrmann, endeavored to show the representatives of the players that they could not change the conditions under which the receipts of the series should be divided. Mr. Johnson pointed out that, had it not been for his efforts in Washington, there would have been no World's Series at all, while Mr. Herrmann emphasized the fact that the commission was powerless to change series' conditions that had been imposed upon it by the National and American Leagues. Mr. Herrmann said the commission could make no change and that if the game was not played it would be up to the players to bear the blame.

PLAY THE GAME UNDER PROTEST

Pres Johnson appealed to Hooper and Mann to influence the players to go out on the field in the interests of the National game and not to disappoint the assembled fans. And, although under protest that they had not been fairly treated, the representatives returned to their clubrooms, and, although the majority of the boys were eager to continue the fight, it was finally decided to go out to play the game, although under protest.

Once the players decided this Ex-Mayor Fitzgerald of Boston, who was one of those present at the meeting, made the announcement from the field that the game would be played, and that the league clubs had temporarily waived their point in order that the fans might not be disappointed.

The game then started, and the contest never for a moment indicated that the ball players even had a thought for the jam they had just been through, but were out to win and without regard to politics and profit cuts.

What will happen today is problematical. The players of both clubs met last night and say they will insist on another meeting with the commission this morning before the gates of Fenway Park are opened. The boys, through their representatives, say they will devote all their share of the receipts to the Red Cross if the commission will accept this proposition and give them what they declare should be their share.

The club owners, Weeghman of Chicago and Frazee of Boston, doubtless will declare themselves in on today's affairs. Both, it is understood, are willing to meet the players halfway in order that the baseball public may not be disappointed and that the series may proceed.

The situation stands as follows: The commission contends that the arrangement for the division of the player share of the receipts of the series [will] not be changed except by consent of the magnates in the respective leagues.

The players contend that they understood that the winner's share of the major post-season games should be $2000 for each man and $1400 for each loser's share, regardless of what the other, first division clubs receive.

This is still the ball players' point of view. The boys say they are going to fight to the limit, and will not go to the ball park today until some satisfactory adjustment is made.

17. Papa, the Gipper, and the Cubs

MANY CELEBRITIES, such as comedian Bill Murray and actors Jim Belushi and John Cusack, have associated themselves with the Cubs in some fashion, but perhaps no public figures larger than Ernest Hemingway and Ronald Reagan have a direct connection to the Cubs. In fact, the Cubs helped both get their careers started. With regard to "Papa," this is reflected in the first selection, an article about Hemingway and his work covering the Cubs for the *Kansas City Star*. The second selection takes a look at the importance of sports, the Cubs in particular, in the life of Ronald Reagan, as well as at the increasingly poignant role sports have played in American culture.

Grover Cleveland Alexander in 1918: A New Kansas City Piece by Ernest Hemingway

George Monteiro, *American Literature*, March 1982

Most of the stories Ernest Hemingway filed with the *Kansas City Star* in his seven months with that newspaper (October 1917 April 1918) will probably never be identified. Indeed, in 1970, Matthew J. Bruccoli reprinted all the *Kansas City Star* stories he could then attribute to Hemingway, a total of twelve.[1] That the collection is far from exhaustive, however, is indicated both by the editorial appendices of "Possible Hemingway Stories" and by the *Star's* assignment sheet for 3 January 1918 (reproduced in facsimile as frontispiece to *Cub Reporter*) showing one day's routine for the twenty-one *Star* reporters therein listed. For Hemingway alone the sheet lists seven assignments. If this surviving sheet can be taken as a typical listing of a day's work for a *Star* reporter, simple multiplication suggests that Hemingway might well cover up to thirty-five assignments in a five-day week, and that would add up to as many as 1015 assignments in his thirty weeks with the *Star*. Even if he averaged no more than one published story per working day, the total would run to 150 stories.

It is now possible, I would suggest, to identify a thirteenth Hemingway contribution to the *Star*. The evidence that he wrote a piece on Grover Cleveland Alexander comes in Hemingway's 14 March 1918 letter to his father, in which he boasted that, having met Alexander during his one-day stopover in Kansas City as he was on his way to spring training with the Chicago Cubs baseball team in Pasadena, California, he had written a story about him.[2] On 13 March the *Star* printed a piece entitled "'Alec' Left With the Cubs," its only story at that time about the famous pitcher.

The individuals mentioned in the story, with one exception, can be found in *The Official Encyclopedia of Baseball*.[3]

'ALEC' LEFT WITH THE CUBS

**The pitcher didn't sign, but he checked his trunk to California.
Kilduff and Hendrix Also Joined the Club Here—
Deal, Wortman and Vaughn Were Greeted by Hand Shaking Friends.**

Grover Cleveland Alexander joined the Cubs en route to their California training camp here today.

The mighty "Alec" didn't sign a contract, but he checked his trunk through to California. Grover Cleveland may not sink his fins into any portion of that $10,000 bonus he is demanding for attaching his monogram to a Chicago contract, but he isn't passing up any free trips to California.

The Cub special, no accent on the special, as it consists of only two cars hooked onto a Santa Fe regular train, reached Kansas City about 11 o'clock this morning.

Alexander, Pete Kilduff, balking infielder, and Claude Hendrix, pitcher, were waiting in ambush for the Cub "special." Alexander told Kansas City friends that he wouldn't sign unless given the $10,000 he asks. Manager Mitchell of the Cubs told friends here that he had absolute power to deal with "Alex," so the guessing is now on as to what station along the route will flash the news that Grover Cleveland has ornamented a contract with his own peculiar style of hieroglyphics.

There is only a little matter of $250 between Pete Kilduff and harmony with the Cub pay wagon, so Manager Mitchell didn't anticipate great difficulty in inducing Peter to sling some ink.

Among the first spring trainers to hop off the Cub rattler were Charley Deal, "Chuck" Wortman and "Hippo" Vaughn, former Blue athletes, who found a reception committee waiting to shake them by the salaried flippers.

The two cars of Cub pennant prospects were last seen some half hour after their arrival cabooshing out of the station on the Santa Fe regular with Manager Mitchell's right arm about the mighty "Alec's" shoulder and his left patting the recalcitrant Kilduff on the back.

Ronald Reagan: Above All, the Gipper was a Good Sport

Gary Peterson, *Knight Ridder/Tribune News Service*, June 5, 2004

Ronald Reagan wasn't the first United States President to recognize the advantages of aligning himself with competitive athletics. That tradition dates back to at least 1892, when Benjamin Harrison became the first President to attend a major league baseball game.

William Taft expanded on the theme, delivering the ceremonial first pitch that launched the 1910 season. Later that day, the 300-pound President inadvertently birthed the seventh-inning stretch when he stood up to stretch his legs. Thinking he was leaving, fans stood up out of respect. Seeing that he wasn't, they sat back down.

Dwight Eisenhower expanded the presidential sports horizon beyond the baseball diamond, golfing the 1950s away. John Kennedy was a touch football maniac. Richard Nixon had a bowling alley installed in the White House basement, and diagrammed a play for Washington Redskins coach George Allen, suitable for use in Super Bowl VII. Gerald Ford played a game resembling golf, only far more violent.

Jimmy Carter jogged.

They knew, as Reagan came to find out, that even the most superficial connection with sports gave them a healthy and vigorous sheen. It provided vitality by association. They also understood the diversionary benefits of shaking hands with Walter Johnson, knocking it around with Billy Casper and trying to embellish the home team's Super Bowl game plan.

They helped pioneer the concept of the presidential sportsman. Reagan perfected it.

And he began long before he even considered a career in politics. Reagan, according to legend and lore, worked as a lifeguard at Lowell Park in Tampico, Ill., as a young man. He may not have had David Hasselhoff's supporting cast, but his rescue numbers were nothing to sneeze at.

Young Master Reagan, it says in the history books, saved 77 people from drowning.

His first paying job after graduating from Eureka College in 1932 was as a sportscaster with NBC working in Iowa. One of his assignments was to re-create Chicago Cubs games from a studio, using accounts of the game delivered by telegraph.

Telegraphy was nearly as unreliable as the Cubs' starting pitching in those days. During one game late in the 1934 season the line went dead with Augie Galan at the plate in the ninth inning of a tie game between the Cubs and the St. Louis Cardinals. Reagan had no choice but to launch into the kind of seat-of-the-pants, long-winded oration that every aspiring politician eventually must master.

"I had a ball on the way to the plate and there was no way to call it back," he recalled later. "So, I had Augie foul this pitch down the left field line. He fouled for six minutes and forty-five seconds. My voice was riding in pitch and threatening to crack—and then, bless him, (the telegrapher) started typing. I clutched at the slip. It said: 'Galan popped out on the first ball pitched.'"

In 1937, while in California covering spring training, Reagan signed with Warner Brothers and began a career in acting—another vocation that would serve him well in politics.

"One day at Catalina, Charlie Grimm, the Cubs' manager bawled me out for not even showing up at the practice field," Reagan said. "How could I tell him that somewhere within myself was the knowledge I would no longer be a sports announcer?"

Reagan's first big role as an actor was playing ill-fated Notre Dame football star George Gipp in the 1940 classic, "Knute Rockne, All-American."

Gipp did for Reagan what Augie Galan never could, spring-boarding the young actor to fame and prominence. Reagan even appropriated Gipp's nickname. Half a century after the release of the movie, Reagan was still being referred to as The Gipper.

Less celebrated was Reagan's role as pitcher Grover Cleveland Alexander in the 1952 movie, "The Winning Team." The studio described it as the story of a man who, "through determination and the love of a good woman, overcame alcoholism, illness and misfortune."

Forty years later, of course, that would be the perfect career synopsis for half the members of Congress. In the innocent '50s, it earned Reagan accolades for his athletic prowess. Several major leaguers had cameos in the film, and all praised Reagan for his ability to pass himself off as a ballplayer.

In time, Reagan left acting for politics, was elected governor of California, and later President. Here is where he hit his stride as American's First Fan.

Reagan liked to surround himself with champions. He invited scores of newly minted championship teams to the White House rose garden. Invariably they showed up with one of their own uniforms, bearing No. 1 and the name "Gipper" on the back.

He also popularized the congratulatory telephone call to the winning locker room. When Baltimore beat Philadelphia to win the 1983 World Series, Reagan called the triumphant (and lubricated) Orioles in their clubhouse.

The phone was passed around until it came to catcher Rick Dempsey, apparently several bubbles deep into his celebration.

"Mr. President," Dempsey said, "you tell those Russians we're having a great time over here playing baseball."

Five years later, the Berlin Wall fell. Coincidence? Or just another example of life imitating baseball? In 1984, Reagan addressed the opening ceremonies at the Summer Olympics in Los Angeles. In 1988 he came full circle. On Sept. 30 he threw out not one but two ceremonial first pitches before a Cubs–Pittsburgh Pirates game. He broadcast an inning and a half, then left after three innings.

"You know," he told announcer Harry Caray, "in a few months I'm going to be out of work and I thought I might as well audition."

He never did return to broadcasting. But he finished his second term as

President without incident. His retirement was marred almost immediately by the onset of Alzheimer's disease, which detracted from his quality of life and contributed to his death Saturday at age 93.

Looking back over Reagan's life as a presidential fan, and a sportsman in the truest horse-riding, wood-chopping sense of the word, Rick Dempsey's sentiment resonates as powerfully now as it did then. Mr. President, you tell those people where you are that we're having a lot of fun down here playing baseball.

18. Humble Beginnings, Majestic Life

WILLIAM WRIGLEY JR. was born into humble means about five months after the start of the Civil War. By the time of his January 26, 1932, death at the age of 70, America had industrialized, Chicago had boomed, and he had become one of the Midwest's wealthiest men, as well as owner of the Chicago Cubs. He built his far-flung business empire, moored by five-cent-a-pack gum, upon crafty advertising and other methods of ingenious salesmanship. After gaining controlling interest in the Cubs in 1922, he helped guide the team to a World Series appearance in 1929. Actually, you could argue he oversaw two World Series appearances, given that the year he died the team made it there as well. And he warrants credit for hiring and keeping on William Veeck Sr. as club president. Veeck served in that capacity from 1919 to 1933.

It was late 1918 when William Wrigley Jr. asked to meet with Veeck Sr., who at that time was a *Chicago American* journalist who had written a number of critical articles about the Chicago Cubs under the pen name "Bill Bailey." While the tone of these articles was critical, Veeck had also offered suggestions for improving the team and readers seemed to like his bent. So too, apparently, did Wrigley Jr. At their meeting, Wrigley Jr. asked, "If you think you can do any better, then why don't you try it?" Without so much as thinking about it, Veeck said, "All right. I will."[1]

By December of that year the sports journalist-turned-executive was named the Cubs vice president, second in command to new president Fred Mitchell. When Mitchell decided to manage the ballclub the following year, Veeck completed his unlikely journey to Cubs president.

A change agent with a sharp business sense, Veeck in time got Wrigley Jr. to embrace "Ladies' Day," which brought droves of women to Wrigley Field on a weekly basis, and he pushed Wrigley Jr. to pay top dollar for talent. To

A wide shot of the Cubs' spring training diamond on Catalina Island, 1928. Photographer: *Chicago Daily News*. Courtesy Chicago History Museum.

boot, Veeck had a keen eye for ballplayers. He is considered the architect of the Cubs' three pennant winners of the 1930s. As for managers, it was Veeck that pushed for the hiring of Joe McCarthy and for the firing, late in the 1932 season, of Rogers Hornsby in favor of Charlie Grimm, who proceeded to lead the Cubs on an assault of the standings and ultimately to that year's National League pennant.[2]

It was William Veeck's son, Bill Veeck Jr., who would cement the family legacy as baseball innovators. As club treasurer in 1937—under the ownership of Wrigley Jr.'s son P. K. Wrigley—Veeck Jr. earned credit for bringing ivy to Wrigley Field's walls. He also oversaw the construction of Wrigley Field's manually operated scoreboard. As if not enough, later with the rival White Sox Veeck Jr. conjured the first exploding scoreboard, put players in shorts, had Harry Caray stretch it out in the seventh inning with a rendition of "Take Me Out to the Ball Game," and oversaw the infamous Disco Demolition Night.[3]

In addition to Veeck, Wrigley also hired manager Joseph McCarthy in 1926, and did other noteworthy things as the Cubs owner, such as hosting spring training twenty-seven miles off the coast of Los Angeles on Catalina Island, which he had purchased whole. All told, the former hustling soap man lived quite a life.[4]

Wrigley did catch some baseball flack, though. While he hired McCarthy as manager, he also basically let go of McCarthy just a year after he had guided the Cubs to the 1929 World Series. McCarthy then went on to manage the "Bronx Bombers" to seven World Series titles from 1931 to 1946.

McCarthy was dismissed in 1930 partly for hiring, ironically enough, former Cubs icon Joe Tinker to scout the Athletics before the 1929 World Series. Supposedly this resulted in Tinker giving "bad information" that hurt the Cubs' strategy. In addition, suggestions arose after the 1929 season that McCarthy allowed his players to live on an "elaborate scale while on the road."[5]

Ultimately there were fans that saw Wrigley's ownership reign as decidedly mixed. This selection, from the *Chicago Daily News*'s Jim Crusinberry, however, largely applauds Wrigley for making the Cubs his passion.

Wrigley Spent Fortune to Make Cubs Champs

Jim Crusinberry, *Chicago Daily News*, January 26, 1932

AS OWNER OF NORTH SIDE TEAM
HE WAS ONE OF GAME'S BOOSTERS

William Wrigley Jr. entered baseball quietly and unheralded in 1916 and became the biggest booster in the game.

When he went into the sport the Cubs were down and in debt. He not only built the team into a champion but made it the biggest moneymaker in the major league.

It was in December, 1915, that peace was made between organized baseball and the Federal League. Charles Weeghman, Chicago restaurant man of that time had been the president of the Chicago Federal League team. The

Cubs were owned by Charles P. Taft of Cincinnati. When peace was made the Federal League passed out of existence. Weeghman, with a number of associates, bought the Cubs from Taft and combined them with the Chicago Federals to make a new team of Cubs in the National League.

BACKED WEEGHMAN VENTURE.

For some two months it wasn't known who had gone in with Weeghman and his partner William Walker of the Federal League team in purchasing the Chicago Nationals. Finally it was announced that the men behind the new move were William Wrigley Jr., J. Ogden Armour, A. D. Lasker and a number of others.

But Weeghman remained as president of the team for three more years or until the end of the season of 1918.

By this time Mr. Wrigley had become greatly interested in the game and in the team. He went into it at the start only through civic pride. The Cubs had been owned by a Cincinnati man. He believed Chicago men should be back of them. And for that reason he put up his money with Mr. Armour and Mr. Lasker and some half dozen others to make the Cubs a purely Chicago owned club.

BOUGHT CATALINA ISLAND.

At the time he had no thought of taking an active part in the operation of the club. The first year he was in, 1916, the team went to Florida to train in the spring. Before the season was over, Mr. Wrigley began to get the baseball fever. He started going out to the games. And the following year he induced Weeghman to take the club to California for the spring training trip. The Cubs have trained in California ever since.

For the first three years out there—1917, 1918 and 1919—the training was done in Pasadena. But in 1919 Wrigley bought Catalina island and built a permanent training camp on the island, with the finest baseball diamond in America, even though the team couldn't use it more than three or four weeks in the year. He built the practice field at a cost of nearly $60,000, which he paid out of his own pocket and not out of the ball club's funds.

It was not until the end of the world war that Mr. Wrigley became the moving spirit in the operation of the Cubs. The team had won the National League pennant in 1918, but there was no great celebration over it because the whole country was thinking of nothing but the war. But when the following season opened the war was over and Mr. Wrigley took up baseball as his hobby.

Even after winning the pennant the club was deep in debt. When the 1918 season was over the club owed the banks approximately $250,000. It was at that time that Charles Weeghman resigned as president. Fred Mitchell, who was manager of the team, was made president and William L Veeck, then a baseball writer in Chicago, was engaged as business manager. Mitchell acted as president for one year. Then Veeck was made president and has held the office ever since.

It was not until 1922 that Mr. Wrigley gained a controlling interest in the club. From 1916 until that time there had been friction between him and A. D. Lasker in dictating the policy of the club. Finally it became apparent that the two men couldn't agree, so Wrigley succeeded in buying enough of the Lasker and the Armour stock to give him control. It is believed he controlled more than 60 percent of the stock.

Since he gained control Wrigley acted as chairman of the board of directors, but has left the running of the ball club to President Veeck. The club became a moneymaker as soon as the new organization went into effect. The debt was entirely paid off in two years. And in 1928, 1929, 1930 and even last year the Cubs outdrew all others in the National League and all clubs in either major league for at least two of those years.

BUYS ALEX AND KILLIFER.

The first move of importance in rebuilding the Cubs after Wrigley and his associates entered the game was the purchase in the spring of 1917 of Grover Alexander and Bill Killifer, the crack battery of the Phillies. Since then the Wrigley bankroll always has been on hand for the purchase of any star who might help the club to be a winner. It is estimated that something more than $1,000,000 has been spent in the effort to make the team a champion, but it was not until 1929 that it succeeded. During, that time the team tried many managers. Seven men have had the position since Wrigley entered the game. The first was Joe Tinker who was taken over from the Chicago Federal League team. Then came Fred Mitchell, Johnny Evers, Bill Killifer, Rabbit Maranville, George Gibson, Joe McCarthy and Rogers Hornsby.

It was a great disappointment to Owner Wrigley when the Cubs were beaten in the world series of 1929 by the Athletics. It wasn't so much the defeat as the manner in which the Cubs were beaten. McCarthy then was the manager, but after one more year McCarthy was let out and the job turned over to Hornsby, who holds it at the present time.

MINGLED WITH HIS PLAYERS.

Probably there never was an owner of a ball club with such enthusiasm for the game as Wrigley. He mingled with the players, especially during the training period on Catalina island, where he had his winter home.

Back in the spring of 1924 on the training trip there happened to be a number of the players who were musically inclined. They dug up some instruments on the island and formed an orchestra with eight pieces.

One night they went up to the Wrigley home and serenaded him. It pleased Mr. Wrigley so much that the next day he went over to Los Angeles with the team to an exhibition game, took the eight musicians to a music store and equipped them with new instruments. The Cubs orchestra of that season gained nationwide publicity, but it didn't get anywhere in the pennant race so the following year the orchestra was disbanded at Mr. Wrigley's request.

OUTSPOKEN IN BASEBALL.

Wrigley was outspoken in his baseball connections. During the season of 1930 he had decided to let McCarthy go and make Hornsby the manager. But it was not to be announced until the end of the season. However, he couldn't help letting some of his associates know, and the story leaked out a couple of weeks before the season was over causing McCarthy to resign.

Last summer, about Aug. 1, Mr. Wrigley grew vitriolic regarding the flop of Hack Wilson, who had been the leading slugger the previous year. He stated plainly that he hoped he wouldn't have to look at Wilson another season as a member of the Cubs. This brought about the trading of Hack last month after he had been suspended without pay for the last four weeks of the season.

19. Baseball Man

FROM 1926 TO 1950, with the Cubs, Red Sox, and Yankees, manager Joe Mc-Carthy won over sixty-one percent of his games. But most startling, as a big league manager he won seven world series titles—all as the head of the famed "Bronx Bombers." In the '30s and '40s it was painful enough for Cubs fans to know that one of its former managers was winning title after title, but it was doubly so in years when those titles culminated with World Series victories over the Cubs, which happened in 1932 and 1938.

Born in Germantown, Pa., McCarthy immersed himself in baseball. As Hall of Fame New York Yankee shortstop Phil Rizutto, who considered Mc-Carthy the greatest manager he ever played for, put it, "Joe McCarthy's life centered around baseball. I think that's why he felt that everyone else's life should be the same."[1] But even though McCarthy lived and breathed the game, as a player he never got as much as a cup of coffee in the big leagues, spending fifteen years in the minors. How he went from that to baseball's most revered skipper with the Yankees—after having been let go by the Cubs, no less—is a remarkable tale. Joe Williams covers it well in the following 1939 *Saturday Evening Post* article.

Busher Joe McCarthy

Joe Williams, *Saturday Evening Post*, April 15, 1939

The Louisville Colonels, of the American Association, were up to their large, fluttering ears in the thick of a furious pennant fight in early September of 1920. They were playing a vital game with St. Paul and it was closer than a handful of fingers in a red mitten.

Near the end of the game a St. Paul player, one Bert Ellison, was caught off first base, and one of those interminable run-downs followed, with the trapped player shuttling back and forth trying to escape, his tormentors trying equally hard to put the ball on him.

Finally the player made a daring dash for second and the Colonels' first baseman, instead of throwing, gave pursuit. And then seeing he was being outfooted he made a quick, jerky throw. The ball hit the second baseman on the chest and bounded off into short center field.

Joe McCarthy went into a purple rage. "Why, you big kraut head! What made you do a stupid thing like that? Why didn't you give me the ball sooner?"

Jay Kirke, a fabulous minor-league character, looked the manager of the Colonels in the eye and imperiously said: "What right have you got trying to tell a .380 hitter how to play ball?"

McCarthy was hitting only .220 at the time, so instead of becoming outraged he bowed to the logic of Mr. Kirke's criticism, and that night he announced his retirement from baseball as an active player. From that point on he would sit on the bench and tell the players what to do. Maybe Mr. Kirke was right. He had gone back too far to put on personal demonstrations—and he realized he never had very far back to go, even from the height of his career.

WHEREIN FATE BREAKS A KNEECAP

This incident was the turning point in what is probably the most remarkable managerial experience in the history of baseball. Step by step, it led to distinctions no other manager has ever been able to achieve. Such as the winning of championships in both the National and the American Leagues and the winning of the world series three times in a row. And yet Joe McCarthy, who is now gunning for his fourth straight championship with the New York Yankees, never was good enough to play a single game in the big leagues. A broken kneecap as a sandlot player in his home town of Germantown, Pennsylvania, doomed him to the bushes forever as a player. The closest he ever got to anything resembling a big-league assignment as a player was a contract with the Brooklyn club of the Federal League, an outlaw organization which collapsed before he was due to report in 1916.

More than half of McCarthy's baseball life was spent in the brambles of mediocrity. He was the confirmed and perennial busher. He played the tank towns, rode the day coaches, had a gustatory acquaintance with all the greasy-spoon restaurants. He played second base and was an adroit fielder. He hit well enough, especially in the clutches, with men on base. But he was slow. The broken kneecap had left an enduring mark. "If it wasn't for that knee we'd recommend you," the scouts always said.

Like all young men who go into baseball, McCarthy's one blazing ambition was to wear a big-league uniform. And like most young men, he was optimistic; one day the knee would get better, his speed would come back, he'd get his chance to play second in the majors. But the knee never lost its stiffness, the royal command never came—and the first time Busher Joe McCarthy appeared in a big league uniform it was as a manager.

The busher's ambition had been realized in a totally undreamed-of and unplanned manner. Certainly when he was back in dear old Wilkes-Barre digging grounders out of rocks and gravel around second he never imagined he'd make his entrance into the big leagues as the head man of the club. But here he was, in 1926, manager of the Chicago Cubs, and he'd never caught a ball or swung a bat, had never even warmed a bench in the big leagues.

Still, the day Bill Veeck, a reformed sports writer who had taken over the practical duties of the Chicago club, came to him and offered him the manager's job he wasn't altogether dreamy-eyed with surprise. Long ago he had given up all hopes of ever playing in the big leagues, and settled down to a studious examination of managerial material. So McCarthy began a deep, intensive study of the methods and tactics of the masters, of McGraw, Carrigan, Robinson, Mack. Particularly Mack. The busher had a warm devotion for Mack, who was his first hero of the diamond. As a youngster he used to stand at the gate of the old Philadelphia Athletics park and wait for Mack to come out, just to see him close up and to walk shyly but reverently behind him on his way to the streetcar. Even now, after a span of forty years, there is only one manager so far as McCarthy is concerned, and that's the long, hawk-faced, seventy-six-year-old Cornelius McGillicuddy, who is still trying to win one more championship with his beloved A's.

There were many things the busher learned about running a ball club as he sat in the dugout in the years that followed the afternoon Mr. Kirke had told him off. Once a hot-headed, impetuous Irishman, whose urge for truculence dated back to when he managed preliminary fighters around Philadelphia during the off seasons, McCarthy began to develop tolerance and patience. Details became more important to him. Unlike the McGraws, the Macks, et al., he had only a limited amount of cloth to work with and he had to scissor it accordingly, watch for raw, latent abilities, encourage and develop them as he tried to weave loose, unfinished threads into winning combinations.

An important truth he realized early as a busher manager was that in the beginning all great players, even the Cobbs, Speakers, Johnsons, and so forth, started out as green, wide-eyed kids. They had to be developed. Having been a busher all his life, and a frustrated busher at that, McCarthy understood their difficulties. And out of this understanding stemmed a deep, sympathetic, and almost parental interest in the youngsters' ambitions, which, if anything, has grown more vibrant with passing years.

THE GREAT ALEX SOLD DOWN THE RIVER

Anyway, this was the McCarthy who came out of the bushes to take over a Chicago club which had finished last the year before. Very few people suspected it at the time, but McCarthy even then was a great manager. In twenty-one years of managing bush teams he had been out of the first division only once. It was this record which moved the old sports writer to persuade William Wrigley, the chewing gum genius, to turn over his crumbling baseball empire to a man who had never played big-league baseball. McCarthy, as his background suggested, knew about all there is to know about the mechanics of baseball, but he had another and more important gift: an understanding of human nature, a high talent for dealing with miscellaneous personalities and temperaments. This talent was soon to be tested on a hitherto unprecedented scale.

That spring the Cubs ended their exhibition tour in Kansas City. The next day they were to open the regular schedule in Cincinnati. The busher called his first general meeting of the players in a suite in the Muehlebach Hotel. During the winter many changes had been made in the personnel of the club and several of the discards had landed with rival clubs in the National League. This made it necessary to devise a new set of signals.

The great Grover Cleveland Alexander was pitching for the Cubs at the time. He was a law unto himself. He came and went as he pleased, so it was no surprise to the busher manager when he looked around the room and saw the pitcher wasn't there. He went ahead with his discussion of the new signals. Presently the door opened and in walked the Great Alex, listing severely to starboard. The busher was saying "Now suppose we get a man on second base___" He never got to finish the sentence. Alex pulled a cigarette from his parched lips with a shaky hand and observed: "You don't have to worry about that, McCarthy. This club will never get a man that far."

It was an unusual reception for the earnest busher at his first team meeting. He swallowed hard, simulated a smile and replied: "Well, Alex, we're going to try, anyway," and continued as if nothing had happened, while Alex found a chair in a corner of the room and fell asleep, probably troubled by morbid dreams of the 1925 Cubs, who hadn't got many men as far as second, at that.

The season wasn't very old before the virtually unknown busher manager had sold the great Alexander down the river to the St. Louis Cardinals. It was a tough and brave decision to make. Alex was still a great pitcher. He proved it that very year by fanning Tony Lazzeri with the bases full to help the Cardinals win a world series from the Yankees. But Alex wasn't McCarthy's type of man. He didn't mind his intemperance so much, but he deplored his influence and his indifference to team success. The night McCarthy let Alex go he received this wire from Magnate Wrigley: "Congratulations. For years I've been looking for a manager who had the nerve to do that." Instead of being pleased, the busher manager was depressed. He'd much rather have been able to handle the old pitcher, for whom, as an artist, he had the highest respect.

Three years later, still with the Cubs, McCarthy was confronted with another problem, somewhat different, but still one that taxed his restraint, good sense and diplomacy to the utmost. By this time he had pretty well established himself as a big leaguer. He had made fine strides with the Cubs, taken them out of the cellar, developed them into pennant threats, set new attendance records—done everything, in fact, but put the club in the world series. When he first came up, the opposing managers and players ribbed him brutally as he stood in the coaching box at third base. "Ya, big busher, ya." . . . "how does it feel to sleep in a lower berth?" . . . "Say, they tell me you were a big shot in Wilkes-Barre once: is that so?" There was nothing McCarthy could do but take it. As a matter of fact, he had anticipated it. But after three years he was accepted in the hard, wise-cracking, realistic school of baseball leadership; he had proved himself. Only one man was not completely satisfied. This was Wrigley. With this enormously wealthy man the Cubs were both a relaxation and a vanity, and as a vanity fulfillment they still left something to be desired. They hadn't won a championship.

The great Rogers Hornsby was on the market. The Boston Braves would sell for $125,000 and five so-so ballplayers. Hornsby was probably the most remarkable right-hand hitter of all time. For six straight years he led the National league with his bat. Twice in a row he hit over .400. Wrigley went out and bought Hornsby over McCarthy's head. He had been brought up in a more frugal school of baseball. Besides, he was already getting results with hand-picked players from the minors, men like Hack Wilson and Riggs Stephenson, men he had seen play in the bushes: he knew their value and brought them in at bargain-basement prices to help rehabilitate the Cubs as a National League power. Another thing, he was pretty sure Hornsby wouldn't fit in, that he wouldn't be a team player, and team play is the bible of McCarthy's baseball, as his later years of success were to prove.

MANAGER VERSUS STAR PERFORMER

It may be, too, that McCarthy's objections were based on a feeling of personal insecurity. If they weren't they should have been. A likable fellow and a tremendous performer, Hornsby was never meant to play under a manager. Not even McGraw had a more powerful personality. Sooner or later Hornsby had to be the boss; he had to give the orders. This proved to be so in St. Louis, with the Cardinals; it threatened to be so when he was shifted to the New York Giants, and he had been with the Boston Braves less than a year before he took full command. So, from the start, McCarthy must have known he was sitting on a keg of dynamite and that it was only a question of time before the blow-up would come. It came finally in the closing month of the 1930 season, when Wrigley announced Hornsby as his new manager. The year before, Hornsby's virile bat had helped put the Cubs in the world series, and all was well with the Wrigley vanity.

The chewing-gum king didn't realize it at the time, but when he fired the busher who had made him his first million dollars in baseball and brought the Cubs back to a pre-eminent position in Chicago's bitter baseball rivalry, he kicked him upstairs. For McCarthy's next stop was his present one, the Yankees. It so happened that at about this time, Col. Jacob Ruppert, the distinguished glass-a-beer man, was casting about for a new manager, and McCarthy's record with the Cubs impressed him.

Bringing a National League manager into the America League is decidedly an uncommon practice. Generally speaking, the American League remains sternly aloof to National League discards of any character. "I like the way that fellow does things," was the colonel's brief explanation to a startled press. And so Joe the Busher moved into the metropolis. Years before he had had visions of playing there, across the river with Brooklyn, but the league had blown up before he could report. Now here he was in the Big Town as a manager. Life certainly was strange and mighty nice too. Except for one thing—what was McCarthy going to do about Babe Ruth?

ONE PROBLEM AFTER ANOTHER

First it was Alexander, then Hornsby, now Ruth. Three of the greatest players of all time and an impish fate had ordained that a man who had never had a uniform on as a big-league player was to serve as their master. Ruth threatened to be the most acute problem of them all. There wasn't anything he hadn't done in or for baseball. By the violence of his bat he had lifted baseball out of its blackest scandal—the White Sox sellout to the gamblers in 1919; he had broken all home-run records, all slugging records, all attendance records, all salary records; he had built the vast Yankee Stadium, biggest and finest in baseball's history; he was by far and away the most idolized player the national pastime had ever known. And what was more, he wanted to manage the Yankees. He had started to slip and he yearned for new fields, new excitement, new adventures in the only business he had known. He had a large and sympathetic audience when he snorted, "Who is this McCarthy?"

The Yankee fans felt the same way. They welcomed him with boisterous silence at the start. They resented him as an intruder—"one of those National League guys." The press wasn't unanimously friendly either. Dark and dire were the predictions as to what would happen when he tried to handle Ruth. For twenty-one years McCarthy had been in the bushes. A large part of this time he had sat in the dugout studying men, analyzing temperaments, weighing problems that had to do with a curiously scrambled human nature. Ruth was not a new problem, only a more highly publicized problem. Better than anybody else, McCarthy knew how to handle the mightiest hitter of all time; he would simply let him handle himself. And that's how incredibly easy it was. All the time Ruth played under McCarthy he was absolutely his own boss. When he wanted to play he played, when he wanted to take himself out of a game, no matter what the situation, he conferred with nobody but Ruth. If he kept in shape, fine; if he didn't—well, after all, he was the Great Man. Meanwhile, McCarthy went along with the other players. He made them appreciate that Ruth was Ruth and that McCarthy was the boss of everybody else on the club. Ruth could do as he pleased, but the others had to do as McCarthy demanded. He didn't demand very much. Keep in shape, don't gamble, be in bed by twelve and "remember this is a team, so play for the team as a whole." . . .

WHAT THE RECORDS TELL

When McCarthy is forced to let a recalcitrant player go, he does a little private grieving about it. Somehow he seems to feel he has failed to solve the problem and that maybe it's his fault. The records tell a different story.

The way he handled Hack Wilson, for example, and the bleak experience Wilson had after McCarthy left the Cubs to take over the Yankees. Wilson was something of a playboy, but McCarthy managed to keep his ambition alive, his pride vibrant, and at one time the fans of the nation were in high excitement wondering if Wilson would break Ruth's home-run record. That was the year Wilson hit fifty-six home runs, which is still the National League record. Under subsequent managers Wilson was just another fat guy going through a puffy, mediocre routine, and it wasn't long before he was back in the minors . . .

MEET MR. BASEBALL

McCarthy is Mr. Baseball himself. He thinks of little else, has no hobbies, reads few books. All his whims are tied up with baseball. He doesn't like a player who smokes a pipe. In McCarthy's mind this means the player is too contented. He turns purple at the sight of a player in street clothes wearing a cap. Somehow he has figured out this connotes carelessness. No manager in baseball is a greater slave to detail. On the road McCarthy always gets out to the enemy park ahead of his players. He does this to get a line on players he hasn't seen. At the home park the whole squad gets a chance to hit and field. This isn't so when the home team travels. There isn't time enough before the game. Only the regulars get a chance to warm up. So McCarthy gets out to the enemy park early, takes a position in the grandstand back of the batting cage and takes a study of the players he isn't familiar with. Sooner or later he may have to deal with them as regulars.

McCarthy's taste in deathless literature runs largely to box scores and official averages. He studies these agate tables religiously. They keep him informed on what the opposing players are doing. Thus he knows when a .370 hitter is in a slump and when one of the weak sisters is enjoying a red-hot spurt. In such circumstances he will pitch to the .370 hitter and pass the weak sister. Good, sound baseball, of course, but something only the well-informed manager would know about.

There was a time when Roger Cramer and Mule Haas, of the Athletics, used to murder Yankees pitching. They weren't supposed to like high-ball pitching, so when they faced the Yankee pitchers that's all they got—whizzing fast ones right under the chin strap. Studying the box scores McCarthy discovered that Mel Harder, of the Indians, invariably handcuffed the two sluggers. It was an epochal day when they got a loud, angry foul off him. Harder's main reliance is a low curve inside. McCarthy called his battery men together and said "We have been just plain dumb. It's the low one inside those guys can't hit." From then on, that's all they got from the Yankee pitchers, and the murdering stopped. This is not presented as a stroke of genius, but I think it does show how an observing, conscientious, ever-trying manager works.

AN INVALID IN THE SERIES

McCarthy literally sleeps baseball. Outwardly a placid, restrained type—you'd take him for a small-town banker or businessman—actually he is a nervous, restless person who takes the ballgame to his home with him. Let the Yankees drop a tough one and he will walk the floor for hours, smoking big black cigars, replaying the game, looking for the elusive points of failure. There is a legend that he is psychic, that in the wee small hours, eerie, ghostly figures float over his bed whispering magic words of baseball wisdom, which are gratefully received by the docile subject. The genesis of the legend is not altogether obscure, but frequently it is confused. McCarthy knew the great Houdini well, once appeared on the stage with him in a Toledo theatre, and even now delights in performing simple tricks of legerdemain for the amusement—and what he imagines is the astonishment—of his friends. But where the legend takes on substance is in the admission by McCarthy that he frequently makes his most important baseball decisions around dawn. It seems that he just wakes up suddenly and decides he should do this or that. Of course he scoffs at the suggestion he is psychic. "I don't know what the word means," he says. "Anyway, when you give a lot of thought to a problem, you are bound to reach a decision sooner or later. It seems mine just happens to come later." . . .

McCarthy is a hard loser, yet restrained in criticism. The Yankees dropped an exhibition game to the Boston Braves, in Florida, several years ago. That night the colored waiter at McCarthy's table started to discuss the recent unpleasantness. He allowed as how the Yankees had looked pretty awful in spots. "You take care of the food around here," snapped McCarthy; "I'll take care of the ball club." Even when the games don't count, McCarthy is not the most pleasant person in the world to be around when the score goes against him.

He has a sly way of getting his points home to his players. Red Ruffing, the pitcher, had a splendid record last year and the year before. He is a horse for work. When he isn't pitching to the hitters he is chasing flies in the outfield. One day last season McCarthy came into the dugout. Three of his other pitchers were sitting there taking it easy. Ruffing, as usual, was in the outfield. Standing in front of the three pitchers, but addressing no one in particular, McCarthy barked: "Somebody ought to tell that Ruffing to quit working so hard. The way he's going he won't last another ten years in the big leagues." The three pitchers took the hint.

Indirect but effective criticism is a McCarthy trick. On one of the western trips last year the Yankees had played slovenly ball. This was particularly so in St. Louis, where they dropped the last game of the series to the lowly, non-descript Browns. A missed signal had lost the game. That night, on the way back to New York, there was a mild card game in the players' car. McCarthy stopped to watch it. The player who had gummed up the signal wasn't in the game, but was sitting near by. After a few minutes of observation, McCarthy said, "You fellows certainly amaze me. You know every card in the deck, but you don't know a simple hit-and-run sign when you see it." With this he walked to his compartment.

This is a typical example of McCarthy discipline in operation. He never puts an offending player by name in the grease in front of his teammates. He has a little two-by-four office in the Yankee dressing room. When he has something to say to a player of a personal nature, he says it to him there in private, and generally the next day, after he's had time to cool himself off. . . .

Triumphant over the Cubs in the world series last fall and having put three such championships together in a row to reach new heights in baseball, the Yankee players decided to honor their manager. They appointed a committee in businesslike fashion to buy him a gift. This finally took the form of a huge plaque containing a silver engraved likeness of every member of the squad, including the bat boy and the trainer. It was a gift that carried with it genuine admiration, almost affection. It wasn't just something the players had bought as a hasty, patronizing gesture. A lot of thought, planning, and feeling had gone into it.

McCarthy was visibly moved. Very likely his mind went back to his busher days, when he brooded dismally on the busted kneecap that had denied him a chance to play in the big leagues, to get even a tryout. And here was one of the great teams of baseball—Connie Mack had called it the greatest of all time—honoring the perennial minor leaguer as leader and friend. Whatever his thoughts were, all he said was, "Thanks, fellows. This is mighty swell of you."

Modesty and simplicity are two of McCarthy's virtues. Next to Mack, who owns 50 per cent of the Athletics, he is the wealthiest manager in baseball. Yet, until last year, he wouldn't indulge in the conventional luxury of a chauffeur. "Too many guys will say I'm going high-hat." Some of the critics have been reluctant to accept him as a great manager. They hold anybody could win with the Yankees, backed by the Ruppert millions. McCarthy takes this criticism in stride and freely admits the mechanics of the far-flung Yankee system are mainly responsible for his success. "They give me the players and I try to tell 'em how to play," he says.

By a rather interesting coincidence Busher Joe used to say the same thing when he was winning pennants in Wilkes-Barre and Louisville.

20. Haymaker Hack

IN THE PANTHEON OF CUBS ICONS, the five-feet-six, 195-pound center-fielder Lewis "Hack" Wilson sometimes gets overlooked. He should not. With a sharp, square jaw and squatty build, including an eighteen-inch neck but only size six shoes, Wilson looked like a cross between a ballet dancer and a Brahma bull. He still owns one of baseball's most unreachable records, 191 RBIs in a season (originally awarded 190 RBIs, in 1999 an additional RBI that had been mistakenly given to another player was added to his total). He registered those 191 RBIs during a 1930 season in which he produced arguably the greatest offensive output ever. In addition to the RBIs, Wilson hit 56 home runs, batted .356, and led the league in walks with 105. And bear in mind that this was during a 154-game season, not a modern 162. The 56 home runs remained a National League record until the infamous Mark McGwire, Sammy Sosa, and Barry Bonds era. Whether or not any or all three of them used performance-enhancing drugs, the only drug Wilson seems to have used was, unfortunately, alcohol. It led to his death at the age of forty-eight.[1]

In addition to his gaudy numbers, Hack helped lead the Cubs to the 1929 World Series. During that series the Cubs got down to the Philadelphia Athletics 2–0 in games, but Cubbie hopes rose when the Cubs won game three in The City of Brotherly Love's Shibe Park and then took an 8–0 lead in game four. But then the bottom of the seventh arrived. By inning's end, the Cubs would surrender ten runs. Hack alone lost two fly balls in the sun. By the time he returned to the dugout, tears were in his eyes and the Athletics led 10–8.

His gargantuan season of 1930, however, helped make up for the lost fly balls, and it landed him a National League–leading $33,000 contract for 1931. But '31 didn't go so well.[2] Rumors of too much boozing swirled. After the 1931 campaign, in January of '32, the *Sporting News* asked Hack what went wrong. In

Robert "Hack" Wilson, Rogers "The Rajah" Hornsby, and Hazen Shirley "Kiki" Cuyler standing on a step in the Cubs' dugout in 1930. Not a bad trio.

his hometown of Martinsburg, West Virginia, Wilson said the newly thickened baseballs probably played some role and that perhaps he'd pressed too much to live up to his $33,000 contract. But he also said, despite simultaneously downplaying murmurs that there had been issues between him and new manager Rogers Hornsby, "When Joe McCarthy was manager of the Cubs, he always had me hitting when the call was three balls and one strike or two balls and no strikes. That meant I could hit the ball if it was good and gave me an edge over the pitchers, but Hornsby usually had me 'take' the next pitch, and it just seemed that every time that situation came along, the pitcher would give me one that I thought I could have socked and I had to take it. And that didn't help my temper or my confidence any."[3]

What Wilson didn't blame his slumping numbers on was fast living. He shook-off such speculation by saying: "Some people said I was a batting flop because I was carousing around too much. That was all wrong. I went out occasionally, but not as much as I did the year before when I was hitting all those home runs. You have to do something for recreation, but I was in condition to play every day. They told me at Chicago that I would have to quit this and that, but I'm not signing any pledges. I have a wife and boy and baseball is my livelihood and I'm not going to do anything that will prevent me from earning my living that way. But I am not going to sign any pledge or make any drastic change in my mode of living."[4]

Years later, though, a week before his premature death in 1948, a basically penniless Wilson admitted that, leading up to the 1931 season, he'd "started to drink heavily. I argued with my manager and with my teammates." And he said, "I spent the winter in taprooms. When spring training rolled around I was 20 pounds overweight. I was suspended before the season ended. I drank more than ever." They'd expected him to break Babe Ruth's home run record, but he hit only thirteen of them.[5]

In fairness, after his relatively paltry 1931 campaign Hack installed in his home a rowing machine, punching bag, and a set of weights. He also employed the use of an "electric belt, designed to reduce his embonpoint by vibration." And he did rebound in 1932 by driving in 123 runs and belting 23 homers with the Brooklyn Dodgers. But that was followed by two notably less productive seasons, along with more drinking, and then retirement.[6]

Throughout his career, Hack Wilson played for four different teams, but he played for the Cubs the most, spending roughly half of his twelve years in the big leagues with the Northsiders. During his 1926–31 seasons with the Cubbies, all of which ironically came during prohibition, he hit .319 and averaged more than 35 home runs, 128 RBIs, and 77 walks per season. Those numbers include that poor 1931 campaign in which Wilson hit only .261 with just 13 home runs.[7]

It's hard to believe that this tough competitor with such gaudy stats went from the top of the baseball world to the minors and then the poorhouse in a matter of years.

In the following article Hack Wilson's feistiness is on full display. In it the *Chicago Daily News* regales readers with the story of his eventful July 4th of 1929, during which he delivered three hits and two brawls.[8] The first brawl happened during a game when Wilson left first base to rush Pitcher Ray Kolp in the Reds' bullpen; the second at a train station as the two teams readied for a trip to New York.

Hack Wilson Fined $100

Chicago Daily News, July 6, 1929

HEYDLER DISCIPLINES SLUGGING OUTFIELDER

Chubby Hitter Explains Fracas to Magnate in Long-Distance Call.

> **Something Doing!**
> Cincinnati, O., July 6.—(AP)—Before leaving for Pittsburgh Jack Hendricks, Reds' manager, referring to the Wilson–Kolp, Wilson–Donohue–Critz–Stephenson affairs at Chicago said, "When the Cubs come here for a double-header Aug. 25 there will be something doing for a certainty."

Hack (K.O.) Wilson, center fielder of the Cubs was fined $100 and handed a three-day suspension beginning today for displaying his pugilistic ability on the Cincinnati players Thursday by President John Heydler of the National league.

Hack is now in Boston with his teammates to open the second eastern invasion against the Braves but today, tomorrow and Monday he will be among those missing. His absence will be felt to a considerable extent by the pennant aspiring Cubs but fortunately the Bruins are playing Boston instead of Pittsburgh or New York.

HACK TALKS TO HEYDLER.

When the Cubs arrived at Boston this morning Wilson found a notice at the hotel to call Mr. Heydler in New York and Hack did so even before having his coffee.

Heydler simply desired to hear Hack's side of the story of the battle on the field Thursday afternoon when Hack left first base and ran to the Cincinnati bench to punch Ray Kolp.

Heydler didn't ask Hack for the particulars of the fight at the railway station that night when Hack knocked Pete Donahue of the Reds down when the latter dared him into battle.

"What did Kolp call you?" asked Heydler over the long-distance phone.

"Well, really, Mr. Heydler," answered Hack, "I wouldn't want to repeat the words over the phone. The operators might overhear them and it was no language to say in the presence of ladies. You just think of the vilest words you ever heard and that's what it was."

"I understand," said Heydler.

HOW RUMPUS STARTED.

The start of the rumpus in which Hack came to the fore as a pugilist took place during the afternoon game on the July 4 program of two contests at Wrigley field. Wilson had poked out a single and while resting on the initial sack took exception to remarks being made about him by the players in the Cincinnati dugout. Ray Kolp, a pitcher, seemed to be the worst offender.

Hack stood the abuse as long as he could, but finally with his neck exceedingly red, he dashed over to the dugout and with great rapidity and éclat busted Mr. Kolp in the eye. Not satisfied with this he proceeded to swing his fists like a windmill on all and sundry persons occupying the bench and ceased only when his teammates dragged him from the fray.

WILSON WAXES BOLDER.

That evening the Reds and Cubs were boarding a train in the Union station, heading for points east, when Pitcher Pete Donahue of the Reds began talking out of turn. He told Hack to play safe and not enter the Reds' car. Hack wanted to know who would stop him. Donahue claimed he would and was immediately popped on the chin twice with a skillful one-two punch. Peace was quickly restored and the Reds and Cubs went their separate ways much to the joy of Mangers Hendricks and McCarthy.

While Hack is enjoying or not enjoying his enforced three days' rest it is expected that Cliff Heathcote will take his place in the garden. Cliff probably is the world's greatest relief outfielder and the Cubs should not find it difficult to keep on winning games with Heathcote batting for Wilson.

PART IV

FROM DEPRESSION-ERA GREATNESS TO THAT DARN GOAT

Season	Wins	Losses	Winning Percentage	Games Behind	Attendance	Ballpark	Owner
1930	90	64	0.584	2	1,463,624	Wrigley Field	William Wrigley, Jr.
1931	84	70	0.545	17	1,086,422	Wrigley Field	William Wrigley, Jr.
1932	90	64	0.584	—	974,688	Wrigley Field	Philip K. Wrigley
1933	86	68	0.558	6	594,112	Wrigley Field	Philip K. Wrigley
1934	86	65	0.570	8	707,525	Wrigley Field	Philip K. Wrigley
1935	100	54	0.649	—	692,604	Wrigley Field	Philip K. Wrigley
1936	87	67	0.565	5	699,370	Wrigley Field	Philip K. Wrigley
1937	93	61	0.604	3	895,020	Wrigley Field	Philip K. Wrigley
1938	89	63	0.586	—	951,640	Wrigley Field	Philip K. Wrigley
1939	84	70	0.545	13	726,663	Wrigley Field	Philip K. Wrigley
1940	75	79	0.487	25½	534,878	Wrigley Field	Philip K. Wrigley
1941	70	84	0.455	30	545,159	Wrigley Field	Philip K. Wrigley
1942	68	86	0.442	38	590,972	Wrigley Field	Philip K. Wrigley
1943	74	79	0.484	30½	508,247	Wrigley Field	Philip K. Wrigley
1944	75	79	0.487	30	640,110	Wrigley Field	Philip K. Wrigley
1945	98	56	0.636	—	1,036,386	Wrigley Field	Philip K. Wrigley

21. Rajah in Charge

WILLIAM WRIGLEY SACKED manager Joe McCarthy at the end of the 1930 season, paving the way for Rogers "The Rajah" Hornsby, one of the greatest hitters of all time and certainly the greatest right-handed hitter, to become the Cubs' player-manager.

One season prior to becoming manager, Hornsby, a chronic gambler who played the horses, won the National League MVP award as he helped the Cubs to the pennant by hitting .380 with 39 home runs and 149 RBIs. Before that he hit over .400 on three separate occasions for the St. Louis Cardinals, including a still-standing record of .424 in 1924. As a player-manager for the Cardinals in 1926, Hornsby led the previously weak organization to an improbable World Series title that culminated in Hornsby's tag-out of Babe Ruth for the final out of the championship. Only one hitter, Ty Cobb, boasts a better career batting average. And like Cobb, Hornsby's personality could rankle. That helps explain how such a talented hitter played for six different teams between 1926 and 1934.

This 1930 article by the stalwart journalist Jim Crusinberry predicts that Cubs President William Veeck would indeed fire Joe McCarthy at the end of that year's campaign, which ended with the Cubs out of the playoffs, and replace him with Rogers Hornsby. Both things happened. And the article reflects how William Wrigley did not do much to quell such speculation.[1]

Ironically, less than two years later, in early August of 1932, Hornsby and the Cubs parted ways. Veeck tired of Hornsby's suspicions about the club's capabilities, and what he thought was an abrasive personality on the part of "Rajah" toward him.

As it happened, within two weeks of Hornsby's firing front-page headlines ran in the *Chicago Daily Tribune* regarding an investigation by commissioner Judge Kenesaw Mountain Landis into alleged gambling by Cubs players on horse races. In the course of that investigation, Hornsby did not deny that he bet on horse races or that he borrowed money from several Cubs while a member of the team. But he said no other Cubs bet with him, and he and Veeck maintained that the saga had no impact on Hornsby's dismissal.[2]

Hornsby's replacement, mild-mannered first baseman Charlie "Jolly Cholly" Grim, helped spur the Cubs to a dramatic finish to end the 1932 regular season. The Cubs won the pennant, but a 1932 World Series sweep at the hands of the Babe Ruth and Lou Gehrig–led Yankees ended the run.

M'Carthy Likely To Go; Hornsby Rumored For Job

Chicago Daily News, September 22, 1930

BRUINS FIGHT ON IN FINAL GAMES WITH REPORTS FLYING FAST.

MOGULS ARE SILENT

CUBS HOLD GROUND

The Cubs defeated Boston today and remained two and one-half games behind the Cardinals, who defeated Philadelphia. Brooklyn, which was idle, remained in third place four games behind St. Louis. . . .

WRIGLEY WANTS WINNER

William Wrigley Jr., owner of the Cubs, declared today that he must have a winning ball club on the north side and that he was not sure if Joe McCarthy, the manager of the Cubs, could give it to him.

"The fans want a winner," he said. "They do not want any alibis. It is all right to talk about bad luck, injuries to players and so forth, but excuses like that don't go when a pennant is the object.

"The only finish worth while is the one in which you win. The fans want a winner and I want a winner, and I'm going to give it to them. I told my son Phil today that if I didn't live long enough to give the fans another winner, that he should go ahead with the job.

"When McCarthy gets back to Chicago we're going to talk it over."

By James Crusinberry
Special Dispatch from a Staff Correspondent

Boston, Mass., Sept. 22—The McCarthy-Hornsby rumors have created such a smoky atmosphere around Chicago's Cubs that the players are groping their way through the final games of the season in a bewildered manner. There is so much smoke that it's a certainty that there's a fire somewhere.

Nothing definite on the situation can be obtained. President William L. Veeck maintains a discreet silence. Owner William Wrigley has declined to affirm or deny the rumors that McCarthy is to be dropped as manager and that Hornsby is to be appointed. Manager McCarthy declines to discuss the matter and Hornsby says he doesn't know anything about it.

STARTED WITH WORLD SERIES

Having been in close and constant touch with the Cubs, the writer formed an opinion on the situation many weeks ago but kept silent when unable to confirm it through officials of the club. But as opinions are being given freely at this time, another one can do no harm. In our opinion the following steps have led up to the present crisis:

> The plan to change managers was hatched in the seventh inning of the fourth game of the last world series when the Cubs blew an eight-run lead. There was a noticeable change in the attitude of Cub officials toward the manager from then on.

The Cubs' directors decided to live up to the contract with Joe McCarthy, which was to continue throughout the present season and up to Jan. 1, 1931. But they planned to change regardless of the outcome of the present pennant race.

HOW RUMORS STARTED

William Wrigley Jr., chairman of the board and majority stockholder, being an enthusiast of the game, was unable to maintain silence on the plan. He talked to friends. During the August drive that put the Cubs in first place the writer met Mr. Wrigley under the grandstand one day and congratulated him because the team was in first place again. "They ought to be ten games in front," was his disgusted reply. In baseball language, Mr. Wrigley "popped off" and that was how the rumors of the proposed change started.

The change of attitude of the officials toward McCarthy was apparent at the winter meeting last December, as shown by one incident. Ray Schalk was hired as coach of the team and it was evident he was taken on at the insistence of President Veeck and over the veto of Manager McCarthy. Schalk has been with the team all season, but, so far as can be observed, is never taken into the councils on matters of running the team. Manager McCarthy and his first assistant, Jimmy Burke, have handled everything with no assistance.

VEECK TALKS WITH RAJAH

When the team was in Cincinnati in midseason a story by a Cincinnati writer stated Rogers Hornsby would never play ball with the Cubs again even if he did recover from his broken ankle. At the time Hornsby was at his home in St. Louis recuperating. The writer interviewed Manager McCarthy, but the latter denied he had said anything to prompt such a story. President Veeck investigated the source of the story and refuted it with words of praise for Hornsby.

Only recently—on Sept. 12, to be exact—President Veeck was in Philadelphia with the team. In the hotel he was seen in conference with Hornsby. He didn't mention the subject of manager, but he talked about ways of improving the team for next year and got Hornsby's opinion of players who might be obtained in trade or by purchase. He had no conference, so as could be learned with Manager McCarthy. Anyway, the writer asked Mr. Veeck regarding the pitcher for that day, and his answer was: "I don't know. I haven't seen Joe." That night the writer interviewed Mr. Veeck privately and asked him pointblank if he was going to have a new manager. Veeck gave the same reply he has given to others—that the matter of next year's manager would not be discussed; that the team was in a hot pennant fight and that McCarthy had a contract which ran until Jan. 1.

OFFICIALS PRAISE HORNSBY.

At the same interview, in talking about Hornsby and the rumors that had been spread about his quitting, President Veeck stated in most emphatic words that both he and Mr. Wrigley thought most highly of Rogers Hornsby; that these rumors and yarns about him had been investigated and that there was no truth in any of them that reflected upon his conduct; that he thought Hornsby would be as great, if not greater, [a] player in 1931 than he was in 1929; that the Cubs had a lot of money invested in him and believed it was well invested, because in Hornsby they had one of the outstanding men in baseball.

After digesting all the rumors and observations the writer formed the opinion that the Cub officials intended to dismiss Joe McCarthy as manager and offer the position to Rogers Hornsby some time after the season is over. It isn't that they think ill of McCarthy, but simply that they believe a man like Hornsby, who has had years and years of big-league playing experience, is better equipped to handle the difficulties that arise on the ball field during the heat of battle.

Lou Gehrig, Joe McCarthy, and Babe Ruth during the 1932 World Series. Courtesy Chicago History Museum.

22. Did He Call It?

OF THE 50,000 SPECTATORS that came to see the Cubs and Yankees in game three of the 1932 World Series, which involved plenty of bench jockeying (trash talking), those accommodated by the temporary bleachers erected over Sheffield Avenue saw a ball hit all the way to them. The blast came off the bat of George Herman "Babe" Ruth, and it became one of baseball's all-time best-known home runs. Upset that former Yankee Mark Koenig, who was unavailable for the Series, was voted only half a World Series share by his new "cheapskate" Cubs teammates, Ruth had already been jabbering with Cubs players. And some say Ruth called the prodigious home run that reached the temporary bleachers. In this selection, however, journalist Edward Burns, who predicted that the blast would "likely go down as one of the classics of baseball razzing," gave no indication that he thought it would do so because Ruth had called the shot.

Though largely forgotten, that now-iconic blast was not the only Ruthian home run of the day. In fact, two Yankee immortals, Lou Gehrig and Ruth, walloped two shots apiece out of the park, giving the Yankees a 7–5 win and a 3–0 Series lead that the club parlayed into a 4–0 sweep.

With the country reeling from the Great Depression that saw the number of unemployed rise from less than 3 million in 1929 to some 12.5 million in 1932—years that bookended Cubbie appearances in the World Series—baseball fans wanted something to cheer about. Unfortunately for the Cubs, it was the Yankee players who gave much of America a chance to do just that. Still, even at this relatively early phase of the lovable losers' drought, Cubs fans could not help but admire the Bronx Bombers' power. As the *Chicago Daily Tribune* noted in the following article, "If the Cubs had to lose, it was nice for the 50,000 customers that they could see the two great sluggers do their stuff in such gala surroundings." Subsequent woes, including two more World Series losses during the 1930s, made appreciating such things a virtual necessity for Cubs fans.

Home Runs by Ruth, Gehrig Beat Cubs, 7–5

Edward Burns, *Chicago Daily Tribune*, October 2, 1932

EACH HITS TWO IN 3D YANKEE VICTORY.

Babe Ruth and Lou Gehrig knocked two homers apiece yesterday as their modest contribution to the third successive victory of the New York Yankees over the Chicago Cubs in the current world series. These four lengthy hits drove in the first six of the seven runs by which the American leaguers triumphed, 7 to 5.

Even homers by Ruth and Gehrig are poor substitutes for a Cub victory thrill, of course. But after all, if the Cubs had to lose, it was nice for the 50,000 customers that they could see the two great sluggers do their stuff in such gala surroundings.

Babe and Lou did not totally eclipse the Cubs in home run matters, however, for Kiki Cuyler made one in the third inning and Gabby Hartnett knocked another in the ninth. Nice homers they were, too, but somehow homers by the losers never are quite so handsome.

ROOT IS VICTIM.

Charley Root was the victim of all four of the Yankee home runs. There were many who predicted that Charley's style of pitching was such that he would be a setup for the two great sluggers. That was the reason he was not used in either of the first two games.

Ruth's first homer, with two on in the first inning, was his fourteenth in world series competition. The three runs thus accrued got the Chicagoans off to a rather depressing start. Then, to start the third, Gehrig got his first homer of the day, his second of the series and his sixth in the world series business.

RUTH BREAKS TIE.

Even these things did not discourage the Cubs, and at the end of the fourth the Chicagoans had the score tied at 4 all. Thereafter Ruth and Gehrig became bonecrushers for sure. Babe broke the tie in the course of bitter repartee with the Cub bench in the fifth and Lou followed with another on the next pitch after Babe circled the bases. That was the last of Mr. Root.

That tie-breaking second homer of the Babe's probably will go down as one of the classics of baseball razzing.

When Babe came up in the fifth the Cubs were feeling pretty pert. They had come from three runs behind to tie the score. They scented victory on dear old Wrigley field. It looked like one of those old August rough houses was in the offing. Yes, the Cubs were very peppery when Mr. Ruth went to bat with the score tied in the fifth.

The Cub bench jockeys came out of the dugout to shout at Ruth. And Ruth shouted right back. Root got a strike past Babe, and did those Cub bench jockeys holler and hiss! After a couple of wide ones, Root whizzed another strike past the great man. More hollering and hissing and no small amount of personal abuse.

THERE IT GOES!

Ruth held up two fingers, indicating the two strikes in umpire fashion. Then he made a remark about spotting the Cubs those two strikes. Well, it seems that Charley Root threw another good one. Mr. Ruth smacked the ball right on the nose and it traveled ever so fast. You know that big flag pole just to the right of the scoreboard beyond center field? Well that's 436 feet from the home plate. Ruth's drive went past that flag pole and hit the box office at Waveland and Sheffield avenues.

Ruth resumed his oratory the minute he threw down his bat. He bellowed every foot of the way around the bases, accompanying derisive roarings with wild and eloquent gesticulations. George Herman Ruth always enjoys a homer under any circumstances, but it is doubtful if he ever cocked one that gave him the satisfaction that accompanied that second one today.

ADDS TO HIS RECORDS.

Every time the Babe makes a move in this series he adds to a world record. That second homer was his 15th in world series play and brought his new world record to 32 world series runs batted in and 37 runs scored. But that wasn't what tickled the Babe. His thoughts were on his personal feud with the Cubs, inspired, you know, by what Babe considers a niggardly splitting of the Cubs' world series shares.

The actions of those two marauders, Babe and Lou, obviously placed the world series of 1932 in a very sick condition in so far as Cub aspirations are concerned. Unless Guy Bush can lead to a victory this afternoon the big show will be all over and the Yankees will be chortling about taking their third successive world series in four straight.[1]

23. What Depression?
Third World Series in Seven Years

THE CHICAGO CUBS WON twenty games in a row in September 1935 and nipped the St. Louis Cardinals for the National League pennant. On September 4th of that year the Cubs had stood five games behind the Cardinals in the loss column and four behind the New York Giants. Charlie "Jolly Cholly" Grimm managed the team during its unlikely streak.[1]

Upon winning the pennant, the Cubs faced the Detroit Tigers in what became a record-setting World Series—record-setting for frigidity, for the size of player bonuses because of the massive gate, and for the $100,000 Henry Ford paid for radio broadcast rights to it. Also, during the series Grimm, in un-Jolly Cholly-like fashion, got tossed. The heave-ho came in the sixth inning of game three, at the hands of the boisterous American League umpire George Moriarty. To the press afterward, Grimm said, "If a manager can't go out and make a decent kick, what the hell is the game coming to? I didn't swear at him but he swore at us."[2] Ultimately Moriarty and players Elwood English, Bill Herman, and Bill Jurges faced $200 fines leveled by Commissioner Kenesaw Mountain Landis for "vile, unprintable language," and Grimm needed to pony up $200 for his ejection.[3]

In the end, the Tigers won its first World Series, four games to two. The selection here, replete with the *Chicago Daily News*'s Gene Morgan's classic journalistic prose, gives readers (despite a rather unfortunate comment by Morgan about Chinese salmon packers) a sense of the World Series' reach, not just in America but also to distant shores.

All World Thrilled By Big Series

Gene Morgan, *Chicago Daily News*, October 1, 1935

Special Dispatch from a Staff Correspondent

Detroit, Mich., Oct. 1.—"World serious" thoughts while our superb Cubs today gird, gambol, and gallivant for tomorrow's fray with Detroit's white-socked Tigers in Navin Field:

Scene one is the deck of a greasy, grubby, floundering steamship from Alaskan trade bound for Golden Gate. To the eastward loom the elephant back ranges of the lower Sierras. Westward boils the horizon beyond which the Pacific stretches to the orient. Sourdoughs from Nome, lime-juicers returning for a sabbatical drunk in San Francisco, hard men from the open spaces, they retain the reticence of the silent north toward each other and toward tenderfoot strangers.

RADIO MAKES FRIENDS

Suddenly the fountain spurts [as] a school of whales are sighted off the port bow. But the taciturn passengers are immediately distracted. The primitive radio mast starts chattering. First-inning scores of the world's championship baseball series. A rush to the steward's office to place bets. A sudden awakening of fraternal feeling among these men, a quickening of sociability as the tidings that make all Americans kin come over the air waves and transport this soot-coated steamer from a barge of loneliness to a craft of comradeship, with every man jack a baseball fan, excepting some Chinese salmon packers in the steerage—and they don't count worth a can opener.

Scene two renewed in this writer's vivid recollection on this nervous day at the eve of the world series is blood-soaked Central park in Havana. Here the Spanish oppressors crushed rebellion under their iron heel for crimson decades. Here the dictator, Machado, had slain his hundreds, and here the machine guns of a recent uprising raked crowds with the same ruthless ferocity.

AND SCOREBOARDS ATTRACT.

On this day of my memory Central park was packed with a seething, angrily shouting horde of white-coated Cubans. But no machine guns frowned upon the appalling riot. Merely a mechanical scoreboard which featured a rubber ball blithely hopping around the bases. The world series was on in the United States, and all Cuba had dropped thoughts of revolution and revenge to attend by proxy the scoreboard presentation of the game nearest to their exhibit hearth.

And so it goes today, wherever Americans have taken root. In the far-away orient there is the same breathless interest in the world series as in this blessed land. In United States infantry barracks in Tientsin, China, lonesome men in khaki impatiently await the cabled reports that take them home and to the bleachers of Navin field. Yankee business men gathering at the cocktail bar of the American club in Shanghai, artillerymen at Corregidor in Manilla bay, Hawaiians of all shades and colors, but lusty baseball fans all.

WHOLE WORLD LISTENS

In Alaska, as far north as Post and Rogers flew, they are set to hear the great series flung over the ice caps via radio. In the mountain forests CCC camps will thrill to the play by play description, while in the Tennessee mountaineer's hill-balanced shanty, as in a Chicago stockyards district flat, the news of the vital contests is the only thing worth mentioning among young and old. Wistful expatriates in Paris cocktail bars, war correspondents in Ethiopia, American engineers in the great industrial projects on the Russian steppes—all hearts beat in tune with the newsboys at Sate and Madison streets, Chicago, or Woodward avenue and Cadillac square. Detroit, with their armfuls of "poipers," filled with column after column of news about the epic clash.

The world series is one of American's greatest solvents. As Waterloo was won on the playing fields of Eton, so American brotherhood is annually restimulated in the baseball parks where the world series is played, a brotherhood which embraces neighboring countries—Canada, Cuba, Mexico, and others which have fallen under the spell of the noblest of national games.

But there's another not so noble phase to this world series on which the curtain rises here tomorrow. The ticket scalpers are in the saddle—and they are riding hard—a $3.30 ticket says $12 in your money and a $5.50 ticket claims $24 plus sales tax, a retainer and your shirt.

Hotel lobbies are thicker with scalpers than they were with bootleggers in the old days. In restaurants along Trumbull avenue one could get a 15-cent sandwich and a $12 grandstand ticket, mustard thrown in.

As England strives to keep her sea lanes open, so do the local police try to keep open lanes for Manager Charlie Grimm's grenadiers when arriving or leaving the Central hotel, which houses this million dollars' worth of batting muscles, base-running agility, pitching prowess and a bit of tobacco-chewing geniality on the side.

The Detroit fans are curious and somewhat awestruck at the sight of these foemen who a short while ago were just so many visiting baseball employees. Not a "Hello Charlie," for Grimm, or a "How are yah?" for Pitcher Warneke. Just silent and persistent looking 'em over, with an occasional autograph fisherman or a souvenir collector.

BOSSES SET SPENDING PACE

In the meantime Judge Kenesaw Mountain Landis, the daddy of the world's present crop of dictators, and William Harridge, president of the American League, are engaged in a dollar-pitching duel to spend this country back to prosperity. The local prints edified their readers with an announcement that Judge Landis—who dealt in $20,000,0000 court fines before Cavarretta ever got his big toe in his mouth—had registered for a $40-a-day suite in the Hotel Statler.

No sooner has this evidence of judicial prodigality run wild through the streets and alleys than it was learned that President Harridge, who certainly can afford a carriage, had looked over the $60-a-day presidential suite at the Book-Cadillac and found it was good.

The Harridge suite has running water, a radio and hot and cold complaints from disgusted would-be ticket purchasers who thought they had a "pull." However, Judge Landis in his moderate room—world-series scale—is said to be finding the camping out perfectly comfortable, although not as snug as the quarters obtained by some war correspondents which consist of room and a bath for a midget and a half.

THE FLATTENED TIGER

Frank Navin had a new luck-piece, a tiger rug which measures ten and one-half feet by fifteen. And on the face of the steam-rollered tiger is an eighteen-inch grin which makes it look as if it had just enjoyed a satisfying lunch of young bruin meat. Then there are those who are wicked enough to speculate whether the real tiger rugs will not be a bunch of Detroit athletes—and by present weather possibilities, the shoes of Cubs may be plenty muddy.

An assortment of good medicine for the Tigers was fetched to town today by Davy Jones, who was a member of the team in 1907 and 1908, when the Cubs grabbed the world series in both years. Jones is busy running a drug store, and what with selling washing machines and air-conditioned bird cages and preventing clerks from getting bath mats mixed into the club sandwiches, he has been too busy in recent years to keep up with the Tigers' tenacious career.

However, he has abundant memories in his locker, has Davy Jones, and he remembers what Mordecai Brown, pitching for the Cubs, did to the Tigers in those golden years. No Mordecai Brown, no world series for the Cubs, says Mr. Jones, who compounds a bitter pill when he predicts that the Tigers will upend the National League's [champs] in six sorrowful sagas.

24. Sandberg before Sandberg?

ON HIS WAY TO COOPERSTOWN, keystoner Billy Herman, the Cubs' "Ryne Sandberg of the 1930s," hit for a career average of over .300 and registered more than 200 hits on three occasions. Adroit at hitting behind runners, he also skillfully manned second for all three of the Cubs' pennants during the 1930s.[1] Unfortunately, Herman was shipped to the Brooklyn Dodgers in an ill-conceived trade in 1941.

On the eve of Herman's entrance into the Hall of Fame in 1975, Ron Coons of Louisville's *Courier-Journal & Times* reflected on the skinny Herman's rise from a not-so-outstanding high school player in New Albany, Indiana, to among the greatest second basemen of all time to struggling manager. Coons also covers Herman's tumultuous relationship with Leo Durocher, a future Cubs manager.

Well-Spent Dime

Ron Coons, *Courier-Journal & Times*, August 17, 1975

TRIP TO LOUISVILLE STARTED NEW ALBANY NATIVE

BILLY HERMAN ON HIS JOURNEY TO THE HALL OF FAME.

Monday will be the biggest day of Billy Herman's life.

He will receive baseball's highest honor—induction into the Hall of Fame at Cooperstown, N.Y. Others to join the elite group this time are Ralph Kiner, Bucky Harris, Earl Averill and one-time star of the Negro leagues, Judy Johnson.

It was 48 years ago that Billy Herman spent a dime for a round-trip fare from his native New Albany to Louisville to sign a contract with the Colonels.

Oddly enough, he wasn't really that outstanding at New Albany High School as a shortstop and third baseman, but Colonel manager Cap Neal was an astute judge of talent. He moved Herman to second base, where he became one of the best of all time.

After spending an apprenticeship with Vicksburg of the Cotton States League and Dayton of the Central League, Herman joined the Colonels on a regular basis in 1930, hitting .305 and .350 for his two seasons there. John McGraw, the Giants' great manager, however, deemed Billy too skinny to play in the majors.

But the Chicago Cubs thought otherwise. In August 1931, Jack Doyle, veteran scout of the Cubs, handed over a check for $60,000 to William Knebelkamp, the Colonels' owner, for the 22-year-old 150-pounder. It was a bargain.

Billy Herman played in 10 All-Star Games, helped the Cubs win pennants in 1932, 1935 and 1938 and was a big factor in Brooklyn going to the World Series in 1941. One of the shrewdest players ever, he collected 2,345 hits during his 15-year career in the major leagues and compiled a .304 lifetime average.

Second youngest in a family of five girls and five boys, William Jennings Herman was born July 7, 1909. The Hermans lived on a small farm. There was a truck garden to be worked, eggs to be sold, cows to be milked. But William Herman Sr., a left-handed pitcher of local fame, saw to it that Billy and his brothers had time to play ball.

Once Billy's mother entrusted him to take the mortgage money—$250—to the bank. He stopped along the way to play baseball and didn't quit until after dark. All the time he was playing the sackful of money lay on the ground.

At 18, Billy pitched Louisville's New Covenant Presbyterian Sunday School to the amateur championship. As a reward, he saw the first two games of the 1927 World Series between the Yankees and the Pirates at Forbes Field.

If he was awed by the slugging feats of Babe Ruth and Lou Gehrig, he didn't let it influence his own style. A right-handed hitter, he specialized in hitting the ball to right field behind the runner. Many can do it if they get an outside pitch to hit, but Billy was equally adept on the inside pitches.

Pee Wee Reese, a Hall of Fame candidate himself who played for New Covenant a few years after Billy, said, "Even if you pitched out, Herman managed to get a piece of the ball and foul it off.

"Billy was a big help to me. He got me thinking about positioning on a 3–1 count. Should I play a step or two in the hole? In double play situations, should I cheat in the inside? He made me aware where the outfielders were playing and how far I had to go back on a ball. He made me think. Who's the hitter? How fast is he? How fast is the guy on first? I was more in the game.

"Billy was very good at making the double play," Reese added, "Whereas Jackie Robinson, with those strong legs of his, stayed at the bag and dared the runner to knock him down, Herman had many different ways to turn it. Rarely was he taken out of a play."

Billy Herman, too, was one of the very best at stealing signs, once leading Larry MacPhail to remark, "If I were managing a team I'd never let my catcher give signs with Herman on second base. I'd have some other player give them. But even then I couldn't bet Billy wouldn't steal them."

"It wouldn't take Billy long to break a code," Reese said. "As he took his lead from second base, he'd stay down or crouch to tell the hitter a fast ball was coming or stand straight up for a curve. That made it a lot easier for the hitter.

"When Billy coached at third or first, he'd watch the pitcher to see if he was tipping off his pitches. It wouldn't be long before he could tell you what the pitcher was going to throw. If he yelled, 'Be ready,' you could expect a fast ball, or if he hollered, 'Come on,' it would be a breaking pitch.

"Once we knew every pitch Max Lanier was going to throw, but he still shut us out."

For the Cubs, a team comparable to the Cardinals' famed Gas House Gang with the likes of Billy Jurges, Larry French, Charlie Grimm, Gabby Hartnett, Augie Galan, and Charlie Root, Herman had seasons in which he hit .314, .303, .341, .334, .335 and .307. Billy, with managerial aspirations of his own, was disappointed when Jimmie Wilson was named manager to succeed Hartnett in 1941.

Fearing they had a discontented player on their hands, the Cubs, at 2:30 a.m. on the morning of May 6, did a most unreasonable thing. They traded Herman to Brooklyn for outfielder Charlie Gilbert, infielder Johnny Hudson and cash estimated at $35,000. MacPhail felt Herman would be a steadying influence on the Dodgers' young shortstop, Pee Wee Reese.

Everyone involved was awakened in the wee hours of the night to announce the deal. Herman, who was hitting .193 at the time, said, "I'm awfully sorry to leave Chicago and hope I will be of some help to Leo Durocher's team."

That afternoon, Billy went 4 for 4—three singles and a double—against the Pirates' Rip Sewell. The following Sunday he enjoyed a 5-for-5 performance (two triples and three singles) against Philadelphia. Brooklyn went on to win the 1941 pennant in a tough down-to-the-wire scramble with St. Louis.

But Herman, who hit .330—second to Stan Musial in 1943—and then served in military service in '44 and '45, and Durocher had a mutual dislike for each other. Leo thought Billy was after his job. Once he antagonized Herman by chewing him out in front of all the other players in the clubhouse for something that wasn't Billy's fault.

If stories are to be believed, Herman once threw a ball in infield practice that struck Durocher. It looked like an accident, and it was accepted as such until the pair exchanged heated words in which Herman told Durocher to his face that he tried to hit him.

So during the 1946 season, Herman was dealt to the Boston Braves for Stew Hofferth, a third string catcher, a trade that appeared to belittle Herman.

But Billy got his revenge.

On the last day of the season, Herman got a double against his ex-teammates and helped the Braves win 4–0, forcing Brooklyn into a playoff with St. Louis for the National League title. The Cards won two straight games and then beat the Boston Red Sox in the World Series.

The following year Billy Herman was the manager of the down-trodden Pittsburgh Pirates. They finished last, and he was fired.

"I didn't think there was any way he could miss as a manager," Reese said. "But Billy did not believe in curfews. He said the players were over 21. I remember a couple of players coming to the games in tuxedoes!"

Herman's explanation was simply this, "I assumed too much. I was used to playing only with good, smart ballplayers. I thought all major league ballplayers knew how to play baseball. I didn't think it was necessary to tell fundamental things to a player with experience of four or five years in the majors. I found out differently. All players in the majors are not major league ballplayers."

Herman then became manager of the Giants' Minneapolis farm club in the American Association in 1948. But, lo and behold, guess who became the Giants' skipper later that season? That's right. Durocher! And Herman quit at season's end.

He later took over for Johnny Pesky at the Boston helm in 1964 and was let loose two years later. Herman remained luckless as a manager, the Red

Sox finishing eighth once and ninth twice in that span. But one year later Boston won the pennant under Dick Williams.

Billy Herman, who once beat Goren in bridge, who was judged too light to play in the big leagues, who was one of the smartest players ever, who was a real pro, is going to the Hall of Fame. His record shows he deserves the honor.

New Albany, too, is proud. Mayor Warren Nash has proclaimed a special day for Billy Herman on Aug. 25, a week after the induction ceremonies.

25. Speakin' of Hartnett

ON SEPTEMBER 28, 1938, the Cubs were amid an eight-game winning streak and sitting only a half-game behind the league-leading Pirates. However, that day's game was moments away from getting called due to darkness, which could have ruined the club's effort to steal the pennant just as the season was coming to a close. But then the greatest catcher in Cubs history, Charles Leo "Gabby" Hartnett, delivered a mighty blast that rocketed the Cubs to the World Series. The shot occurred with two strikes and no balls, and in its wake pandemonium erupted. Baseball writer Warren Brown, as seen in this 1939 selection, described the scene that "Hollywood's wildest dream will never approach."

Cubs players "Gabby" Hartnett and Charlie "Jolly Cholly" Grimm at spring training on Catalina Island in 1926. Twelve years later, during the 1938 campaign, Gabby would replace Jolly as manager. Courtesy Chicago History Museum.

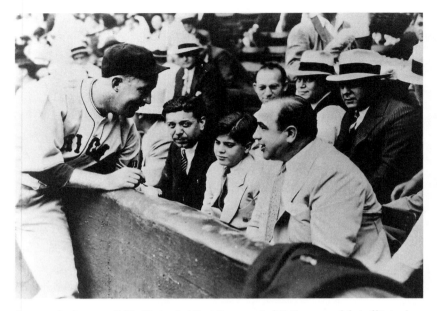

At a 1931 charity game, Gabby Hartnett obliged the request of Al Capone, and that of his twelve-year-old son Al "Sonny" Jr., for an autograph. Capone Sr.'s "minders" sat behind him, protecting his backside. This photo didn't make National League brass too happy.

Brown's essay, which ran in the *Saturday Evening Post*, also explains how "Gabby" got his nickname, his wild popularity with Cubs fans, and his methodical journey to greatness, as well as how he lived. In addition, Brown tells how Hartnett became the Cubs manager—he was already the catcher—only weeks before his monstrous homer that catapulted his team to the World Series.

However, after a disappointing season in 1940, Hartnett, who as a manager "angered easily" and became embroiled in spats with pitchers Dizzy Dean and Clay Bryant, was fired. Still, he remains a celebrated icon in Cubs lore.[1] His career numbers reflect his prowess, and he manned the plate for three Cubs World Series appearances from 1932 to 1938 (he also pinch-hit in the 1929 World Series but spent most of that season inactive with a sore arm). The stellar fielder landed six All-Star nods, won the NL MVP in 1935 and finished as runner-up in 1938. His career ended with an impressive .297 batting average. But numbers alone do not explain how he became the "people's choice." This article helps shed light on that.

Gabby Likes 'Em Hot

Warren Brown, *Saturday Evening Post*, February 11, 1939

A Skinny, red-faced youngster, going three thousand miles away from his New England home and fireside to seek his baseball fortune in a major-league training camp, sat huddled in a Pullman, observed everything, but spoke nary a word, from the city of Chicago to the island kingdom of the Wrigleys, Catalina.

A newspaperman, as Irish as the lad he had been studying, stood the silence as long as he could, and then blared forth, that all might hear: "There's the gabbiest guy that ever went on a spring-training trip."

Thus entered into the ranks of the Chicago Cubs, the National League, and eventually, unless a great many baseball folk are wrong, into Baseball's Hall of Fame, Charles Leo (Gabby) Hartnett.

That was in 1922. That same Hartnett, no longer reserved, but bubbling over with energy that at times seems explosive, having established a major league catching record for steady service that will likely endure, is now the manager of the Cubs, and, with the lone exception of the scout who found him, the sole survivor of seventeen frenzied baseball years.

In the fall of '37 he completed with the Cubs the thirteenth season in which he caught more than 100 games. Only Ray Schalk, of the old Chicago White Sox, had ever done anything like that in major-league baseball. And not even Schalk, or Johnny Kling, Jimmy Archer, or any of the other storied catchers of Chicago baseball history ever came close to Gabby Hartnett in a hold on the paying public.

Perhaps this was best illustrated in the sudden appointment of Hartnett as manager of the Cubs last season, succeeding Charlie Grimm. It was a sudden move on the part of the owner, P. K. Wrigley, but it was not unexpected. For years, Hartnett seemed destined one day to manage the club with which his entire major-league playing career had been bound up. Indeed, as things went none too well for Grimm in the last few seasons, there was what amounted to an insistent demand that Hartnett be appointed manager. In 1937, when Grimm became ill, late in the season, the club was turned over to Hartnett. It went into a winning streak at once, and gained the top of the league. Grimm returned later, and for one reason or another the Cubs folded and the Giants came on to win the pennant.

During the winter, Wrigley expressed the opinion that the Cubs probably would have won had Hartnett remained as manager. He was not prepared then to make the managerial change. He decided that in mid-season of last year.

"Hartnett was entitled to the job," Wrigley said, "and he was Grimm's logical successor. But he was not made manager for those reasons. I wanted to be sure, first, that he was the best man for the job. I studied the situation, myself. I questioned hundreds of persons—fans, baseball people of every capacity, players, other managers, league executives, club owners and officials, even umpires. Their opinion was unanimously for Hartnett."

One of Gabby's managers—he has played under six—has not hesitated in calling Hartnett the greatest catcher the game has ever known. This manager speaks with some authority, too, for he is Joe McCarthy, of the old school, present manager of the New York Yankees, and the only man who has ever won pennants in both National and American leagues.

As a ball player, Gabby is definitely old school. Some players pick their spots. Some like 'em hot, some like 'em cold. Gabby never picks his spots. But he likes 'em hot. Where the going is toughest, that's where Gabby wants to be. He's the kind of competitor who delivers in the clutch.

The events of the most dramatic baseball afternoon of last year will prove that. Hollywood's wildest dream will never approach the dramatic climax reached on the afternoon of last September twenty-eighth in Wrigley Field, Chicago.

Gabby was still a debutante manager. His Cubs were half a game behind the reeling Pirates, having embarked on a winning streak of eight straight games. The score was tied at five to five in the last half of the ninth. Two out, nobody on base. Manager Hartnett stepped to the plate.

There never was a tighter clutch. Night was blacking out the field. It was clear to all of the 34,465 tense fans in the stands that, after Gabby's turn at bat, the game would be called on account of darkness.

Mace Brown, relief star for the Pirates, tossed a curve. Gabby's bat didn't leave his shoulder. Strike one. Gabby swung on the next one and missed. It looked as though Gabby, mighty Gabby, might emulate Casey, mighty Casey. Brown uncorked his fast one.

Gabby swung again. Everybody in the park heard the crack as bat met ball. The ball rocketed into the night. And it seemed as though everybody in the left-field bleachers was reaching for it the next instant. As Gabby circled the bases, thousands rushed for him. Half of Chicago accompanied him as he surged across home plate in the darkness. Scores of rooters fought to touch his dirty uniform.

THE HIT THAT WON A PENNANT

That blow sank the Pirates. That blow put the Cubs out in front and catapulted them into the World Series with the Yankees. Catcher Hartnett had delivered for Manager Hartnett in the tightest of clutches. Catcher Hartnett had made Manager Hartnett a miracle man by bringing home the bacon with his own big bat.

Gabby's very presence on the ball field commands attention. His infectious smile, his roaring greeting to friends that he counts by the thousand in every city he visits, his career-long policy of asking no quarter and giving none are reminiscent of what baseball's graybeards are pleased to term the "good old days." But Hartnett is essentially modern, good-natured, and well qualified to know his way around in any company, anywhere. In Chicago, which has not been without its baseball heroes from Pop Anson's time down, Hartnett is the people's choice and the returns from outlying precincts of the major leagues show him piling up huge majorities in the popularity poll.

Capitalization on Hartnett's great personal popularity began with his appointment as manager. It is a matter of record that the first half-dozen games played after his taking charge were witnessed by a crowd total greater than any other half-dozen-game period in all Cub history.

It was undoubtedly the suggestion of the old school about Hartnett that attracted him to a Cub scout, or vice versa, while a member of the Worcester club in 1921. Hartnett had been rescued by Worcester from a county-fair game at Uxbridge, Massachusetts.

The scout was gnarled Jack Doyle, one-time flame thrower for the rough-and-ready Baltimore Orioles that had given to baseball John McGraw, Hughey Jennings, Willie Keeler and others of the sort who would willingly have given a lion the first two bites before regarding the contest as even.

Doyle, still scouting the canebrakes and the tall uncut for the Cubs, always has fancied big men, and Hartnett was big, if rawboned, in those days. He has acquired some aldermanic proportions since, and there was even a time, a few years ago, when his teammates called him "Puffy."

Doyle, unbeknown to Hartnett, rode beside him on a car to the Albany ball park.

"He had a strong puss," says Doyle, who is inordinately proud of having discovered Hartnett. "Puss" is Baltimore Oriole for face, and in order to appreciate how that figures in Doyle's calculations, we must detour for a moment.

A few years ago, Doyle recommended a pitcher to the Cubs. Seemingly, the pitcher had all that was needed in the way of fast ball and curve. He was big and strong. But he had a great difficulty in getting anyone out.

One day in the Polo Grounds, New York, Hartnett was out of uniform because of a finger injury. He sat with Doyle and the two watched the pitcher, who was making another try, and failing, against the Giants.

"I've been looking at that guy close," said Doyle, "and he's got a weak puss. I should have noticed that when I saw him in the minor leagues. That's the only way to tell whether a guy will battle for you. Look at that Frank Demaree. There's a strong puss for you. When he sticks his jaw out like that, he'd scare anybody.

In the ball game at Albany, Doyle saw Hartnett block a runner at the plate. He wasn't spike-shy. He had what it takes. That was enough for Doyle. He likes men who like the hot spots, men who go where the fighting is.

That evening, Hartnett, like all youngsters in their first year of professional baseball, a bit shy on funds, approached his manager and asked for a couple of dollars "eating money."

"He gave me five," says Hartnett, "and told me to send it back to him from Chicago next year. That was the first I knew I had been sold to the Cubs."

It would be nice to relate that Hartnett was a tremendous success from taw. But that would not be accurate.

When the spring-training exercises at Catalina Island were over, manager Bill Killefer brought the Cubs to Los Angeles to begin an exhibition series. Present at the time were Bill Veeck, the club's president, John O. Seys, then traveling secretary, and Doyle, the scout. Of the three, only Doyle is now alive.

Killefer approached them and announced that he was going to send Hartnett away. He was reporting to Veeck, of course, but the voices of Doyle and Seys were raised in protest.

"But he hasn't caught a game," they said. "Why not give him that chance?" Killefer agreed, if reluctantly.

Hartnett caught that afternoon, well enough to stay the descent of the spring-training ax. That was the nearest he has ever been to leaving the Cub pay roll since the day his name went on it.

In his early days as a Cub regular, Hartnett, a free swinger, struck out a lot, and was the target for plenty of jeering from Cub fans, who are a bit notorious for their hot-and-cold natures. However, many of those same scoffers remained to become charter members of the Hartnett Cheering Society, whose entire roster now will not admit that Gabby can do a wrong.

There is something of a contradiction in Hartnett's nature. On the field, effusive noise and a magnificent actor of his star part, Gabby's private life is very much its own. Unlike most ball players, he is a resident and taxpayer in the city he represents on the field. And the Hartnett home life is the Hartnetts'. Married in 1929 to Martha Marshall, Hartnett has two children, Charles Leo, Jr.—otherwise Buddy—and Sheila Ann.

Buddy is nine, and Sheila Ann is four. Buddy hasn't paid much attention to baseball, as yet. He is too busy in his spare time constructing model airplanes.

A NEW ENGLAND CHAMPION

"I'm not worried about him in that regard," says Gabby. "Why, when I was ten, and living in Millville, Massachusetts, my greatest ambition was to be known as the champion berry picker of New England. I'm not sure that I wasn't either. I sold as many as sixty quarts I picked to one lady. Got fifteen cents a quart too. [I had the reputation as a clean berry picker. No greenies or crushed berries.]"

The Hartnetts do little or no entertaining at home. And Mrs. Hartnett, unlike most wives of ballplayers, and especially star ballplayers, can take her baseball or leave it alone.

"If I were driving a truck," says Hartnett, "I'd not expect my wife to be riding on the seat beside me to see how I was doing, would I? Well, baseball's just as much my business, and the ball park is the place for that. When I'm home, that's where I enjoy being with my family. They are not a part of baseball, and that's the way it's going to be."

In his off-season stretches, Hartnett likes to play bridge and pinochle. He belongs to a club or two that specialize in each. He will play a friendly pinochle game, or take part in a hand or two of bridge. But not when there is much betting.

"I don't believe in that," he says. "Ballplayers that bet high on cards have too many things on their minds. I always say that if you show me a ballplayer who saves his money, I'll show you a good ballplayer."

For that reason Hartnett rarely makes a bet on a horse race.

Most ballplayers, and especially Cubs since Hornsby's time, like huge steaks. Rogers Hornsby, while managing the club, advocated steaks as a means to a high batting average. Hartnett doesn't go much for steaks. He likes roasts, though.

He likes to play golf, and is a fine golfer, but rarely indulges in the game in the regular baseball season. Once a year, in the period between the close of one baseball season and the opening of another, he goes on long hunting trips. He has no choice of quarry.

"I like to hunt pheasants and ducks," he says. "And I like to hunt deer. After the season, I generally go on a trip to shoot elk, moose and bear. I can't go much for that goat shooting at Catalina. Too much like firing at a cow."

Hartnett regards his former clubmate, Pat Malone, as one of baseball's best rifle shots.

Lon Warneke, also a former Cub, is another good shot. "But the boys built him up into a sort of latter-day Deadeye Dick," says Hartnett. "Lon isn't that good with a rifle. But with a baseball—"

Hartnett broke into the major leagues on the top floor, as it were.

When the 1922 season opened at Cincinnati, the youngster was playing his first major-league ball game. More than that, he was seeing his first major league ball game, since that was the first time he had ever been in a major league park.

"Was I scared?" He says. "Of course I was. I had never seen that many people at a ball game in my life. And I had to catch Alex. Not that there was anything tough about that. You could sit in a rocking chair and catch Old Pete, for there never has been a pitcher that I have seen who could put the ball where he wanted it like Alex could. It will always be a regret to me that when I came up with the Cubs, Alex was beginning to fade. He must have been as great as the greatest when he had it. I'll always be grateful to him, for, after I had caught him that first time, he went to Killefer, the boss, who had caught him so many times, and said, 'Bill, the kid's all right.' I've had a good many nice things written about me and said about me in fifteen years, but that little speech of Old Pete is the one I remember. I've still got the ball that was in play when that game ended, and treasure it, as I do the glove I used. Alex fanned Babe Pinelli for the last out. That's how I happened to get the ball."

If Hartnett had his thrill over his first major-league game, he had another one coming. That was the time when he registered his first hit in the big show.

"We were playing at St. Louis," says Hartnett, "and Killefer sent me in to bat in the pinch for Vic Aldridge. I got hold of one and drove it out to right center. I lit out for first, all excited, and was still watching the ball when I rounded the base. My feet caught in the bag and down I went, plowing up a couple of feet of ground with my face. I got up and got as far around as third, at that."

HUB, THE GIANT KILLER

These incidents are described by Hartnett as worthy of his remembrance, but if properly cross examined, he will always return to the 1934 All-Star game.

Hartnett was the National League's No. 1 catcher in the first five of these games. With his own manager, Charlie Grimm, directing, and three other Cubs, Bill Herman, Augie Galan and Frank Demaree in action, Gabby helped win the 1936 game, the first the National League ever won.

He doesn't talk much about that, but likes to go back to Carl Hubbell and 1934.

He will go over, pitch by pitch, that memorable two innings of the All-Star game in which Hub fanned, in succession, Babe Ruth, Lou Gehrig, Jimmy Foxx, Al Simmons and Joe Cronin.

Does he then rate Hubbell as his all-time greatest?

Not exactly.

"I'll have to take Dizzy Dean," says Hartnett; "and that isn't because he is now one of our pitchers either. I felt that way about him when he was with St. Louis. But I do want to say that, sore arm or no, since he has been with us, I can regard some of the games he has pitched as the greatest in his career. He is a great competitor, the greatest of all baseball's showmen.

"I might straddle the issue and call Hub the greatest left hander, and Old Diz the greatest right hander. But I'll still take Old Diz. Alex, of course, was on the downgrade when I caught him."

Hartnett, incidentally, had more than a little to do with the urging of

Owner Wrigley to acquire Dizzy Dean. It was suggested at a conference at the Catalina training camp, last spring, Hartnett voicing the opinion that the club needed another ranking pitcher.

It cost Wrigley $185,000 and three players to get Dean, and there is no available estimate how much more it cost in medical surveys for the time Old Diz remained in idleness, his sore arm sharing the publicity glare with the growing conflagration that was to burn away the managerial portfolio held by Grimm.

DEAN'S ACHILLES TOE

Old Diz—the man of a few thousand words, generally about himself—broke a few seconds' silence after he had first pitched to Hartnett, in one of the All-Star games.

"If I had that guy to pitch to all the time," said Diz, "I'd never lose me a game."

The time came, and in the 1937 All-Star game, when Old Diz, along with Hubbell, Mungo, Grissom, and practically all the rest of the National League except President Ford Frick, was so rudely handled by a parcel of New York Yankees and some other fellows in the guise of American League All-Stars.

Old Diz explained his misfortune in that game as directly due to his "shaking off" Hartnett on a pitch. He was hit on the toe with a rifle shot from an American League batsman.

His own analysis is that all his troubles for the rest of the 1937 season and the early part of 1938 were due to that.

When he joined the Cubs he would have no catcher but Hartnett, and before and after his twelve-week layoff from pitching duty, Old Diz, no longer "fogging 'em" by the batters, pitched solely to Hartnett's signals. Given perfect control, in one of his games against the Giants—whom he allowed but five hits—Old Diz threw just 88 balls in the nine innings. It was that game which Hartnett, then Dean's manager as well as catcher, characterized as one of the greatest exhibitions Dean had ever given.

It began to look then, since that was Dean's fifth win for the Cubs, without a defeat, as if there was something to his statement of a few years back that, with Hartnett as his catcher, he would never lose a game.

It was Hartnett's ill luck that the first World Series that he ever attended in the uniform of one of the contestants was the one in which he couldn't play.

That was in 1929, when he was out all season with a sore arm that threatened to close his entire career. His few appearances for the Cubs that year were restricted to pinch hitting.

He characterizes the seventh inning of the fourth game of that series as having caused him more suffering than all other evils that have befallen him, including the debacle of Manager Hartnett's Cubs in the dreary World Series of last fall. That was the inning in which the Athletics fell upon the Cubs, and kept falling until they had wiped out an 8 to 0 lead against them, scored ten runs on ten hits and won the game.

Charley Root, still with the Cubs, had held the Athletics to two hits. Al Simmons, first up in the seventh, hit a homer. Jimmy Foxx singled. So did Bing Miller. Jimmy Dykes singled, and Foxx scored. Joe Boley singled, and Miller Scored. George Burns, a pinch hitter, popped out.

"I was sitting beside Joe McCarthy, on the bench," said Hartnett. "Up to then, he wasn't worried much. We still had a big lead. But when Max Bishop got a hit, and scored Dykes, making it 8 to 4, McCarthy chased Art Nehf out to pitch. Mule Haas was the hitter. He banged a kind of line fly right out at Hack Wilson, in center. Hack never did see that ball in the sun. When he finally got it back, two more runs were in and Haas was on second. McCarthy ordered Mickey Cochrane passed, and sent Sheriff Blake in to pitch to Simmons, up for the second time. Simmons hit one and scored Haas. Then Foxx hit one and Cochran scored the tying run.

"I was pretty excited, but I can still hear McCarthy asking no one in particular, 'What can I do?' But I didn't know either. Pat Malone went in to pitch. He soaked Miller with a pitch, and the first thing we knew, Dykes unloaded a double, two runs scored, and it didn't matter much that Malone did fan the last two men. I never want to see anything like that again. You can talk all you want about New York Yankee power, but I'll bet that even McCarthy, who is directing it now, will never forget the Athletics of 1929.

To McCarthy, Hartnett gives his sincere praise as the greatest all-around manager for whom he has ever worked, in a list which began with Killefer and ranged through Rabbit Maranville, George Gibson, McCarthy, Rogers Hornsby, and on to Grimm.

ONE-PLAY GABBY

"I think McCarthy knew more about baseball than any other manager I ever saw in action or worked for," says Hartnett. "But that was only part of it. He knew how to handle men. He had understanding, and he was a great disciplinarian, while never losing his standing with all of us as a great guy. If there is system to baseball, as there is to football, I'd say McCarthy's is best. At all events, I think his record comes close to proving it, doesn't it?"

Grimm, whom Hartnett supplanted as manager, went his way singing the praises of his successor. There was always a strong bond of friendship between the two, and even the internal turmoil of a baseball situation that has had few parallels in the major leagues could not snap that bond.

To Grimm, as to all the other managers from whom he has played, Hartnett gave everything he had, and all knew that.

"Let's assume that he's the greatest catcher you or I will ever see," said Grimm, "and let me tell you about the time he played first base. I was with Pittsburgh then. It was in 1923 and we were playing the Cubs. There was something the matter with the regular first baseman, and who walked out for practice but Hartnett. In fielding practice he looked like Stuffy McInnis grown up. He shifted his feet, fired that ball around as only Hartnett can. He handled the ball like a right-handed Hal Chase. We were properly impressed.

"Well the game began. The first man up for us was Bigbee. He dribbled one of those mean, slow, twisting rollers down the line. Hartnett came charging in. The pitcher came charging over. Bigbee came tearing down the line. All four—Hartnett, the pitcher, Bigbee and the ball—got to the same place at the same time. Everybody piled up. Hartnett's glove went one way. He went another. They never did find his cap. Finally order was restored, Hartnett announced that he was ready, and play went on. Or started to. But out from the Cubs' dugout came Killefer, and called 'Time!' A new first baseman was put into the game. Chicago fans should be grateful that One-Play Hartnett finished his career as a first baseman there and then. I'll guarantee you he'd have been killed in action if Killefer hadn't taken him out there and then."

But Hartnett doesn't list that as his funniest experience. He goes into the Polo Grounds in John McGraw's time for that.

"You know," he says, "how McGraw used to eat his Giants alive if they let themselves be nailed in double plays? Well, we're playing them one day and Heinie Mueller was on first base with two out. He forgot that. All he was thinking about was that even if he got forced at second, he must prevent the double play. The batter hit one down to Sparky Adams, who was playing second for us. Adams gave it to the shortstop, Cooney, forcing out Mueller and retiring the side. But just from force of habit, Cooney started his throw to first base. Side out or not, Mueller saw that throw start. He leaped in the air to block it, and was hit squarely in the mouth. I guess he was the only man in baseball history who ever broke up a double play for McGraw after the side had been retired.

Hartnett regards Joe Medwick, of the St. Louis Cardinals, as the most formidable hitter he has ever attempted to help a pitcher outguess.

"Hornsby was the tops, until Medwick really began to hit," says Hartnett. "We've been trying everything on Joe for years, and it doesn't seem to do much good. His weakness, as the saying is, is a base on balls."

POISON PITCHERS

Hartnett's idea of an ideal ballplayer, smooth working, effortless, but highly efficient, is Charley Gehringer, of the Detroit Tigers.

"That guy hits Hubbell like he owns him," says Hartnett, which is tops in praise for a National Leaguer.

Baseball folks generally look on Hartnett as a worthy batsman himself, even though his lack of speed afoot makes him earn every hit he makes.

"I don't think of, offhand, one pitcher I like to hit more than another," he says. "But I can tell you three that I was glad to see get out of the league. They were Burleigh Grimes, Art Nehf, and Ray Kremer. Oh yes, don't forget that Lefty Grove. Remember how he fanned me those couple of times I batted in the 1929 series, and again in the first All-Star game? Still, I caught up with him, finally. I got a hit off him in spring training in 1936 and a triple in the All-Star game that year. But Grimes, Nehf, and Kremer didn't hold still long enough for me."

The toughest base runner to corral?

"Never could be anybody else but Pepper Martin, of the Cardinals," says Hartnett. "Why, if that guy could steal first base, he'd beat you out of a ball game all by himself."

Since handling his own pitchers and trying to detect weakness in opposing hitters is a large part of a catcher's job, listen to Hartnett on these matters.

"When a new player comes along and hits us, we start working different things on him. So do the other clubs, if he is still going good. Word gets around the league that way. Only trouble is, then, getting your pitchers to put the ball in the right spot. Lack of that kind of control has ruined more pitchers than anything else I can think of, except one thing, and that is lack of heart. I've always said that if it were possible to cut Charley Root's heart up into twenty-five chunks and transplant them in that many other pitchers, I'd have twenty-five great pitchers in no time. You can develop curves and fast balls, change of pace, sinkers, screw balls, knucklers, and everything else. But you're either born with a heart or without one. You don't acquire one."

For many years Hartnett has been invaluable to the Cubs in helping out the youngsters, especially the catchers who have come up to the Cubs, year after year. As a player he always was willing to share the secrets of his catching technique with anyone.

A few years ago, while the Cubs were in California for spring training, Gabby went out to a night game at Los Angeles between the Seattle Club and a Japanese All-Star team.

Hanging around the ball park in the afternoons and acting as bat boy for the Cubs was a Japanese schoolboy named "Yosh"—which was a near as any of the Cubs could get to his entire name. Yosh was in his element when the Japanese All-Stars appeared, and was very much on the job.

Gabby watched the Japanese catcher in action for an inning.

"That fellow will get every finger on his throwing hand broken," he observed. The Japanese catcher was extending his right hand with the fingers outspread.

Gabby called to Yosh, who spoke English well, and told him about the catcher's lack of protective knowledge.

Yosh carried the message away, and in a moment was back with the catcher, who was grinning from ear to ear at meeting Hartnett.

It took about five minutes of gesturing, with Yosh acting as interpreter, but finally the Japanese catcher learned that he was to keep his fingers closed, more or less fistlike, until the ball thudded into his glove, and then open the fingers over the ball.

Hartnett's fee for the expert advice was a baseball autographed by the Japanese players—in Japanese. He treasures that one.

Charley Root, the Cubs' veteran pitcher, who has been around since 1923, is best qualified to discuss Hartnett's methods in handling pitchers.

"He gets it out of you," said Root. "If you're letting down, or inclined to get grumpy like Pat Malone used to do, Gabby will fire that ball back at you like a shot. Believe me, that wakes you up. My own experience with him catching is that he always calls for the right pitch. Many times, I've stood out there and figured that the thing to do was come in with a curve. I'd look for the signal, and that's what Gabby wanted. He was forever on the alert, and I think he has broken up more steals and more hit-and-run plays by calling for pitch-outs than any other catcher in baseball. He is daring at all times, and sure of himself. He makes a pitcher feel that way too."

A BALLPLAYER'S BALLPLAYER

Hartnett himself catches one pitcher about as another. He has expressed himself on the subject of tough pitchers to handle. He thinks Sheriff Blake was the worst. Blake had a tremendous lot of stuff and was wild. That always makes for a rough day for the catcher. Hartnett termed Lon Warneke one of the easiest pitchers to handle, largely because of Warneke's superb control.

There isn't a player on the Cub squad who doesn't like Hartnett, and some of the youngsters even idolize him. Every one of them looks upon him as the ideal managerial type.

Augie Galan, a comparative youngster in the big leagues, tells of the first day Hartnett took over the management of the club in 1937, when Grimm was stricken and had to enter a hospital.

"When we had our meeting before the game," said Galan, "Hartnett couldn't keep from laughing. He wanted to be serious, and he was serious. But every once in a while it struck him as funny. Still he ran the ball club, as we all knew he would. He had his own way of doing things. Nobody got bawled out in the dugout, or even spoken to for doing something wrong. But the next day at the meeting there wasn't a thing Hartnett had missed. He went over all the mistakes and talked about them. In that way we were all pretty much on guard against making that mistake again."

When Hartnett was made manager in the midst of last year's race, his players actually exceeded their own ability in an effort to show how they felt about Gabby.

That went from the biggest star to the lowliest rookie. But for our purposes, perhaps the expression of Tony Lazzeri, now no longer a Cub, had best be reported.

A GALAXY OF STARS

Lazzeri came to the Cubs after the 1937 season, in which he was a World Series hero with the Yankees. Many felt that he was being groomed for the management of the Cubs. All were certain that his presence would lead to complications. All were wrong. From the first, Lazzeri, who sees much and says little, hit it off with Grimm, and hit it off with Hartnett, who had been designated as a coach as well as player, when the 1938 season began.

When Hartnett was named manager, there was a big demand of the photographers for posed pictures of Hartnett and Lazzeri, together.

Lazzeri wasn't very affable about that.

"I know what they've got in mind," he said. "They want to write under them something about how Gabby and I are going to get along, or aren't going to get along. They don't say nothing, but I know what they've got in mind. But all I've got to say about this is that Gabby ought to have been made manager long ago. All I hope is that he'll find some place for me to get into the games every day so I can show him where I stand. Gabby knows. He's my friend, and he's going to be a great manager."

Looking back over his major-league career, Hartnett is willing to pick his own All-Star team, with a few ideas on American Leaguers gained from All-Star games, spring-training exhibitions and World Series play.

He lists Gus Mancuso, of the New York Giants, as the best National League catcher he has seen.

His first baseman is Bill Terry, manager of the Giants. His second baseman is Frankie Frisch, former manager of the Cardinals. His shortstop is Frank Crosetti, of the Yankees. His third baseman is Pie Traynor, now manager of the Pittsburgh Pirates. His outfield gave him some thought, but he settled for Medwick, Chick Hafey and Ross Young, deceased, once a star of McGraw's Giants.

"Crosetti showed me more shortstopping in that last World Series than I ever want to see against me again," Hartnett says. "I know now who is the spark of that ball club. I hesitated a bit about naming Frisch over Billy Herman. Frisch, though, was a wonder when he was at his best with the Giants and later with the Cardinals. Not so good as Gehringer, of Detroit, though. I like Lou Gehrig, of the Yankees, too, but I'll need some argument to put him on my team over Terry. I guess we'd have to make a place for Babe Ruth on the team, and I know we would for Joe DiMaggio. He's the best ballplayer in the game today, doing anything. As long as we didn't get him, I'm glad my old boss, McCarthy, did."

Dizzy Dean, Hubbell and Van Mungo, at their best, were his pitching selections.

Which one was the fastest pitcher—"fast" in baseball parlance meaning speed of the ball?

"None of them," said Hartnett. "There has been only one fast pitcher in the National League in my time, Dazzy Vance."

"We had a little fellow named Clyde Beck on our club, years ago, when Vance was at tops. When Brooklyn was in town, Beck would come out on the field cautiously and peek around. If he saw Vance taking batting practice, which meant it was his turn to pitch, Beck would pick up his own bat and put it under the bench.

"Hack Wilson would come storming out on the field, and start yelling at Vance, telling him what we were going to do to that 'broken-arm' delivery of his. I don't think Hack ever got a good foul off Vance, but that didn't stop him from trying, or yelling.

"Beck would walk over to Hack and ask him to please be quiet. I can still hear him saying: 'Please Hack, I got to play today too.'"

Hartnett has a way with the umpires too.

At times he seems to be raving and ranting around the home plate, the chief figure in many a heated session. But he seldom gets chased from the games any more. There was a time, though, when he was always getting bounced, especially by Bill Klem.

"McCarthy finally got Klem and me straightened out," says Hartnett. "We get along fine now."

The umpires like Hartnett because he never puts up a squawk unless he thinks there is one coming. Umpires appreciate that.

Indeed, there is on record an incident of a few years back, when Dolly Stark, umpiring behind the plate in a Cub-Cardinal game at Chicago, was felled with a foul tip.

Hartnett steadied Stark as the umpire reeled around.

Stark had to be assisted from the field, eventually, and the first-base umpire prepared to don mask, shin guards, chest protector and what not to go behind the plate.

Out of the Cardinal dugout boiled Manager Frisch, the No. 1 umpire baiter of the league, unsympathetic to the last.

Across the field, he roared: "Never mind putting another umpire behind there! Hartnett's done a swell job of calling 'em so far this afternoon!"

Like umpires?

"They're my pals," says Hartnett. "Do you know that when I was sixteen years old I caught a game pitched by Bill Stewart, now a National League umpire? I had the mumps, and darn near died the next day. I was to get two dollars for catching the game. I haven't got it yet."

But that was all, it seems, in this game of baseball that Charles Leo Hartnett has ever missed.

26. Swoonin'

THE CUBS CAPTURED FOUR pennants from 1929 to 1938 only to find it-self amongst the National League's lower echelons from 1939 to 1943. Midway through World War II, this candid 1943 *Saturday Evening Post* article by Stanley Frank traced the downturn in Cubs' fortunes. Frank noted the fans' impatience by 1943 with owner Philip K. Wrigley, who took over when his father passed in 1932 and had recently tightened the team's purse strings, as well as with the "James boys," general manager James "Jim" Gallagher and manager James "Jim" Wilson, particularly with their handling of Russian power hitter Lou Novikoff. As an indication of the discontent, at a June game that year boos poured down from the roughly 37,000 fans. A sizable decrease in attendance by 1942 had also highlighted fans' weariness. In analyzing the situation, Frank jabbed Wrigley for admitting in 1932 that he knew little and cared little about baseball, and Frank maintained that Wrigley's inclination to think in a business-like fashion, with an emphasis on marketing and "efficiency," had not delivered. Downplay-ing Wrigley's role in the Cubs "stunning" 1935 and 1938 pennant runs, Frank suggested that many fans thought that those pennants came about because of personnel moves made by former general manager William L. Veeck rather than because of P. K. Wrigley. Veeck died in 1933 and, according to the Veeck-effect theory, the impact of Veeck's personnel moves could only last so long.

The Decline and Fall of the Cubs

Stanley Frank, *Saturday Evening Post*, September 11, 1943

Chicago baseball fans, always known as patient, fair-minded citizens reasonably devoted to the home team, threw their reputation and restraint out of the window at Wrigley Field on the afternoon of June twenty-seventh. A crowd of 37,792 reared back on its hind legs and howled its indignation at the floundering Cubs on the field and the blundering in the front office. The customers denounced Philip K. Wrigley for the pinch-penny policy that had squeezed Lou Novikoff, their outraged hero, and they indicated, raucously, and pointedly, that they wanted no part of Jim Wilson, the field manager, and Jim Gallagher, the general manager, whom the *Chicago Times* calls "the James boys."

Old inhabitants of Wrigley Field say it was the most violent demonstration against the Cub management since the wolves attacked Rogers Hornsby in 1932. On that occasion Hornsby crushed the mob by hitting a pinch home run with the bases loaded to beat the Braves. Wilson was powerless to silence the outburst or to make the bleacher clients tear up their signs reading: NOVIKOFF FOR MANAGER—THE BABE RUTH OF 1943—NOVIKOFF—OUST THE JAMES BOYS. The Cubs lost a double-header to the Cardinals, blowing the first game in the ninth inning and the second game in the eighth, to fall within half a game of last place. In the Cubs' next game, three days later in Boston, Wilson put another match to the smoldering antagonism back home by benching Novikoff in the second inning. The Mad Russian was told to sit down after he had struck out and played a pop fly into a double.

What the Cubs were doing near last place in midseason is, in the first place, the most important baseball story of the year. Casual fans are aware that the Cubs, inheritors of the proud tradition founded by Pop Anson, nurtured by Tinker to Evers to Chance and kept alive by four pennants during the decade of 1929–38, have been sagging badly since 1939. But perhaps only the experts, who picked the Cubs to challenge the Cardinals for the pennant this year, realize how complete the collapse has been.

That Jim Wilson himself has a pretty firm grasp on that idea was indicated recently when a friend approached him while he was batting fungoes and informed him that Bucky Harris has just been fired by the Phillies.

"That's strange," Wilson said, lifting a high one to right field. "I thought *I* was the next manager to be bounced."

The significance of the situation extends far beyond Chicago. The financial structure of the National League has been jolted severely by the sharp nosedive into the second division of the legendary Cubs and the Giants—McGraw's Giants—the good providers of the other members. It is very well to say that constant circulation of the pennant is a fine thing for stimulating interest, but if the league is to prosper, it must have strong, contending teams annually in Chicago and New York. Once the bitter rivalry between the Cubs and Giants, winners of fifteen championships apiece, invigorated the entire organization. The ancient feudists' dreary struggle to escape the cellar this season has hurt the league where it lives, at the box office.

In 1929 the Cubs established the all-time attendance record by drawing 1,485,166 paid admissions at home, a figure that even the Yankees, with a ball park of twice the capacity of Wrigley Field, never have approached. For five successive years, from 1927 through 1931, the Cubs played to more than a million people in Chicago each season. Last year they barely attracted 600,000 cash customers.

Harsh critics assert, however, that the Cubs last year did as well on the balance sheet as some of the old pennant winners. The answer to this riddle is that Wrigley, who formerly paid whopping salaries and fancy prices for new players, has put the team on a stringent budget, a practice rarely successful in baseball. The defense says Wrigley ran his team on a loose, lavish basis and dissipated a small fortune without getting results. Quick as a flash, the prosecution retorts that Wrigley still would have his money and a good team if he had not been a gold-plated sucker who spent, among other things, $185,000 for Dizzy Dean and $115,000 to acquire, then get rid of, Chuck Klein.

The Decline and Fall of the Cub Empire is ascribed to reasons that represent every evil from absentee ownership to amateur meddling: blanket indictments charge incompetent management from the front office to the dugout. Apologists mutter morosely about the terrible luck that has dogged the team in its player deals and claim the rough ride Phil Wrigley, the owner, has been getting is a very bum rap against a good guy. Ultimately though, the squalling baby no one wants to acknowledge is left on the doorstep of Wrigley, the wealthiest and least-known executive in the National League. The chewing-gum magnate is astonishingly naïve in baseball matters and is given to impulsive decisions which seem to be splendid ideas at the moment, but never work out.

Wrigley has no genuine affection for baseball. He admitted as much when he assumed control of the Cubs in 1932 upon the death of his father,

William Wrigley, Jr. In an interview with two newspapermen, P.K. said he knew little about baseball and cared less for it. The newspaperman persuaded Wrigley to withdraw the statement, pointing out that the customers hardly could be expected to show more enthusiasm for the team than the fellow who owned it.

Once Wrigley was in baseball, however, he made every effort to cultivate an interest in the game, an attitude consistent with the two principles that have motivated his life. Wrigley worships the memory of his father and detests inefficiency. The elder Wrigley was an ardent baseball nut and made his son promise he would carry on with the Cubs. For eleven years P.K. has taken an active leadership in the affairs of the team and he has given more time to it than the investment or the pressure war work warrants. That the net result is a worsening mess is the hair shirt in the Wrigley wardrobe. Every other enterprise in the vast Wrigley holdings is self-supporting.

Although the turmoil and publicity of baseball are alien to Wrigley's temperament, he made a careful study of the game after his father's death and tried to apply to it the methods that sold gum. Constant repetition of advertisement had created a desire for gum in the public consciousness; Wrigley ran ads in Chicago papers in the dead of winter exhorting the patrons to look ahead to Happy Hours with the Cubs the following summer. Another bright idea was hiring psychologists and efficiency experts for the team. Nothing came of it. The learned gents could not teach the hairy heroes how to hit or throw a curve ball.

The most important innovation Wrigley brought into baseball was his insistence that his product be presented in a clean, attractive package. His ball parks in Chicago and Los Angeles are by far the most beautiful and comfortable in the country. He ripped several thousand seats out of the Chicago park to relieve congestion and he tore down the unsightly red-brick outfield wall, replacing it with a graceful, vine-covered fence. His ushers were outfitted in smart uniforms and performed their duties with military precision. The enormously profitable food-and-drink concessions—retained by the ball club—established new standards of quality and cleanliness. Wrigley gave his product a resplendent wrapper, only to make a rather discouraging discovery. The customers weren't buying the inferior product, a slipping ball club, he was selling.

Wrigley today is up to his ears in war work, but the team is a chronic headache that makes demands upon his time and attention. His wrapping machinery is packaging articles for the armed forces, in millions of units, it never handled before. Yet P.K. had to take time out to carry on the final diplomatic negotiations in the Novikoff holdout and early in June he was so distressed by the team's miserable slump that he called a secret meeting in the clubhouse. "Forget the pennant" was the gist of his speech to the players. "Let's try to upset applecarts from now on."

Historians trace the decline of the Cubs back to October, 1933, to the death of William L. Veeck, who had been the shrewd, tough general manager of the team since 1919. Veeck had covered baseball for the *Chicago American*, writing under the name of Bill Bailey, and was a loud and caustic critic of the elder Wrigley. His accurate sniping annoyed Bill Wrigley and during one of those "put-up-or-shut-up" arguments Veeck was offered the job of running the ball club. Much to everyone's astonishment, Veeck proved to be an unusually capable executive. During his regime the Cubs supplanted the Giants as the ranking team and gold mine of the National League.

Veeck's passing, following within a year the death of the first Wrigley, left the Cubs without an experienced baseball head. Phil Wrigley appointed William M. Walker, a fish-and-oyster man who was a member of the board, president and general manager. The setup lasted a year. Walker wanted Gabby Hartnett to succeed Charlie Grimm as manager. P.K. insisted on retaining Grimm, who had been appointed by his father. When Walker resigned, P.K. assumed the presidency of the club with Charles "Boots" Weber reluctantly agreeing to serve as general manager. Weber speaks in a whisper and suffers from claustrophobia, an ailment that prevented him from traveling with the team.

The Cubs pulled a stunning stroke to launch P.K.'s regime in style. They won twenty-one straight games in September, 1935, to overhaul the Cardinals for the pennant two days before the close of the season. In 1938, after Hartnett displaced Grimm, the Cubs gave the same dose to the Pirates, who had completed all World Series arrangements down to printing the tickets and building a new press box. Baseball people were of the opinion, however, that these successes were founded upon the players Veeck had brought to Chicago. They looked upon Wrigley as a lucky dilettante.

When the Cubs, in 1940, fell into the second division for the first time in fifteen years, P.K. made two moves, inspired by sheer hunches, which generally are regarded as the causes of the present difficulties. He turned the operation of the team over to Gallagher and Wilson. They have yet to finish in the first division.

In pulling Gallagher out of a hat, P.K. undoubtedly was influenced by his father's fortunate choice of Veeck. The analogy is striking in every detail. Gallagher, like Veeck, was a baseball writer for the *Chicago American* and pulled no punches in upbraiding the management. Like Veeck, Gallagher had no business or executive experience. The anvil chorus says the parallel ends abruptly at this point.

The first deal Gallagher made was an ill-advised transaction that provoked the antagonism of the clients, who take extensive pleasure in reminding him of it at every opportunity. Gallagher probably presented the pennant to Brooklyn in May, 1941, by trading Billy Herman, the best second baseman in the league, for Charley Gilbert, Johnny Hudson and $12,500. Neither Gilbert nor Hudson finished the season with the Cubs and Mr. Wrigley needs $12,500 as urgently as you need another neck.

Wilson was sprung on the populace as a total surprise. If it had not been for six dramatic days in the 1940 World Series, he still would be a coach at Cincinnati. Although it was obvious that Hartnett was no ball of fire as a manager after 1938, Wrigley expressed his approval of him. In response to a direct question, Wrigley told John Carmichael, of the *Chicago Daily News*, that Hartnett would be re-engaged for 1941. Wrigley always has been absolutely truthful and forthright in his relations with the press, but something happened between his vote of confidence in Hartnett and the unexpected hiring of Wilson.

That something was the World Series, which brought Wilson out of obscurity and made him the most arresting human-interest sport story of the year. Wilson had put in five seasons as manager of the Phillies, during which time the team finished no better then seventh, and was jolly well satisfied to be relieved of his cross in 1938. He had settled down to the uneventful life of a coach when an ankle injury to Ernie Lombardi, Cincinnati's first-string catcher, catapulted him into the spotlight.

The Reds virtually had clinched the pennant, but they had no catcher other than Bill Baker, a rookie, for the World Series. Wilson then was past forty and had appeared briefly in only seven games during the two preceding years, but he laboriously got into shape and did a remarkable job in helping the Reds defeat the Tigers. He caught six of the seven games, hit a robust

.353 and accounted for the only base stolen in the series. Wilson suddenly found himself back in circulation as a potential manager. He was perfectly happy in Cincinnati, but Wrigley's offer to manage the Cubs was too good to be refused. It was a two-year contract calling for $25,000 a year.

The trade's regard for the ability of the James boys is, frankly, not too high. Insiders claim Gallagher is not adroit in the delicate matter of juggling talent and temperament; opponents point to his three-year tenure as proof that a big league team cannot be run on an inflexible budget. Wilson was considered the best "second man," or coach, in the business, but the players say he lacks patience with young men and tends to panic in a jam. They suspect that the five blank years he spent with the Phillies ruined him as a winning manager.

Critics sum up the bill of particulars against Gallagher and Wilson with the Novikoff affair, which saw the management lose more good will than it could afford. Few players have come up to the major leagues with a flossier build-up than that which preceded Louie Novikoff. He did not embark on his career until he was twenty-two, but after his first professional year he was the batting champion of every minor league in which he played. Novikoff is built along the general lines of a hydrant and has a personality as rugged and gushing. Purveyors of light literature in Chicago hailed him with gladstone cries and said he might be the best right-handed hitter to enter the league since Joe Medwick.

THE MAD RUSSIAN'S HOLDOUT

Novikoff had been celebrated on the Pacific Coast as the Babe Ruth of softball, for both his batting and his pitching prowess. He hit several drives with the softball that measured 350 feet, equivalent to a 500-foot belt with a hard baseball. In one game he fanned twenty-two batters in eight innings. Asked how he would pitch to himself, Novikoff charmed the interviewers as follows: "If I didn't brain myself with a pitched ball, I might kill myself with a line drive through the box. I'd be a bum and a hero at the same time. Ha-ha. I don't get it."

The quaint youth, who spoke nothing but Russian until he was ten years old, joined the Cubs in 1941. Purists were horrified by his form. He was in imminent danger of being skulled when he went after a fly ball and his favorite pitches for hitting purposes were balls he picked off the ground or his ear. The Cubs tried to have Novikoff cut a more presentable figure, but soon despaired of getting him to think. He was sent to Milwaukee on option early in the season when his average was flirting with .200. Louie was disconsolate.

"I'm so lousy," he wailed, "that I couldn't get a hit if the pitcher walked past the plate holdin' the ball in his hand. But I'll be good soon and then no bum will get me out."

He was exaggerating only slightly. Novikoff led the American Association in hitting with .370. Brought back to the Cubs in 1942, the Mad Russian once more had an awful time untracking himself. He was hitting less than .260 in May, but presently he got good again and was among the first five hitters of the league when his average rose to .316 in August. He finished the year hitting .300 on the nose.

Novikoff was not the people's choice until Gallagher sent him a contract for 1943. It was for $6000, a raise of only $500. Novikoff hollered bloody murder and said the affront to his honor would cost the team $10,000. The pronouncement did not drive the war off Page 1; it appeared to be the kind of holdout that is settled with an aura of sweetness and light ten days before opening game. Novikoff, however, still was absent when the season opened. At the same time it was revealed that Wrigley was investing $100,000 in a girls' softball league in the Middle West.

People began to wonder out loud why the rich Mr. Wrigley spread his largesse among girl players, but wouldn't give a popular athlete more than coolie wages. Gallagher scotched all rumors of a trade by stating he would not accept any other player in the league for Novikoff, adding that the fellow represented an investment of $80,000 to the Cubs. Again, people thought it strange that Novikoff, who was worth so much to the ball club, was not worth another $1500 or so to himself. The questions became more pertinent late in May when the Cubs lost nine straight games on their first Eastern trip. The slump put Novikoff in the driver's seat and the club finally capitulated on May twenty-first, ending the longest holdout in recent years. It is believed Louis got about $7500, which would have averted all the unpleasantness had it been offered to him originally.

Opinion concerning Novikoff as a ballplayer is divided so sharply that there never will be a meeting of the minds. Those who see him occasionally believe he has the makings of a tremendous hitter. Others insist the guy is an overrated oaf who never will learn to field adequately and will hit only when a game already has been won or lost beyond saving. It is significant that the Cub players concur in the latter viewpoint.

The Novikoff case served to emphasize one point that does much to explain the club's present policy. The honeymoon is over for the Cubs. The happy days, when fifteen-game pitchers received $20,000 a year, and good, but not great, infielders got $17,500, are gone. Such benevolence ended with the Gallagher appointment. The Cubs no longer are the plutocrats of the profession; they are paid on the same scale observed by all teams but the perennial weak sisters. Gallagher has been blasted for adhering to the budget too slavishly, but he has done an outstanding job of creating a farm system, something the Cubs never had, and which made it necessary to spend huge sums for good players.

Still the Cubs lose when they win. Lefty O'Doul, San Francisco manager, needled Gallagher early in the season with a crack to the effect that Chicago has its best team in Los Angeles. "You can bet your last dime," O'Doul said, "the Angels wouldn't be eighth in the National League." When the Cubs began to play ball in July—without Novikoff—the wolfpack yelled that the winning streak merely proved the team had the stuff to win from the beginning. Even if the Cubs should finish fourth this year, 1943 will be written off as a disappointment in Chicago, where greater expectations flowered last winter.

There must be times when Mr. Gallagher wished he were behind the firing end of a typewriter once more. That old feeling probably steals over him when he looks at a daily feature in the *Chicago Times*, a box on the sport page headed, What Ex-Cubs Did Yesterday. The box is a "must" ordered by Gene Kessler, the sports editor who worked on a South Bend, Indiana, paper with Gallagher, and the purpose is to remind the fans of the honors pulled in trades by the Cubs. The Times hardly gives the Gallagher-Wilson administration the best of it. In the last decade the Cubs have made most of the deals that are held up as horrible examples of gullibility, bad judgment and worse luck. Like their predecessors, Gallagher and Wilson have been guilty of mistakes and they have been plagued by the persistent jinx which bedevils the Cubs. In July, for instance, they released Dick Barrett, a thirty-five-year-old pitcher who had lost four games while failing to win one all season. A few days later Barrett turned up with the Phillies and pitched a fourteen-inning shutout to beat Cincinnati, 1–0. In his next start, Barrett whipped the Giants, 9–1. Happens all the time—or so it seems.

The two classic stickings of the Cubs were, of course, the Dizzy Dean and Chuck Klein episodes. Everybody in baseball knew Dean was suffering with a bad arm early in 1938, but Wrigley gave the Cardinals $185,000 and Pitchers Curt Davis and Clyde Shoun and an outfielder, Tuck Stainback, for the Great Mouthpiece. Dean won the grand total of sixteen games for Chicago in three years. Davis won forty-two games during the same period and Shoun, a workhorse relief man, appeared in 147 games for the Cardinals. Wrigley did not protest the Dean deal to Judge Landis on the ground that a sore-arm pitcher had been palmed off on him. Some folks are unkind enough to suggest that Dean brought $185,000 worth of extra business through the games and, besides, the whole thing was priceless publicity for the gum company.

DOINGS OF THE ALUMNI

Davis was involved in two transactions representing a cash outlay of $300,000 and all the Cubs received from him was ten winning games. In 1933 Chicago gave Philadelphia $65,000 and three players for Klein, then the batting champion. Two seasons later Chicago paid Philadelphia $50,000 to take Klein back in return for Davis and Ethan Allen. Wrigley may not miss the $115,000 spent on Klein's changes of scenery and the $185,000 Dean cost, but the Cubs could make splendid use of Davis, still a winning pitcher.

Lon Warneke, the pitching ace on two pennant winners, was traded to the Cardinals in 1936 for Rip Collins and Roy Parmelee, who did not start a second Chicago fire with their exploits. Last year the Cubs gave the Cardinals the waiver price for Warneke, who had enjoyed five big years in St. Louis. In 1934 the Cubs acquired Frank Hurst from Philadelphia for Dolph Camilli and ubiquitous Joe Cash. Hurst hit .228 for Chicago and dropped out of sight. Camilli became a star of first magnitude. Augie Galan was released to Los Angeles in 1941 and was purchased by Brooklyn for the waiver price. Galan is a Dodger regular.

The occurrence at Ebbets Field on July fifth last was one of the little things that depress Cub fans. On that day Brooklyn swept a doubleheader with Chicago. Ex-Cub Bobo Newsom was the winning pitcher in the first game and Ex-Cub Higbe was more of the same in the second contest. Galan's triple with bases full won the first game and his home run with bases full clinched the second. Herman and Camilli also were among those present for the Dodgers.

Sitting there with Branch Rickey, the Brooklyn brain, we asked him to explain the sad plight of the Cubs. Rickey pondered for a moment, then expressed—with rotund overtones, of course—the general opinion of most baseball men.

"This team has to approach cooperative perfection to remain in the shadow of last place," the Reverend Rickey pontificated. "There is artistry in ineptitude, too, you know."

27. Maybe Next Year?

THE FOLLOWING ARTICLE, from the *Chicago Daily News,* describes the gala atmosphere that accompanied the 1945 World Series on the eve of its first pitch in Detroit.

People in both Chicago and the Motor City seemed unconcerned that the major leagues still faced a major shortage of talent due to big-leaguers serving in the armed forces—a situation that led famed sportswriter Warren Brown to opine, "I don't think either one of them can win it [the World Series]." (Brown even titled a chapter about it in a book on the history of the Cubs, "World's Worst Series.")[1] Nor did people seem overly burdened that just two months earlier atomic bombs fell on Japan to end World War II, a war that caused more than fifty million deaths worldwide, including over 400,000 Americans. It might seem hard to imagine the Cubbie revelry in the wake of such anguish, but many had worried long enough—it was a time to celebrate. In fact, the 1945 World Series became the most lucrative to that date, with over $270,000 in revenue and with players' shares approximating the average major league salary. Mutual Broadcasting Corporation paid $100,000 for exclusive broadcast rights and record attendance totaled over 333,000.[2]

For Chicago fans, the excitement grew after game three in Detroit, when, behind a one-hit pitching performance by Claude Passeau against the Tigers, the Cubs went ahead in the World Series two games to one. Cubs fans could just about taste the world title. In fact, by the time the Cubs made it to Chicago for game four (the 1945 World Series maintained the three games away, four home wartime format) players found a city absolutely giddy with anticipation. All night long people waited in line at Wrigley Field for bleacher tickets, and many of those seeking hotels needed to find accommodations in distant suburbs.

The festive atmosphere came to an end for Chicagoans in game seven at

Wrigley Field when the Cubs lost to the Tigers 9–3. Compounding matters, for those inclined to such superstitions, the 1945 Series brought with it the "Curse of the Billy Goat." As lore has it, Billy Goat Tavern–founder William Sianis put the curse on the Cubbies when Cubs management banished his goat from the stadium. A *Chicago Sun* account from the day of the event says Mr. Sianis and his goat were never let in Wrigley Field, and another account claims that the two paraded around the grounds for a few innings until P. K. Wrigley kicked them out because of the goat's stench, while yet another holds that the two were asked to leave after the goat ate some fans' hot dogs.

Although it did not end well, the *Daily News*'s John P. Carmichael shows that Cubs fans were thinking rather optimistically at the start of the 1945 World Series. That hope remains well into the new millenium.

Back Cubs with Heavy Betting:
O'Neil's Hope in Southpaws, Tiger Pilot
Will Shift to Trucks if Newhouser Fails

John P. Carmichael, *Chicago Daily News,* October 2, 1945

Detroit—If Hal Newhouser beats the Cubs tomorrow in the first game of this 1945 World Series, then "Stubby" Overmire will get the call in the second game. But if Newhouser should be shaded by the National League champions, then Virgil "Fire" Trucks will go in the no. 2 affair.

That is the pitching program and principle of Manager Steve O'Neill of the Tigers, who won the American League pennant.

"If we can stop the Cubs' lefthanders, we'll continue to do so," he said. "If we can't, we'll try something else."

In other words the Detroit pilot will throw southpaws . . . like Newhouser and Overmire . . . against the Cubs until they prove they're not effective.

———

In any event, according to O'Neill's plans, Paul "Dizzy" Trout, the Detroit fast-ball expert, will work the opening game at Wrigley Field in Chicago next Saturday. Chances are he'll face either Hank Wyse or Ray Prim, but as Charley Grimm greeted newspapermen today [he said] "We aim to win 'em one at a time. My team has played great ball to win the pennant; I see no reason why it should let down now."

The Cubs were to work out late today at Briggs Stadium.

––––––

Fellows like Claude Passeau, who probably will pitch the second game of the series, and Andy Pafko and Bill Nicholson and "Peanuts" Lowry and Don Johnson have never seen a World Series game before, let alone played in one.

When you consider that every one of those men are key figures in the Cub scheme of things, it is no wonder that pitcher Paul Derringer remarked: "Hell, we'll win this pennant three straight years . . . we're just getting acquainted."

Nine of the Cubs, including their wives, were billeted to Great Lakes ships tied up to the dock. That's how the hotel-room shortage affected everybody.

––––––

This town is a madhouse. There are no seats. There are no rooms. There isn't anything but a lot of 8–5 money on the Tigers which some sharp Chicago dough is snapping up here and there in big chunks.

The Cub bettors are wagering that Newhouser will get beat, despite his impressive record, and that once he's through Detroit hasn't anything but its last-ditch prestige to stand it in good stead.

This is Manager O'Neill's first flag as a pilot. He was with the Indians in '20 as a catcher, but never before managed a winner.

General Manager Jack Seller of the Tigers is having trouble getting people to call for their seats and the weatherman says that rain may or may not be in evidence for tomorrow's opening.

In other words, this is something the Tigers have had to do for the first time in five years and they're swamped with prognostication calls for tickets and the possibility of being extended over the weekend.

––––––

They can get 56,000 people into Briggs Stadium. If they had room, they could have sold 300,000 tickets in this sports-mad town. The same goes for Chicago.

This can be the biggest World Series from the standpoint of interest, money and attendance that has been held in many a year.

Only Stan Hack and Phil Cavaretta played in the last Cubs-Tigers series, but the fact is all the more menacing when it is considered that they are the two big hitters of this Chicago team. Cavaretta won the batting title and Hack was in the first five hitters.

Notes

1. TITLE TIME?

1. "Second Defeat of the Mutuals," *Chicago Tribune,* November 2, 1870, pg. 3; "The Proposed White Stocking–Mutual Game Off," *Chicago Tribune,* November 4, 1870, pg. 4.

2. "Sporting: The Great Baseball Event of the Season of 1870," *Chicago Times,* October 14, 1870.

3. Timothy J. Gilfoyle, "Millenium Park," *New York Times,* August 6, 2006.

4. Glenn Stout and Richard A. Johnson, *The Cubs: The Complete Story of Chicago Cubs Baseball* (New York: Houghton Mifflin, 2007), 81.

5. "Sporting: The Great Baseball Event of the Season of 1870," *Chicago Times,* October 14, 1870.

2. BASEBALL, CELEBRATED AND LAMPOONED

1. Joel Zoss and John Bowman, *Diamonds in the Rough: The Untold History of Baseball* (Lincoln: University of Nebraska Press, 2004), 67.

4. "CAP"

1. Peter Golenbock, *Wrigleyville: A Magical History Tour of the Chicago Cubs* (New York: St. Martin's Griffin, 1999), 20–90; David Pietrusza, Matthew Silverman, and Michael Gershman, *Baseball: The Biographical Encyclopedia* (New York: Total Sports, 2000), 29–31.

2. David L. Fleitz, *Cap Anson: the Grand Old Man of Baseball* (Jefferson, N.C.: McFarland & Company, 2005), 192.

3. Ibid., 193.

4. Dave Wilton, "Charley Horse," Wordorigins.org, May 31, 2006, http://www.wordorigins.org/index.php/site/comments/charley_horse/ (accessed March 31, 2010).

5. THE $10,000 BEAUT!

1. Glenn Stout, Richard A. Johnson, *The Cubs: The Complete Story of Chicago Cubs Baseball* (New York: Houghton Mifflin, 2007), 81.

6. FROM TEETOTALING TO EGYPT

1. Peter Levine, *A.G. Spalding and the Rise of Baseball: the Promise of American Sport* (New York: Oxford University Press, 1985); Mark Lamster, *Spalding's World Tour: The*

Epic Adventure That Took Baseball Around the Globe—And Made It America's Game (New York: Public Affairs Press, 2006), 275, 276; Neal Conan, "When Baseball Went Global: Spalding's World Tour," *Talk of the Nation (NPR)*, 2006, *HighBeam Research*. Feb. 22, 2009 (http://www.highbeam.com); "Spalding's World Tour: The Epic Adventure That Took Baseball Around the Globe—And Made It America's Game (book review), *Nine*, September 22, 2007, *HighBeam Research*. Feb. 22, 2009 (http://www.highbeam.com).

2. David L. Fleitz, *Cap Anson: the Grand Old Man of Baseball* (Jefferson, N.C.: Mc-Farland & Company, 2005), 189.

7. HOT TIME AT THE HOT SPRINGS

1. "Faywood Hot Springs History," http://www.faywood.com/History.htm, accessed March 31, 2010.

2. "1906–1942: The Early Years," http://www.springtrainingonline.com/features/history_1.htm, accessed January 29, 2008.

3. Glenn Stout, Richard A. Johnson, *The Cubs: The Complete Story of Chicago Cubs Baseball* (New York: Houghton Mifflin, 2007), 81.

8. CHI-TOWN FANDEMONIUM

1. Hugh S. Fullerton, "'Sox' Join 'Cubs,' Pennant Is Won," *Chicago Tribune*, October 4, 1906.

2. Ibid.

3. As Cubs historian Arthur A. Ahrens has noted, up to 1942 the Cubs and Sox slugged it out on twenty-six separate occasions in the City Series, and fans often responded to the games with ribald enthusiasm, pushing scalper prices sky high. Arthur A. Ahrens, "Chicago's City Series: Cubs Versus White Sox," *Chicago History*, Volume 5, Issue 4, 1976, pgs. 243–52.

4. Lenny Jacobsen, "Charles Murphy," *SABR.org* [on-line] http://bioproj.sabr.org/bioproj.cfm?a=v&v=l&pid=16915&bid=912: accessed February 3, 2011; "Baseball Pioneer Dead," *New York Times*, July 19, 1919.

5. Jacobsen, "Charles Murphy"; "C.W. Murphy, Cubs' Owner in 1906–1914, Dies," *Chicago Tribune*, October 17, 1931, pg. 21

6. Jacobsen, "Charles Murphy."

9. EVERS ON THE GLORY YEARS

1. Joe Williams, "A Chat with 'Crab' Evers," (1937) accessed from the *Baseball Hall of Fame Archives*, Cooperstown, NY, "John J. Evers file."

2. Ed Sims, "Touching Second: Reviewed by Ed Sims, former president of SLA and professor emeritus of English at Springfield College," *Sport Literature Association,* http://www.uta.edu/english/sla/br050424.html, accessed July 8, 2009.

3. John J. Evers and Hugh S. Fullerton, *Touching Second: The Science of Baseball* (The Reilly & Britton Company: Chicago, 1910), 56.

11. CUBS, CHAMPIONS!

1. George F. Will, "Perfect Season," *New York Times*, April 1, 2007.
2. Ibid.

12. CENTENNIAL BROWN

1. "Three-Fingered Immortal" reprinted with permission, copyright SPORT Gallery Inc.

13. POLITICS AT THE PARK

1. "Frantic Rooters Crowd the Field," *Chicago Tribune*, October 15, 1906.
2. "Interview: Paul Dickson talks about his book on presidents and baseball," *NPR Morning Edition*, April 2, 2001, http://www.highbeam.com/doc/1P1-43188311.html (accessed February 28, 2009); *Washington Post*, July 12, 1993; Michael Aubrecht, "Seventh-Inning Sretch," *Baseball Almanac*, http://www.baseball-almanac.com/articles/7th_inning_stretch.shtml (accessed February 28, 2009).

15. GROVER'S HIGHS AND LOWS

1. Alexander's Philadelphia teammate, Hans Lobert, recalled that Alexander had epileptic seizures throughout the years Lobert played on the Phillies, 1911–15. Lobert remembered that Alexander had to be held down and his tongue grabbed to prevent choking. Brandy was kept on the bench to be poured down his throat in case a seizure occurred. Lawrence S. Ritter, *The Glory of Their Times* (Collier Books, New York, 1978), 186. Ironically, the Yankees' Tony Lazzeri also suffered from epilepsy.
2. *The Sporting News*, November 15, 1950.
3. *St. Paul Phonograph*, October 13, 1926; *St. Paul Republican*, September 19, 1907; *Ord Journal*, September 19, 1907.
4. *Central City Nonpareil*, July 2, 1908.
5. Green's Nebraska Indian baseball team was organized by Guy W. Green, a Lincoln resident, in the 1890s. Supposedly comprised of Native American baseball players, the team actually had a majority of white players. A photograph of the team in the [Nebraska State Historical] Society's collection substantiates this.
6. *Galesburg Republican-Register*, April 13, 1909.
7. *Galesburg Evening Mail*, April 14, 1909.
8. Ibid., May 18, May 21, 1909; *Galesburg Republican-Register*, May 21, 1909.
9. *St. Paul Phonograph-Press*, May 21, 1909.
10. *Galesburg Republican-Register*, June 18, 1909.
11. Ibid., July 20, 1909.
12. Ibid., July 3, 23, 1909.
13. Ibid., July 23, 1909.
14. Ibid., July 26, 1909.
15. *Galesburg Evening Mail*, August 19, 1909.
16. Ibid., August 5, 1909.

17. *Galesburg Republican-Register*, August 19, 1909.

18. *St. Paul Phonograph-Press*, August 27, 1909.

19. Ibid., October 8, 1909.

20. *Syracuse Post-Standard*, July 21, 1910.

21. *Syracuse Journal*, August 29, 1910.

22. *St. Paul Phonograph-Press*, September 23, 1910.

23. Ibid. It is interesting to note that the catcher for these games was Leslie Nunamaker, a native of Malcolm, Nebraska. Nunamaker had a twelve-year major league career as a reserve catcher for the Boston, New York, St. Louis, and Cleveland teams of the American League, 1911–22.

24. *St. Paul Phonograph*, April 13, 1911.

25. Ibid., June 1, 1911.

26. Ibid., June 22, 1911.

27. Ibid., October 12, 1911.

28. Ritter, *Glory*, 200.

29. *St. Paul Phonograph*, May 9, 1918.

30. *The Sporting News*, May 2, 1951.

31. Alexander acquired the nickname "Old Pete" from Bill Killefer during a hunting trip in which Alexander fell into a pool of alkali and mud. Killefer at first called Alexander "Alkali Pete" after a cartoon character, but the name was shortened to "Pete" by Alexander's teammates.

32. Tom Meany, *Baseball's Greatest Pitchers* (New York, A.S. Barned, 1951), 8.

33. *The Sporting News*, June 14, 1969.

34. *Omaha World-Herald*, October 17, 1926.

35. *St. Paul Phonograph*, October 13, 1926.

36. Ibid., November 3, 1926.

37. *Omaha World-Herald*, October 4, 1929.

38. Known as the "Whiskered Wizards" and the "Bearded Beauties," the House of David traveling baseball team barnstormed throughout the Midwest during the 1920s and 1930s. The House of David was a Protestant sect founded by Benjamin Purnell in 1903. The players on the House of David baseball team, like all members of the sect, kept their hair and beards unshorn "in emulation of Jesus." The extra hair and beards proved not to be a hindrance, as the House of David teams routinely beat the best of the local teams sent to face them.

39. According to an interview with Alexander's niece, Elma O'Neill of St. Paul, Alexander's salary also went towards the support of his widowed mother and other members of the family. Interview with Mrs. O'Neill took place on February 23, 1989. Tape available in Nebraska State Historical Society Archives.

40. *Omaha World-Herald*, September 25, 1930.

41. Ibid., August 4, 1936.

42. *St. Louis Globe-Democrat*, August 22, 1944.

43. *Omaha World-Herald*, June 27, 1948.

44. *St. Paul Phonograph*, May 31, 1950.

45. *The Sporting News*, April 25, 1951.

46. "Focus," *Lincoln Journal and Star*, March 31, 1974.

16. SHARE SQUABBLE AT THE SERIES

1. "Lucky Charlie Weeghman Is Dead at 64," *Chicago Daily Tribune*, November 3, 1938, pg. 1; Andy Oakley, "Boys in the Hoods," *Chicago Reader*, September 26, 1996, http://www.chicagoreader.com/chicago/boys-in-the-hoods/Content?oid=891620 (accessed February 2, 2011).

2. "Lucky Charlie Weeghman Is Dead at 64," *Chicago Daily Tribune*; Andy Oakley, "Boys in the Hoods," *Chicago Reader*.

3. "World's Series Players May Contest to Sept. 15," *Chicago Tribune*, August 24, 1918.

4. Meredith Goad, "In 1918, Different Time, Same Outcome," *Portland Press Herald*, October 28, 2004.

5. I. E. Sanborn, "World's Series Big Guessing Problem," *Chicago Tribune*, September 1, 1918.

6. Goad, "In 1918, Different Time, Same Outcome."

7. "Jangle Over Money Retards Game Hour; Means' Series Knell," *Chicago Tribune*, September 11, 1918.

8. "1918 World Series," *Baseball-Reference.com,* http://www.baseball-reference.com/postseason/1918_WS.shtml (accessed July 8, 2009).

17. PAPA, THE GIPPER, AND THE CUBS

1. *Ernest Hemingway: Cub Reporter* (Pittsburgh: Univ. of Pittsburgh Press, 1970).

2. MS, John F. Kennedy Library, Boston, Mass. He claimed further that the story had been picked up by the Associated Press and the United Press, but I have not yet located any story on Alexander at this time credited to either the AP or UP.

3. Hy Turkin and S.C. Thompson, *The Official Encyclopedia of Baseball*, 9th ed. Rev. by Pete Palmer (Garden City, N.Y.: Doubleday, 1977). The exception is William A. "Swede" Johnstone, who made a prophet of the young Hemingway by never making it to the major leagues.

18. HUMBLE BEGINNINGS, MAJESTIC LIFE

1. "William Veeck Dies of Blood Ailment, *Alton Evening Telegraph*, October 5, 1933, pg. 24.

2. Ibid.

3. Michael Maher, "Minor League Spotlight: The Veeck Connection," *Baseball Digest*, June 17, 2010, http://www.baseballdigest.com/2010/06/17/mls-veeck-connection/ (accessed February 8, 2010); Peter Golenbock, *Wrigleyville: A Magical History Tour of the Chicago Cubs* (New York: St. Martin's Griffin, 1999), 269, 270.

4. "Wrigley Rites Tomorrow in Pasadena Home," *Chicago Daily Tribune*, January 27, 1932, pg. 1.

5. Irving Vaughan, "Hornsby Gets Job," *Chicago Daily Tribune,* September 23, 1930, pg. 1.

19. BASEBALL MAN

1. Randy Schultz, "Joe McCarthy Ranks Among Baseball's Greatest Managers," *Baseball Digest*, August, 2005.

20. HAYMAKER HACK

1. Ira Berkow, "On Baseball; Hack Wilson's Lesson Still Valid," *New York Times,* September 5, 1998.

2. Ibid.

3. J. Roy Stockton, "Wilson, Buffeted by Cubs and Cards, Striving for a Comeback," *Sporting News*, January 21, 1932; Cliffton Blue Parker, *Fouled Away: The Baseball Tragedy of Hack Wilson* (Jefferson: McFarland & Company, 2000), 125–41.

4. Stockton, "Wilson, Buffeted by Cubs and Cards, Striving for a Comeback," *Sporting News.*

5. Parker, *Fouled Away: The Baseball Tragedy of Hack Wilson*, 2; Berkow, "On Baseball: Hack Wilson's Lesson Still Valid," *New York Times.*

6. Berkow, "On Baseball: Hack Wilson's Lesson Still Valid," *New York Times*; Parker, *Fouled Away: The Baseball Tragedy of Hack Wilson*, 142–64.

7. Berkow, "On Baseball; Hack Wilson's Lesson Still Valid," *New York Times.*

8. "Hack Wilson as Pugilist Has a Big Day," *Chicago Daily Tribune*, July 5, 1929, pg. 1.

21. RAJAH IN CHARGE

1. This can also be seen in: Irving Vaughn, "Hornsby Gets Job," *Chicago Daily Tribune*, September 23, 1930, pg. 1.

2. Edward Burns, "Hornsby Removed By Cubs: Grimm Takes Up Manager's Duties Today," *Chicago Daily Tribune*, August 3, 1932, pg. 1.

22. DID HE CALL IT?

1. "Home Runs by Ruth, Gehrig Beat Cubs 7–5" from Chicago Tribune. © 1932 Chicago Tribune. All rights reserved. Used by permission and protected by the Copyright Laws of the United States. The printing, copying, redistribution, or retransmission of the material without express written permission is prohibited.

23. WHAT DEPRESSION? THIRD WORLD SERIES IN SEVEN YEARS

1. "How They Did It," Edward Burns, *Chicago Daily,* September 28, 1935.

2. "World Series," *Time,* October 14, 1935, http://www.time.com/time/magazine/article/0,9171,755165,00.html (accessed January 26, 2008).

3. "World Series Aftermath," *Time,* November 4, 1935, http://www.time.com/time/magazine/article/0,9171,755297,00.html (accessed January 26, 2008).

24. SANDBERG BEFORE SANDBERG?

1. Jerome Holtzman, "Cub Legend Billy Herman Takes Stroll Down Memory Lane in Cooperstown," *Chicago Tribune*, August 2, 1988.

25. SPEAKIN' OF HARTNETT

1. Charles N. Billington, *Wrigley Field's Last World Series: The Wartime Chicago Cubs and the Pennant of 1945* (Chicago: Lake Claremont Press, 2005), 58–59.

27. MAYBE NEXT YEAR?

1. Warren Brown, *The Chicago Cubs* (Southern Illinois University Press: Carbondale, 2001).

2. Charles N. Billington, *Wrigley Field's Last World Series: The Wartime Chicago Cubs and the Pennant of 1945* (Chicago: Lake Claremont Press, 2005), Chicago, 271.

Index

Page references in italics refer to illustrations.

Armour, Ogden, 184, 185
Arrants, Aimee (Mrs. Grover Cleveland Alexander), 164, 166, 167, 168
Averill, Earl, 223

Bailey, Bill. *See* Veeck, William, Sr.
Baker, Bill, 252
ballparks: Dexter Park, 13, 14, 15, 16; Ogden Park, 14; South Side Park, 65; South Side Park II, 75; 23rd Street Grounds, 11, 29; West Side Park I, 11, 50, 65, 75, 82; West Side Park II, 65, 75, *83*, 86, 145; Wrigley Field, 10, *83*, 145, 169, 170, 182, 203, 205, 213–16, 248, 249, 250, 259–60
Baltimore Orioles (American League), 179
Baltimore Orioles (National League), 123
Barnes, Ross, 23, 25, *30*, 32
Barrett, Dick, 255
Baseball, The Early Years (Seymour), 57
"Baseball's Sad Lexicon" (Adams), 99, 133–34, 147
base-running. *See* statistical analysis
Beck, Clyde, 245
Bielaski, Oscar, 31–32
"billy goat curse," 10, 260
Bishop, Max, 239
black players, 5–6, 39–40
Blake, "Sheriff," 239, 243
Boley, Joe, 239
Bonds, Barry, 199
"bonehead" play (Merkle), 109–20, *121*, 135, 147
Boston Beaneaters, 35, 49, 50, 54–58, 60–61, 69–71. *See also* Boston Braves; Boston Red Stockings
Boston Braves, 147–48, 191, 192, 226. *See also* Boston Beaneaters; Boston Red Stockings
Boston Red Sox, 164, 170–74, 226–27
Boston Red Stockings, 4, 23–24, 25,

123. *See also* Boston Beaneaters; Boston Braves
Bradley, George, *30*
Bressler, "Rube," 163
Bridwell, Al, 8, 109, 112, 113, 116, 117, 118
Briggs, Herbert, 47, 107
broadcast rights, 217
Bronx Bombers. *See* New York Yankees
Brooklyn Dodgers, 201, 223, 224, 225–26, 256–57
Brotherhood of Ball Players, 5, 41, 27, 57. *See also* National League
Brown, Mace, 232–33
Brown, Mordecai Peter Centennial ("Three Finger"), 9, 125, *128*, 141; birth of, 3, 130; and the Chicago Cubs, 6–7, 100, 104, 127, 132, 133–37, 221; and the Cincinnati Reds, 137; death of, 137; hand injury of, 6, 127, *128*, 129–31, 133; and Christy Mathewson, 127, 132–33, 134–35, 136–37; in the minor leagues (Coxsville), 131–32; nicknames of, 132; statistics of, 6–7, 127, 134, 136–37; and the St. Louis Cardinals, 104, 133
Brown, Warren, 229–30, 259
Bruccoli, Matthew J., 175
Bryant, Clay, 230
Burke, Jimmy, 210
Burkholder, Ed, 127
Burns, Edward, 213
Burns, George, 239
Burns, Tom ("Tommy"), 43, 72, 78, 79
Bush, George, 140
Bush, George H. W., 140

Callahan, Jimmy, 77, 79, 151, 152
Camilli, Dolph, 256
Campton, Al, 149
Capone, Al, *230*
Cappio, Alfred P., 51, 54–55
Caray, Harry, 179, 182
Carmichael, John, 252, 260

Casa de Consuelo (House of Comfort), 75, 76, 77. *See also* spring training

Casey, "Doc," 104, 106, 107

"Casey at the Bat" (Thayer), 55, 56, 58

Catalina Island, *182*, 183, 184, 186, *229*, 234–35. *See also* spring training

Cavarretta, Phil, 10, 262

Central City, NE, 159–60

Chadwick, Henry, 23

Chance, Frank, *100*, 122, 137, 155; and Mordecai Brown, 133–34, 135, 136; and double plays, 99; firing of, 82–83, 147, 149, 152, 154; as first baseman, 7, 99, 104, 125; as manager, 6, 9, 82, 96, 100–101, 104, 106–8, 123, 124, 125, 133, 135, 136, 147, 151; and President Taft, *142*

"Charley Horse," 36, 45–48

Chicago, IL: and board of trade fans, 86; and the "City Series," 81, 147, 151–52, 154, 264n3; and fan control, 115; and founding of Cubs, 2–3; Great Fire in, 3, 14, 29; and immigration, 17; Palmer House, 49–50, 69; and popularity of baseball, 14, 81, 84–90, 92–97; population of, 14, 17, 67; and World Series between Cubs and Sox, 7, 81, 83–84, 87, 90–97, 134. *See also* Chicago Cubs; Chicago White Sox

Chicagoans. *See* Chicago Cubs

Chicago Colts. *See* Chicago Cubs

Chicago Cubs: and abstinence pledges, 5; attendance, 11, 13, 15, 16, 55, 65, 84, 86–87, 115, 123, 139, 145, 185, 205, 213, 247, 249; and "buying" of players, 4, 25, 38, 100–106, 185; and celebrities, 175–80; and championship win (1870), 13–16; as the Chicagoans, 13; and the "City Series," 81, 147, 151–52, 154, 264n3; as the Colts, 5, 41–43, 45–48, 67, 70, 84; and "Cubs" as official name, 6; and the

"Curse of the Billy Goat," 10, 260; and farm system, 255; founding of the, 2–3; "golden age" of the, 1, 2, 4–5, 6–9; inaugural season of the (1870), 13–16; and "Ladies' Day," 181; and the Merkle "bonehead" play, 109–20, *121*, 135, 147; name changes, 2, 3, 5, 6, 13, 41, 43; and the National Association, 24–25; and the National League, 25, 102; as the Orphans, 43, 75–79; and profitability, 81, 97, 185; records held by, 40; as the Remnants, 6; scouts for the, 101–2, 103, 104–5, 106, 108, 224, 233–34; and spring training, 4, 35, 41, 75–79, *182*, 183, 184, 186, *229*, 234–35; and President Taft, 139, 140–43; and Tinker-Evers-Chance double plays, 99–100; and the University of Illinois, 103; and Charles Weeghman, 169, 170, 184; as the White Stockings, 2, 3, 4, 13–16, 29, 31–33, 35, 38–41, 123; win-loss records, 11, 29, 39, 40, 65, 145, 147, 205; and World Series losses: 1906, 7, 81, 83–84, 87, 90–97, 122, 134, 147; 1910, 147; 1918, 169, 171; 1929, 186, 199, 238–39; 1932, 187, 208, 213–16; 1935, 217–21; 1938, 187; 1945, 259–60; and World Series wins: 1907, 7, 100, 108, 122, 135, 147, 221; 1908, 9, 100, 108, 121, 122–26, 136, 147, 221; during World War II, 247–57, 259. *See also* ballparks; individual player names

Chicago Cubs pennant wins, 69, 123, 147; **1880s**, 4, 5, 29, *30*, 31, 39, 40; **1906**, 7, 84, 108, 134; **1907**, 108; **1908**, 7–9, 108, 109–11, 116, 118, 122, 123, 135–36, 147; **1910**, 9, 137; **1918**, 9–10, 184–85; **1929**, 9–10; **1932**, 9–10, 182, 208, 224; **1935**, 9–10, 182, 217, 224, 247, 251; **1938**, 9–10, 182, 224, 229, 232–33, 247, 251; **1945**, 9–10

Chicago Orphans. *See* Chicago Cubs

Merkle "bonehead" play, 8, 110–11, 112–13, 117–18, 119, 120; in the minor leagues, 103; salary of, 153; as second baseman, 7, 8, 99–100, 103–4, 112–13, 119, 120, 125, 126, 147–49, 152–53; and Joe Tinker, 99–100; *Touching Second,* 100–108

fans, 90–91, 93–95, 124, 141
Federal League, 83, 152, 153, 169, 183–84, 188. *See also* National League
Field, Eugene, 37
fielding chances. *See* statistical analysis
Fleitz, David, 69
Ford, Henry, 217
Foxx, Jimmy, 237, 239
Frank, Stanley, 247
Freedman, Andrew, 43
French, Larry, 225
Frisch, Frankie, 244, 245
Fullerton, Hugh S., 81; *Touching Second,* 100–108

Gage, George, 11
Galan, Augie, 178, 179, 225, 237, 243, 256
Galesburg, IL, 160–61
Gallagher, James ("Jim"), 247, 248, 252, 253, 254–55
gambling, 14, 15, 16, 20, 89, 207–8, 236; buggy ride bet, 83–84, 95; fixing games, 5
Gehrig, Lou, 208, *212,* 213, 214–15, 216, 237, 244
Gehringer, Charley, 241
Gibson, George, 185, 239
Gilbert, Charlie, 225, 252
Gill, Warren, 113–14, 117
Gleason, "Kid," 152
Glenn, John, *30,* 32
Grace, W. G., 68
Graham, Andrew R., 75, 77
Great Fire (Chicago, IL), 3, 14, 29
Green, Guy W., 265n5

Griffith, Clark, 41, 79
Grim, Jack, 103
Grimes, Burleigh, 241
Grimm, Charlie ("Jolly Cholly"), 220, 225, 238, 239, 244, 251, 260; and the All-Star game, 237; and pennant wins, 182, 208, 217; replacement of, as manager, 229, 231–32, 240; and Ronald Reagan, 179
Grove, "Lefty," 241

Haas, "Mule," 195, 239
Hack, Stan, 262
Hafey, "Chick," 244
Hanlon, Ned, 72, 108
Harder, Mel, 195
Harridge, William, 220
Harris, Bucky, 223, 248
Harrison, Benjamin, 177
Hart, James A., 42–43, 46–47, 65, 81, 102, 105; and sale of Chicago Cubs, 106–7
Hartford Dark Blues, 25
Hartnett, Charles Leo ("Gabby"), 10, 214, 225, 233–37, 239–41; and the All-Star games, 237, 238; as manager, 230, 231–33, 243–44, 251, 252; marriage of, to Martha Marshall, 235; nickname of, 231; opinion of, regarding pitchers, 241–43, 244–46; and pennant wins, 229, 232–33; popularity of, with fans, 230, 231, 233, 235; statistics of, 230
Hartnett, Martha Marshall (Mrs. Gabby Hartnett), 235
Healy, John, 72
Heathcote, Cliff, 203
Hemingway, Ernest, 175–77
Hendricks, Jack, 202, 203
Hendrix, Claude, 176
Herman, Bill ("Billy"), 217, 223–27, 237, 252, 256
Herman, William, Sr., 224
Herrmann, August, 142